D1582297

FRENCH KITCHEN

To Céleste and Sasha,
for bringing me so much joy and inspiration

SERGE DANSEREAU

FRENCH KITCHEN

CONTENTS

FOREWORD

Serge's beautiful new book, *French Kitchen*, is a wonderful reflection of his abilities and personality; it is informative and inspiring — an impressive collection of the most delicious recipes to prepare at home. Serge's French background influences his food, and in this book he produces some of his most refined but simple French recipes. From the lemon crêpes to the baked salmon with leeks, *soupe au pistou* to pot-au-feu, his range is rich and recipes are mouth watering.

I have known Serge for over 25 years, our friendship forged through his constant search for the best produce in Australia and around the world, and his passion for cooking is evident from the pages of this exquisitely produced book. The images are captivating and they will inspire people to seek great produce and cook with the techniques he explains so vividly and clearly. One look at the John Dory with fennel and capers or the chicken confit, and you instantly realise that this is the right way to cook. His cooking techniques are simple but assured and his recipes confident.

These simple, classic recipes will give confidence to people who are learning to cook or inspire people who just wish to cook fresh and traditional French food. His duck cassoulet left me in awe, and everyone would love to cook his cherry clafoutis or grapefruit soufflé, such is the beauty of these dishes.

Serge's cooking has always shown his ability to follow seasons and to take advantage of regional and local produce. He is a traditionalist, but his knowledge also gives him the confidence to be creative and to lead the way in making us understand the importance of fresh, regional and hand-crafted food.

Simon Johnson
Providore

INTRODUCTION

Writing this book has been a pleasant and rewarding experience. The recipes are very close to my French heritage and these are dishes that I truly love to cook at home.

Growing up in a typical French–Canadian family in Montréal, I learned from an early age to appreciate simple fresh food, either from my father's large garden, my mother's cuisine or my grandmother's incredible feasts. We ate fresh fish nearly every week, often caught by my father and brothers from the rivers and lakes of the region, and wild game from my father's occasional hunting trips, as well as staples such as boiled ham and baked chicken casserole. Bread was often baked fresh and pies would be filled with rhubarb or cherries grown in the garden. All this helped me realise that there was a whole lot more to food than something that you simply ate for lunch or dinner.

French food has also been a constant in my professional life; it made me understand the importance of freshness and quality, educated me in appreciating flavours and created in me a respect for technique, observation and creativity, but also for simplicity.

These days I visit France more often than my native town of Montréal. In the small country towns of France I am endlessly amazed by the respect they have for their local produce and the classic dishes of their region. It inspires me. I also like the dishevelled French style you find in country French houses; their parquet floors, stone courtyards and scented gardens. I love the dull sheen of old copper pots, rustic platters, porcelain plates and antique silver cutlery. Indeed, I like to collect old French gastronomic object; I feel they enhance the food by their unspoken memories.

There is nothing more satisfying than sharing the preparation of a meal with loved ones and enjoying freshly cooked food at the table. I relish the challenge of cooking in different environments — whether at friends' places or in country houses where I am unfamiliar with the equipment or even in a fireplace or on a wood fire. It stimulates me and forces me to improvise and stretch my skills.

This book is a collection of recipes that are approachable and rich in French tradition. It is the type of food I was either raised on or I learned to cook over the years. It is home food with a rusticity that defines the superb flavours of each dish. There's no need to agonise over the presentation — this is food that celebrates beautiful ingredients and simple techniques. I hope this book will inspire many great meals with your family and friends.

CHEF'S NOTES

It is not a bad idea to follow a recipe to the letter the first few times you make it, but once you understand the cooking principles, have confidence and substitute ingredients according to what you have available. Here are some general notes and tips to keep in mind as you use this book:

Anchovies
Use Spanish anchovies for any delicate dish as they are less salty, plumper and not so pungent. Other salted anchovies can be used for dressings or marinades.

Barbecue grill
Superheat your grill with the cover down (if it has a cover) before you grill any meat. Brush the grill quickly with a wire brush and oil the grill bar with a touch of oil just before setting your fish or meat on it. Do not brush the meat with oil as it might burn once on the grill and create acrid smoke.

Beef
Choose beef that has a firm, very white fat cover with plenty of fatty speckles in its flesh. This ensures the meat is moist and tender.

Butter
I use salted butter in all savoury recipes and unsalted in all sweet ones.

Chopping boards
I use two wooden chopping boards at home — a small oval one and a large rectangular one. If you wash your boards in soapy water after each use, they can be used for fish, poultry, or anything else.

Eggs and chicken
Use free-range eggs and free-range or corn-fed chickens.

Herbs
Establish a small herb garden at home — growing such herbs as parsley, basil, thyme, oregano, dill, mint and chives — either in small pots or planted in a sunny part of your garden, and use fresh herbs in your dishes.

Knives

You only need a few knives, but make sure they are good quality. I mainly use three knives — a paring knife, a chef's knife and a serrated knife. All chefs have their own personal preference for kitchen knives. I like a light blade with a wooden handle, but try various brands to find your favourite.

Meat

If you can, shop at your local butcher, especially if they break whole lamb and beef carcasses into prime cuts.

Take meat out of the fridge and bring to near room temperature before you start searing or cooking it. Dry meat before searing it, and sear when the oil is very hot/smoky. If you wish to avoid a mess, sear large pieces of meat on a barbecue plate outside.

For perfectly tender meat, cook on high heat to create a good crust then reduce to a constant low temperature.

Rest your meat by covering it with aluminium foil and a clean tea towel.

Mayonnaise

I purchase whole egg mayonnaise for home for everyday use, but I often make my own for special dishes. Combine two free-range egg yolks, a teaspoon of Dijon mustard and a teaspoon of white wine vinegar and whisk well. Add a cup of vegetable oil, slowly at first, while constantly whisking. Finish with a squeeze of lemon and some salt and white pepper, and use it on the same day.

Milk

In all cooking I use full-cream milk, but in some cases you could substitute with low-fat.

Mushrooms

When cooking mushrooms, use plenty of oil or butter to start with on high heat, and when that is absorbed add more butter for a great colour and taste.

Oil

Use extra virgin olive oil drizzled on cold dishes and grilled fish, and olive oil to cook vegetables, fish and some meat dishes. Use vegetable oil for searing and sautéeing and to make lighter dressings.

Parsley

Put parsley in a tea towel and rinse and wash under cold running water, then squeeze well to remove any water before chopping. This produces a light, dry, powdery parsley that will last a few days.

Potatoes

I use desiree potatoes for most dishes. Unwashed potatoes will keep longer. Keep them in the fridge or in a paper bag in a dark, cool place.

Pots and pans

Have a couple of thick-based casserole pots, either in stainless steel or copper. Use a good large cast-iron pan to cook most of your pan-fried dishes — from fish and chicken to mushrooms and steak. For small delicate fish use a nonstick frying pan but one with a good thickness in its base.

Salt

Ideally you should keep three types of salt in your pantry: cooking salt for blanching, stocks and large roasts, fine salt for stuffings, dressings and for making dough, and flaked sea salt to finish most dishes, especially fish and grilled meat. Australian brands are good.

Tomatoes

Keep tomatoes in a bowl — not the fridge. They will develop much better flavour and will be perfectly ripe when you are ready to use them.

Vanilla

For custards, crème anglaise or ice cream, I use vanilla beans — split and the seeds scraped in the milk. For recipes that require a liquid form of vanilla, I use vanilla bean paste, which is a natural product.

Vegetables

Use plenty of salted boiling water to cook your green vegetables. Have a bowl of very cold or iced water ready to plunge your green vegetables in, to stop the cooking process. This will keep them crisp and a beautiful green colour. When cooking white vegetables, such as cauliflower or white asparagus, add a touch of milk or a couple of tablespoons of flour to the water to help keep them white.

CONVERSION CHARTS

1 metric tablespoon = 20 ml
1 metric teaspoon = 5 ml
1 cup = 250 ml (8 fl oz)

OVEN TEMPERATURES

°C (Celsius)	°F (Fahrenheit)	Gas mark
120	250	1
150	300	2
160	325	3
180	350	4
200	400	5
220	450	6
240	500	7

METRIC Centimetres (cm) Millimetres (mm)	IMPERIAL Inches (in)
2-3 mm	⅛ in
5-6 mm	¼ in
1 cm	½ in
2 cm	¾ in
2.5 cm	1 in
5 cm	2 in
6 cm	2½ in
8 cm	3 in
10 cm	4 in
13 cm	5 in
15 cm	6 in
18 cm	7 in
20 cm	8 in
23 cm	9 in
25 cm	10 in
28 cm	11 in
30 cm	12 in

DRY AND LIQUID MEASURES

Metric (grams)	Imperial (ounces/pounds)	Metric (millilitres)	Imperial (fluid ounces)
30 g	1 oz	30 ml	1 fl oz
60 g	2 oz	60 ml	2 fl oz
90 g	3 oz	90 ml	3 fl oz
125 g	4 oz	125 ml	4 fl oz
150 g	5 oz	150 ml	5 fl oz
180 g	6 oz	180 ml	6 fl oz
200 g	7 oz	200 ml	7 fl oz
250 g	8 oz	250 ml	8 fl oz
280 g	9 oz	280 ml	9 fl oz
310 g	10 oz	310 ml	10 fl oz
340 g	11 oz	340 ml	11 fl oz
375 g	12 oz	375 ml	12 fl oz
500 g	16 oz/1 lb	500 ml	16 fl oz
1 kg	32 oz/2 lb	1 litre	32 fl oz

BREAKFAST

Breakfast

Most weekends I find myself cooking a special breakfast for Yvette and the kids. It's always a joy to cook crêpes or make a simple brioche to have with homemade marmalade when there are no time pressures. We also love starting the day with friends — whether it's a late breakfast or Sunday brunch the range of dishes is as varied as it is delicious, with an easy relaxed way to serve it.

LEMON CRÊPES

Crêpes au citron

Most Sundays I make pancakes for my son, Sasha, and lemon crêpes for my daughter, Céleste. Instead of making two separate batters I have become expert at thinning down my pancake mix (see page 11) to make delicious crêpes. Having said that, this is a traditional crêpe recipe that I use at work and at home to make a large batch. Crêpes can easily be made in advance and warmed up at a later stage. Serve them simply with lemon and sugar or top them with jam or stewed fruit.

375 ml (1½ cups) full-cream milk

4 free-range eggs, beaten

60 ml (¼ cup) vegetable oil

160 g (1¼ cups) plain flour, sifted

2 tablespoons butter, softened

caster sugar, for sprinkling

2–3 lemons, halved, to serve

Use a whisk to beat the milk and eggs in a bowl. Add 2 tablespoons of the oil and all of the flour and mix well; strain through a fine sieve. Set aside for 1 hour in the fridge to let the batter settle.

Heat a frying pan over medium heat and brush the base of the pan with oil (a paper towel dipped in the remaining oil is the best way). Add a small ladle of batter to the pan to create a thin circle about 20 cm in diameter. The crêpe will cook quickly, in 1–2 minutes — turn it over once it is a nice golden colour on the bottom. Cook for 1 minute further to cook through then remove to a plate.

Repeat with the remaining crêpe batter and oil until it is all used — you should make about 12 crêpes in total. When ready to serve, spread a touch of soft butter on the crêpe with a brush, sprinkle with a little sugar and drizzle with lemon juice and fold into quarters.

If you have any leftover crêpes, cover them in plastic wrap once cool and refrigerate them — they will be perfect for dessert. Similarly, any leftover batter can be stored overnight in the refrigerator and used the next day.

VARIATIONS: You could use these crêpes in many different ways. Serve them as crêpes suzette or simply smothered with cognac and almond marmalade (see page 17). These crêpes could also be made as a dessert using orange instead of lemon with a touch of Grand Marnier for adults.

FRESH CURD CHEESE

Fromage blanc

Makes 700 g (3 cups)

Fresh curd cheese, also known as fromage blanc, is the simplest form of cheese you can make. It could be compared to quark cheese, a very light cream cheese or fresh goat's cheese, although comparisons are hard to make. It is not readily available in shops as it spoils very quickly, which is a pity as it does have a unique texture and taste. The good news is it is easy to make at home and only really requires patience while it sets and drains.

To make the fromage blanc you need to have a curdling agent, such as a junket tablet, yoghurt, buttermilk or lemon juice — each will produce a different final texture. Once set, the whey is slowly extracted to create a yoghurt-like mass, known as curd. The curd is then slowly drained to create fromage blanc. In France it is often served for dessert with fresh berries or alone in a small dish accompanied with a shaker of sugar, but it also works just as well served for breakfast with poached fruits.

---

4 litres (16 cups)
full-cream milk

2 tablespoons buttermilk

Select a large shallow saucepan that will fit inside a deep roasting tray to create a bain marie. Put the milk and buttermilk in the pan. Fill the roasting tray with warm water, about 28°C (or what we call blood temperature). Use a thermometer the first time you do this to gauge the temperature you need to achieve. The more setting surface you have and the wider the tray the more effective it will be to produce the curd. Sit the pan in the water in the tray.

Set aside in a warm place — on top of the refrigerator or close to a stove or oven that has recently been turned off is good. The milk will need 24 hours to set. The idea is for good bacteria in the buttermilk to multiply and set the milk and form the curd mass. The main elements here are time and the correct temperature. The curd is ready when a yoghurt-like mass starts to set at the sides of the pan. The whey (a white liquid) will also be visible.

Line a colander with two layers of washed muslin (cheesecloth) and place over a large saucepan. Use a slotted spoon to gently scoop the curd into the colander making sure you do not crush the mass. Once all the solids are scooped, place in the refrigerator over the pan and allow to drain for about 4 hours.

Once the first drainage is done, gather the ends of the muslin and gently squeeze out the excess liquid and return the muslin with solids to the colander. Return to the refrigerator and leave to drain overnight. You could leave to drain for longer — up to 48 hours — to produce a firmer, dryer curd cheese. The longer the drainage time the firmer the cheese will be.

Once the curd has drained, carefully open the muslin bag and scrape the cheese with a spoon into a bowl. Discard the whey and muslin cloth. Refrigerate the cheese until ready to use. You should use it within a couple of days of making.

Serve the cheese simply spread on buttered toast for breakfast. It also tastes great on a pizza with smoked salmon. You can serve it with poached peaches and a touch of the poaching liquid. It goes perfectly with fresh raspberry, some fine sugar and a little jug of pouring cream.

VARIATIONS: You can add a little salt and chopped herbs to make a more flavoursome curd cheese just before serving. To make quick curd cheese, add a tablespoon of lemon juice to the warm milk — this will make a curd with a firmer texture very quickly. For a slow setting you could use yoghurt or even a junket tablet.

BIRCHER MUESLI

I have been making Bircher muesli for a few decades now, but it doesn't seem to be any less popular at my restaurant or at home. When I first learned to make this breakfast dish, which originally came from Switzerland, it was quite a rarity in a country where bacon and eggs for breakfast was the norm. Now this light and healthy dish has become all the rage.

250 g (2½ cups) rolled oats

500 ml (2 cups) full-cream milk

125 ml (½ cup) pouring cream

100 ml orange juice

1 tablespoon lemon juice

90 g (¼ cup) honey

2 apples, grated

2 oranges, peeled and diced

80 g (⅔ cup) sultanas

60 g (½ cup) slivered almonds, toasted

125 g (½ cup) plain yoghurt

This recipe is best prepared the previous day so the oats are really well soaked.

Put the oats in a bowl and pour over the milk, cream and citrus juices. Add the remaining ingredients to the oats and refrigerate overnight.

Serve with a mixture of diced melons, fresh berries or any stewed fruit. You could also use up any nuts you have at home, such as hazelnuts or pistachios — just roast them first to remove any moisture so they are nice and crunchy.

VARIATIONS: Replace the cream with more milk or a touch more yoghurt to make it lighter.

CARAMELISED HONEY GRANOLA

Céréale rôtie au miel

Serves 8–10 or makes about 4 cups

This granola has been on the menu at the Bathers' Pavilion Café since it opened over 10 years ago. It is extremely popular and tastes great served over yoghurt or with seasonal fruit such as fresh mango, stewed apple or sliced peaches. It can also be warmed up to give it more crispness after a few days of storage.

250 g (2½ cups) rolled oats

50 g (½ cup) desiccated coconut

60 g (½ cup) almonds, roughly chopped

120 g (1 cup) mixed seeds, such as pumpkin and sunflower seeds

100 g (½ cup) brown sugar

150 g (½ cup) honey

60 ml (¼ cup) vegetable oil

½ teaspoon vanilla bean paste

Preheat the oven to 150°C. Line a baking tray with baking paper.

Mix together the oats, coconut, almonds and seeds in a large bowl.

Put the sugar, honey, oil and vanilla bean paste in a saucepan and bring to the boil. Boil for 1– 2 minutes, stirring until the sugar has dissolved. Pour over the dry ingredients and stir to coat — do not overmix, you just need to combine the ingredients until they are wet.

Spread the oats over the prepared tray and cook in the oven for 8 minutes, then use a spatula to flip the mixture over so it cooks evenly on all sides. Continue cooking and turning every 5 minutes or so, for about 25–30 minutes, or until golden and crunchy. Remove from the heat and allow to cool, then break up any large lumps and store in an airtight container for up to 1 week.

VARIATIONS: Experiment with the flavour and texture of the granola by adjusting the seed mix to include a variety of nuts, such as pistachios or peanuts. You can use this mix to dress a cheesecake or strawberry flan, or serve with ice cream.

PEAR AND POMEGRANATE WITH SHEEP'S MILK YOGHURT

Confit de poire et grenade au yaourt   Serves 4

Pomegranates are a beautiful Autumnal fruit but most people are never too sure what to make of them or how to use them. The red fleshy seeds can be added to salads or scattered over fruit for breakfast or dessert. In this recipe the seeds are cooked to make a syrup, which is then used to poach the pears, although you could poach just about any fruit.

4 Corella pears, peeled, cored and halved

juice of 1 lemon

250 g (1¼ cups) caster sugar

2 pomegranates, halved, seeds removed

500 g (2 cups) sheep's milk yoghurt

Put the pear halves in a bowl with the lemon juice and enough water to cover — this will prevent the pears from browning.

Put the sugar and 500 ml (2 cups) water in a saucepan and bring to the boil. Reduce the heat to low and simmer for 2 minutes, stirring at first to dissolve the sugar. Add half the pomegranate seeds and simmer for a further 1 minute.

Add the pears to the pomegranate syrup, then cover with a sheet of baking paper to ensure they cook evenly and cook for 15 minutes. Remove from the heat and allow the pears to cool in the syrup. Strain and reserve the syrup.

To serve, place the pear halves in serving bowls and top with some yoghurt, a touch of the syrup and some of the remaining pomegranate seeds, to garnish.

VARIATIONS: If you cannot find pomegranate, poach 2 rhubarb stalks, trimmed and cut into sticks, in the syrup before you cook the pear and they will still acquire a beautiful pink tinge. Or use 1 tablespoon of passionfruit pulp per person for a similar effect. I also sometimes use a punnet of strawberries, cleaned, halved and poached for 2 minutes, instead of the pomegranate. You can also replace the pears with quince, strawberries or even rhubarb.

ROAST PEACHES WITH HONEY RICOTTA AND PISTACHIOS

Pêches rôties au ricotta à la pistache et au miel   Serves 4

There is nothing more glorious than beautifully ripe peaches during the summer months. When you need a bit of a change from eating fresh, try roasting them quickly with a touch of butter and sugar and serve them for breakfast with sweetened ricotta and nuts. They also taste great served with cake and ice cream for dessert.

3 tablespoons pistachios, roughly chopped

4 large peaches

50 g butter, softened

50 g (¼ cup) brown sugar

200 g soft ricotta cheese

2 tablespoons honey

Preheat the oven to 180°C.

Arrange the pistachios on a baking tray and cook them in the oven for 5 minutes, or until toasted.

Cut the peaches in half and remove the stones. Place on a baking tray, cut side down, and top with a small amount of butter and some brown sugar. Cook in the oven for 5 minutes, then test to see if you can remove the skin — it should easily peel off. If not, continue cooking for another 2 minutes; the cooking time will vary depending on how ripe the peaches are. The idea is to barely cook them so the skin comes off, not to fully roast them. Remove from the oven, peel and discard the skins; allow to cool. Reserve the roasting butter.

Put the ricotta in the bowl of an electric mixer and process on low speed to soften. Add 2 tablespoons of the pistachios and all of the honey and continue to mix by hand for 1 minute until well combined.

To serve, divide the ricotta between small bowls, top with the peach halves and sprinkle over the remaining pistachios. Drizzle over any of the leftover roasting butter from the tray.

VARIATIONS: You can use nectarines, apricots or even mangoes instead of the peaches if you prefer and sprinkle them with caramelised honey granola (see page 7).

CANADIAN-STYLE PANCAKES

Crêpes à la Canadienne

I have been making pancakes most of my life. I always serve them with real maple syrup from Canada, well actually from Québec where I was born. This mix is pretty simple to prepare and can be used virtually as soon as it is mixed. Add a touch of milk if you let it stand, as the baking powder will thicken the batter over a short time. The thicker the batter the more volume the pancakes will have. Make sure the heat is low and the pancakes are cooked slowly if you like them thick and fluffy.

250 g (2 cups) self-raising flour

500 ml (2 cups) full-cream milk

2 free-range eggs, beaten

2 tablespoons baking powder

1 pinch of salt

1 tablespoon butter for frying

Combine all of the ingredients except the butter in a bowl and stir together until well incorporated. I do not mix to the point of a smooth batter, it is better if it is looking a little bit lumpy. Let the batter rest for 5 minutes.

Heat a frying pan over medium heat. Once the pan is hot, spread a small amount of butter, just enough to grease the cooking surface, to the pan. Ladle about ¼ cup of batter into the pan. Reduce the heat to low and let the pancake cook until you see bubbles appear on the surface. Flip the pancake and cook for 1 minute further, or until golden on both sides. Remove to a plate. Repeat with the remaining butter and batter to make four pancakes in total.

Serve the pancakes warm, spread with butter and plenty of Canadian maple syrup.

VARIATIONS: Add diced banana, whole blueberries or chopped strawberries to the batter to make fruit pancakes. You can even add freshly cooked corn to make little savoury pancakes.

MARMALADE FRENCH TOAST OF BRIOCHE WITH FIGS

Pain perdu à la marmelade

This is quite a delicious change from simple French toast. Use thick bread or brioche to make them. The marmalade is sandwiched between two pieces of brioche, soaked in beaten eggs and gently cooked. Once cooked, cut the toast into fingers or quarters to serve.

1 brioche loaf, cut into 8 thick slices (see page 14)

200 g (⅔ cup) orange marmalade

4 free-range eggs, beaten

50 g (¼ cup) caster sugar

2 drops natural vanilla extract

100 ml full-cream milk

butter, for frying

4–8 black figs, pulled apart, to serve

Preheat the oven to 120°C.

Lay four slices of brioche on a cutting board and spread with the marmalade. Cover with the remaining brioche slices and refrigerate while you prepare the eggs.

Beat together the eggs, sugar, vanilla and milk in a large bowl.

Heat a little butter in a frying pan over medium heat. Working with one sandwich at a time, dip the brioche into the egg mixture to completely coat, allowing any excess to drip off. Cook for 2 minutes on each side, or until golden on both sides. Keep warm in the oven and repeat with the three remaining brioche.

Cut the brioche into halves or quarters before serving with the figs alongside.

VARIATIONS: Any berry jam will taste great served with this dish and it is worth trying a homemade marmalade (see page 17) when you can. If you are serving the toast with fresh fruit, use the ripest fruit of the season, such as mangoes and peaches. In Canada, French toast is made with country-style bread and served plain with plenty of maple syrup.

BUTTER BRIOCHE
Brioche

If you do not have a classic brioche mould, use a bread tin instead and make a loaf that can easily be sliced and toasted. To make a perfectly square loaf, sit a flat tray over the tin while it rises and during baking to prevent the brioche from rising — it will produce a denser, flat loaf that is perfect for slicing into canapé bases.

50 g (¼ cup) caster sugar

125 ml (½ cup) full-cream milk

4 free-range eggs, lightly beaten

500 g (4 cups) plain flour

21 g (3 x 7 g sachets) dry yeast

2 pinches of salt

250 g butter, diced, softened

1 free-range egg, well beaten with 1 tablespoon of milk, for glazing

Put the sugar and 1 tablespoon water in a medium-size casserole dish over medium heat and stir to dissolve the sugar. Remove from the heat, add the milk and eggs and mix well to combine.

Put the flour, yeast and salt in the bowl of an electric mixer fitted with a dough hook attachment. Mix on low speed to just combine, then gradually add the milk and egg mixture, stopping from time to time to scrape the sides of the bowl. Increase the speed to medium and work the dough for about 10 minutes — the dough will start to come together and look glossy.

Add the butter in small batches at medium speed, and when it is all incorporated return to high speed to work the dough for a further 10 minutes. The brioche dough is ready when it is glossy and easily pulls away from the sides of the bowl.

Transfer the dough to a clean bowl, cover with plastic wrap but do not seal the bowl, and lay a clean tea towel over the top. Use a pen to mark the dough level on the outside of the bowl — it will need to prove in a warmish place so it doubles in volume. Depending on the ambient temperature it might take 1–2 hours to rise.

Lightly grease two brioche moulds or one 22 x 12 x 10 cm loaf tin and eight small fluted brioche moulds with a little oil spray. Knock back the dough by pressing with your fist to remove excess air and cut it into two even-sized portions. If you are making two classic brioche, remove a small amount of dough, about the size of a 50 cent piece, from each half and set aside. Roll each of the large halves of dough into even balls

with your hand and set in the classic moulds. Then roll each of the two smaller pieces of dough into perfect little balls. Make a dent in the top of each of the larger balls and set the small balls on top. If you are making one loaf in a bread tin and eight smaller loaves, press one dough portion into the prepared tin; you will need to divide the remaining portion into quarters, then halve again, and press into the small brioche moulds. Make dents in the top of each and roll small pieces of dough into little balls and set on top if you wish. Cover with plastic wrap and set aside to prove again for a further 1 hour, or until doubled in volume.

Preheat the oven to 180°C.

Glaze the top of the brioche with the egg wash and bake in the oven for 20 minutes for small brioche, and 35–40 minutes for large brioche. If you are making a rectangular loaf, place a tray over the tin to prevent the loaf from rising in the oven. To test if they are cooked, remove from their tin, taking care not to burn yourself, and knock on the base of each loaf — it should sound hollow and feel cooked, light and dry. If they are not ready, return to the oven for a further 5 minutes.

VARIATION: You could make a brioche with a high-quality sausage in it, like pistachio sausage or even a blood pudding sausage. This is best baked in a loaf tin to form the brioche, without using a cover. Simply place the cooked sausage in the centre of the dough before cooking. When the brioche is cooked and rested, cut into slices to reveal the sausage.

COGNAC AND ALMOND MARMALADE

Marmelade d'orange d'amande et cognac

Makes about 1 kg or 4 x 250 ml jars

Marmalade is a good jam to make but don't be afraid to add different ingredients and vary the flavour. Try grapefruit, lemon or small sour oranges, or pineapple or apple with the orange, or even ginger or rosewater. The almonds in this recipe add some crunch and texture. If you feel the marmalade is too runny, strain some of the liquid and let it set separately as an orange jelly.

500 g oranges

100 g flaked almonds, toasted

500 g (2½ cups) caster sugar

1 tablespoon cognac or brandy

25 g jam setting powder (optional)

Wash the oranges, dry them well, then cut each orange in half. Slice the oranges, then chop into small even-sized pieces. Remove as many seeds as possible and place the seeds in a square of muslin (cheesecloth), tying securely with kitchen string to make a little bundle — this will allow you to extract the pectin from the seeds during cooking, which helps the jam to set.

Put the sugar and 125 ml (½ cup) water in a heavy-based saucepan over medium heat. Stir until the sugar dissolves, then add the oranges and the muslin bundle. Bring to the boil, then reduce the heat and simmer for 30 minutes, stirring regularly to prevent the jam from burning and sticking to the base of the pan. Add the almonds, cognac or brandy and the jam setting powder, if using. Remove the muslin bundle, cool and squeeze to extract any pectin from the seeds, then discard the bundle. Cook for another 15 minutes, or until the marmalade coats the back of a spoon. To test when the marmalade is ready, place a small spoonful on a plate and refrigerate for 5 minutes to see if it sets. If not, cook a little longer.

Cool the marmalade and place in sterilised airtight jars. The marmalade will keep for up to 2 weeks out of the refrigerator and up to 4 weeks in the refrigerator once opened.

VARIATIONS: You can use tangelos, mandarins, cumquats or grapefruit for a change, or even a mixture of fruit, such as figs and blood oranges. Similarly you can experiment with the flavour by replacing the cognac with whisky or calvados.

Brunch with Friends

Pear and pomegranate with
sheep's milk yoghurt

Butter brioche with
cognac and almond marmalade

Ratatouille with crispy fried egg

Baked salmon with leeks, potatoes
and cream

Paris-style apple tarts

Blood-orange juice

LEMON BREAD

Pain au citron

Lemon bread is another breakfast favourite of mine. The kids love it for morning tea or to go with their school lunches. This recipe requires you use quite a bit of lemon zest, so to avoid wasting the lemons it is a good idea to use the juice of the lemon to prepare fresh lemonade, make a lemon tart (see page 309) or lemon cream (see page 319).

4 free-range eggs

300 g (1½ cups) caster sugar

2 pinches of salt

200 g (1⅔ cups) plain flour, sifted

½ teaspoon baking powder, sifted

finely grated zest of 3 lemons

125 ml (½ cup) pouring cream

100 g butter, melted and cooled

Preheat the oven to 180°C. Lightly grease a 25 x 12 x 10 cm loaf tin with oil spray and line with baking paper.

Put the eggs in the bowl of an electric mixer with a whisk attachment and mix for 1 minute. Add the sugar and salt and beat for about 2 minutes on high speed until thick and creamy. With the mixer on low speed, slowly add the flour and baking powder to combine, then add the lemon zest and cream alternately to avoid creating lumps. Add the melted butter, scrape the sides of the bowl and mix well until combined.

Pour the batter into the prepared tin and smooth the top. Bake in the oven for 1 hour. Check to ensure the centre is cooked by testing with a wooden skewer — if it comes out clean the bread is done. If it is still wet, cook for a further 10 minutes. If the bread browns too quickly on top, cover with a sheet of baking paper. Allow to cool for 10–15 minutes in the tin before turning out onto a wire rack to cool completely.

VARIATIONS: You can use finely grated orange or grapefruit zest instead of the lemon. If serving as a dessert, a citrus ice cream makes a nice addition.

ALMOND BREAD
Pain d'amande

Makes 1 loaf

I started making this almond bread after cyclone damage devastated the banana crops of Northern Australia, resulting in some very expensive fruit. This bread does not toast as well as banana bread so any bread eaten a day or two after it is made should be spread with some soft butter.

225 g softened butter

150 g (¾ cup) caster sugar

3 free-range eggs, beaten

250 g (2 cups) self-raising flour, sifted

100 g (1 cup) ground almonds

finely grated zest of ½ lemon

125 ml (½ cup) milk

Preheat the oven to 170°C. Lightly grease a 22 x 12 x 10 cm loaf tin with oil spray and line with baking paper.

Cream the butter and sugar together in the bowl of an electric mixer until it is white and creamy. On low speed, add the eggs one at a time. Add the flour and ground almonds, then add the lemon zest and lastly the milk to avoid creating lumps. Scrape the sides of the bowl and mix until well combined.

Pour the batter into the prepared tin and smooth the top. Bake in the oven for 45 minutes. Check to ensure the centre is cooked by testing with a wooden skewer — if it comes out clean the bread is done. If it is still wet, cook for a further 15 minutes. If the bread browns too quickly on top, cover with a sheet of baking paper. Allow to cool completely in the tin to avoid breaking it.

When the bread is cool but still warm cut into thick slices and serve with butter. You can also serve it as a dessert with some softly whipped cream and berries or poached fruit.

VARIATIONS: It is easy to add dried fruit, like dates, or dried blueberries, cranberries, apple or mango, to the mix. Just soak approximately 2 tablespoons of dried fruit in 2 tablespoons of boiling water for 15 minutes. Drain and then mix into the almond cake batter to combine before pouring into the tin. You could also make the bread in small muffin tins.

BANANA BREAD

Pain à la banane

Makes 1 loaf

This classic banana bread has been cooked in every kitchen I have ever worked in — that's how good it is. Enjoy it at home, cut into slices and warmed under the grill, then smothered with butter — delicious! For the best results use overripe bananas.

300 g ripe bananas

300 g (1½ cups) caster sugar

3 free-range eggs

300 g plain flour, sifted

2 pinches of salt

1 tablespoon baking powder

125 ml (½ cup) full-cream milk

80 ml (⅓ cup) vegetable oil

Preheat the oven to 180°C. Lightly grease a 25 x 12 x 10 cm loaf tin with oil spray and line with baking paper.

Put the bananas and sugar in the bowl of an electric mixer and mix on medium speed for a few minutes, or until combined. Reduce the speed to low and add the eggs, one at a time, until combined. Mix well at medium speed. Reduce the speed, add the flour, salt and baking powder, then add the milk and vegetable oil and mix at medium speed for 4–5 minutes, or until you have a smooth batter.

Pour the mixture into the prepared tin and bake for 90 minutes. Check to ensure the centre is cooked by testing with a wooden skewer — if it comes out clean the bread is done. If it is still wet, cook for a further 5 minutes. If the bread browns too quickly on top, cover with a sheet of baking paper. Allow to cool for 10–15 minutes in the tin before turning out onto a wire rack to cool completely. The bread will keep for 1 week refrigerated.

When the bread is cool but still warm, cut into thick slices and serve with butter or a dusting of icing sugar. Banana bread is also great when toasted under a grill and spread with butter.

VARIATIONS: Add some dried dates, toasted walnuts, pecans or hazelnuts, or even a cup of shredded coconut to the mix.

BLACKBERRY BRAN MUFFINS

Muffins au son et aux mûres   Makes 6 large muffins or 12 standard muffins

These days muffins are quite easy to purchase from just about any bakery or café,
but there is nothing like making your own. Vary the mixture by adding fresh berries,
chopped bananas, cooked apples, seeds or even cinnamon.

250 g (2 cups) plain
flour

1 tablespoon baking
powder

2 pinches of salt

100 g (½ cup) brown
sugar

60 g butter, melted and
cooled

1 tablespoon vegetable oil

2 free-range eggs

2 tablespoons molasses
or treacle

250 ml (1 cup)
full-cream milk

100 g (1½ cups) bran
flakes

150 g blackberries or
raspberries

Preheat the oven to 200°C. Lightly grease a 6-hole large muffin tin or
a 12-hole standard muffin tin with oil spray, line each hole with a square
of baking paper and spray again.

Sift the flour, baking powder and salt into a bowl and stir in the sugar to
combine.

Put the melted butter, oil, eggs, molasses or treacle and half of the milk
in the bowl of an electric mixer fitted with a whisk attachment and mix
well to combine. Add the flour mixture, in batches, until combined,
then gradually add the remaining milk, mixing at low speed. Stop the
mixer, remove the whisk and use a wooden spoon to gently stir through
the bran. Add the berries and fold in, to evenly distribute through the
muffin batter.

Fill each muffin hole about two-thirds full. Bake for about 20 minutes.

Check to ensure the centres are cooked by testing with a wooden skewer
— if it comes out clean the muffins are done. If it is still wet, cook for
a further 5–10 minutes. Allow to cool for 10 minutes in the tin before
turning out onto a wire rack to cool completely.

VARIATIONS: Replace the berries with chopped walnuts or flaked or
toasted almonds. The recipe can be adapted to use just about anything
healthy — try grated carrot or zucchini for something different.

PARIS-STYLE APPLE TARTS

Tarte aux pommes Parisienne

I always loved the apple tarts made by the legendary French baker Lionel Poilâne in Paris. They are unadorned, with a pure apple taste that is perfect served for breakfast or as a midday snack. At Poilâne the apple tarts are cooked in a wood-fired oven on the last bake of the day when the oven is cool, so this recipe could never have the same cachet of eating his tart in Paris, but at least you can understand a little of the genius of the best baker that France has ever seen.

500 g sugar pastry
(see page 26)

plain flour, for dusting

4 Granny Smith apples, peeled, cored and cut into eighths

1 tablespoon full-cream milk

Lightly grease four 10 cm round tart tins with oil spray.

Take the pastry out of the refrigerator about 10 minutes before you wish to start rolling so it is easier to work with. Lightly flour the work surface. Cut the pastry into four equal portions and roll each portion out to make 15 cm circles, about 2–3 mm thick all over. Gently push the pastry into the base of each tart tin, making sure you leave no pockets of air around the base. Refrigerate for 2 hours.

Preheat the oven to 180°C.

Arrange 8 apple pieces in the base of each tart. Fold the overhanging pastry partly over the apple towards the centre and refrigerate for 10 minutes to firm up.

Just before cooking, brush the pastry edges of each tart with the milk and bake for about 30 minutes, checking after 20 minutes, or until the crust is golden. Remove from the oven and allow to cool in the tins. These are best served warm.

VARIATIONS: Experimenting with different apple and pear varieties will produce varying results. If you wish to make a different shape you could make a long, narrow flan.

SUGAR PASTRY
Pâte sucrée

Makes 750 g

This is a very soft pastry that needs to be rested in the refrigerator after you line your mould or after it is laid out each time to prevent it from shrinking when cooked. It will produce a deliciously sweet and crispy pastry, ideal for using in many desserts, especially tarts, although it also makes a terrific base for some cakes, including baked cheesecake (see page 302). The dough will need to be rested for 4 hours or overnight in the refrigerator before rolling.

150 g (¾ cup) caster sugar

160 g butter, diced and softened

¼ teaspoon vanilla bean paste

2 free-range eggs

320 g plain flour, sifted

Put the sugar and butter in the bowl of an electric mixer fitted with a paddle attachment. Mix on low speed for 4 minutes. Add the vanilla, then the eggs, one at a time, and continue mixing on low speed until well combined. Add the flour and mix on low speed until just combined to avoid the dough becoming elastic. Gather into a ball, wrap in plastic wrap and refrigerate for 4 hours or overnight.

When you are ready to use the pastry, simply cut off the portion required (make sure you weigh it for accuracy) and roll as directed in each recipe.

Any leftover pastry can be frozen for up to I week. I recommend separating the pastry into two portions and re-wrapping in plastic wrap — press it with your hand to have a squarish slab which will make it easier to defrost and roll.

VARIATIONS: You can add I teaspoon finely grated lemon zest to the dough or scrape some vanilla seeds from the bean directly into the dough. You could also add 50 g ground almonds and reduce the amount of flour used.

BOILED EGGS WITH SMOKED SALMON AND FROMAGE BLANC

Oeufs mollets au saumon fumé et au fromage blanc   Serves 4

I love soft-boiled eggs — they take about 6 minutes to cook and can be difficult to handle and peel unless plunged in iced water for a short time. Another 2 minutes and you have a firm egg with a soft, nearly runny yolk, which also tastes delicious. Another 2 minutes and you have a perfect hard-boiled egg. You can make your own fromage blanc, which will transform this simple dish.

4 large free-range eggs

4 slices sourdough bread

50 g butter

100 g (⅓ cup) fromage blanc (see page 4) or cream cheese

200 g smoked salmon

A few sprigs of chervil or chives

Put the eggs in a small saucepan, being careful not to crack them. Pour in just enough boiling water to cover the eggs and place over medium heat. Cook the eggs for 6–8 minutes — they should be firm with a soft yolk.

Meanwhile, toast the slices of sourdough bread and spread with the butter. Spread the fromage blanc over the top and cover with slices of smoked salmon.

When the eggs are cooked, plunge them into a bowl of iced water for 10 seconds, then peel and cut each egg in half. Season with sea salt and finely ground black pepper and arrange the egg halves over the salmon. Garnish with the chervil or chives.

VARIATIONS: You could easily substitute the smoked salmon with slices of ripe tomato, or even replace the fromage blanc with ricotta or cottage cheese.

RATATOUILLE WITH CRISPY FRIED EGG

Oeuf en croûte à la ratatouille

Texture is an important part of eating and in this recipe the eggs are cooked in a surprising way to achieve a different taste and texture experience. To bite into a crunchy egg with a runny yolk is quite a unique experience.

250 ml (1 cup) extra virgin olive oil

2 garlic cloves

1 eggplant, diced into 3 cm cubes

1 onion, diced

1 red capsicum, seeded and diced into 3 cm cubes

1 green capsicum, seeded and diced into 3 cm cubes

2 zucchini, peeled and thickly sliced

4 bay leaves

2 thyme sprigs

½ bunch basil

½ bunch oregano, leaves only

2 tomatoes, cored, each cut into 8 wedges

olive oil, for deep-frying

100 g (1 cup) dry breadcrumbs

125 ml (½ cup) parmesan cheese

4 free-range eggs, poached (see page 31)

1 free-range egg, well beaten, for egg wash

Heat the extra virgin olive oil in a large heavy-based saucepan. When the oil is smoking, add the garlic and fry for 1 minute, or until golden. Remove the garlic from the pan using a slotted spoon and finely chop and set aside.

In the same pan, fry the eggplant for 5 minutes, or until the eggplant is brown on all sides. Remove the eggplant using a slotted spoon or tongs and drain on paper towels. Add the onion and cook until golden brown, then remove to a plate.

Add more oil to the pan if necessary and fry the capsicums for 3 minutes. Remove and drain on paper towels. Add the zucchini and cook for 5 minutes, or until they are golden and partly cooked. Put all the vegetables back into the pan with the herbs, garlic and tomato and cook over high heat for a few minutes.

Fill a deep, heavy-based saucepan one-third full of olive oil and heat until a cube of bread dropped into the oil browns in 15 seconds.

Mix the breadcrumbs and parmesan in a small bowl and dip the poached eggs firstly into the beaten egg and then into the parmesan crumbs to evenly coat all over. Gently lower the crumbed eggs into the oil and fry for 1 minute, or until golden brown. Remove with a slotted spoon and drain on paper towels.

When you are ready to serve, season the ratatouille with salt and pepper and spoon into four serving bowls. Sit an egg over the ratatouille and serve.

CORN CAKES WITH FRENCH FRIED EGGS

Gâteau de maïs aux œufs frits

Serves 4

I love corn and corn cakes. I even add corn to my pancake mix from time to time (see page 11). These corn cakes are very versatile and can be served for breakfast or lunch. They are best made for a maximum of 4 people as the eggs are quite fragile and the yolks can easily break.

250 g (2 cups) plain flour

1 tablespoon baking powder

250 ml (1 cup) milk

1 handful watercress, trimmed, blanched and refreshed

2 corn cobs, cooked and kernels removed

4 free-range eggs, separated

1 pinch of salt

2 tablespoons vegetable oil

1 tablespoon butter

150 ml peanut oil or vegetable oil

4 free-range eggs

1 handful flat-leaf parsley leaves, to serve

Mix together the flour, baking powder and milk in a bowl and season with salt and pepper. Roughly chop the blanched watercress and add to the batter. Add the corn and season well. Set aside.

Put the egg whites in the bowl of an electric mixer fitted with a whisk attachment (making sure the bowl is clean). Add the salt and whisk until stiff peaks form. Taking small amounts at a time to retain the airy texture, fold the egg whites into the corn mixture.

Heat a little of the oil and butter in a frying pan over medium heat. Drop a few spoonfuls of the corn mixture into the pan at a time to make small corn cakes. Cook for 2 minutes on each side, then remove to a plate and keep warm in a low oven. Repeat with the remaining batter to make eight corn cakes in total.

Heat the peanut oil in a frying pan over high heat until it is nearly smoking. Add one egg and tilt the pan to gather the oil. The egg will start to fry; use a tablespoon to fold the white over the yolk. Once the white is crisp, flip the egg over to cook the other side. Drain on paper towels to remove any excess oil. Repeat with the remaining eggs.

When all the eggs are fried, add the parsley to the oil (being careful not to splash yourself) and fry for a few seconds. Remove the parsley with a slotted spoon and drain on paper towels.

Divide the corn cakes between warm plates, top with a fried egg and garnish with the fried parsley.

VARIATIONS: Use poached eggs (see page 31) instead of the fried eggs, or serve the corn cakes with a fresh watercress and avocado salad.

POACHED EGGS WITH HERBS AND ASPARAGUS

Oeufs pochés aux fines herbes et aux asperges

Serves 4

This is an old-fashioned recipe where the poached eggs are simmered in herb butter. The butter is melted over low heat, the herbs are added and then the already poached eggs are tossed in the butter before serving over freshly cooked asparagus.

8 free-range eggs

100 ml white vinegar

150 g butter

1 handful mixed herbs, such as flat-leaf parsley, chervil, tarragon or chives, chopped

4 bunches asparagus, about 175 g per bunch, peeled and trimmed into 12 cm lengths

To poach the eggs, put 1 litre (4 cups) water in a saucepan over high heat. Add the vinegar and bring to a simmer. Break an egg into the water and gently allow it to sink to the bottom of the pan. Gently move the egg with a slotted spoon in a circular movement to ensure the white evenly coats the yolk. Cook for a touch longer than 2 minutes for soft or 4 minutes for medium and firm. Poach two eggs at a time and once cooked, remove with a slotted spoon and plunge immediately into a bowl of iced water to stop the cooking process and to firm them up. Neatly trim the edge of each egg.

Melt the butter in a frying pan over low heat and add the chopped herbs, then the eggs. Immediately remove from the heat (the idea is to warm up the egg but not cook the yolk) and season with salt and pepper.

Blanch the asparagus in a saucepan of salted boiling water for 2 minutes, then drain well.

Arrange the asparagus spears on serving plates. Turn the eggs in the herb butter to coat, then place two eggs on each plate and drizzle with the herb butter.

VARIATIONS: You can add shaved parmesan to the top of the eggs before pouring the butter over. The eggs can also be served on blanched spinach, wilted rocket or watercress instead of the asparagus. You could make soft-boiled eggs instead of poached and toss them in the herb butter. Using anchovy paste instead of the herbs provides a different flavour.

NOTE: You can serve poached eggs straightaway or prepare them ahead of time — they can be kept in the refrigerator for up to a day. You will need to gently reheat them before serving. To do this simply plunge them in salted simmering water.

POACHED EGGS WITH SMOKED OCEAN TROUT AND HOLLANDAISE SAUCE

Oeufs poché à la truite fumé, sauce hollandaise

Serves 4

Smoked ocean trout, or for that matter salmon, and eggs make a great food combination. Céleste, my daughter, is a lover of smoked salmon or ocean trout and for a real treat I sometimes make a hollandaise sauce to go with her breakfast.

Hollandaise sauce

50 ml white wine vinegar

2 French shallots, finely chopped

1 tarragon sprig

1 pinch white pepper

4 free-range egg yolks

400 ml clarified butter (see Note page 203), lukewarm

juice of 1 lemon

50 g butter

250 g watercress or baby English spinach

1 French baguette, cut into thick slices, toasted

200 g smoked ocean trout

8 free-range eggs, poached (see page 31)

To make the hollandaise, combine the vinegar, shallots, tarragon and pepper in a saucepan, bring to the boil and simmer until reduced by half. Remove from the heat and cool.

Place the egg yolks and vinegar reduction in a stainless steel bowl over a saucepan of simmering water or on top of a double boiler on low heat. Whisk for about 3 minutes, or until thickened and creamy. You must be careful to avoid overcooking the eggs or they will scramble and the sauce might become lumpy.

Remove from the heat and slowly incorporate the clarified butter — at first a little at a time and then more as the volume of your sauce increases. If the sauce becomes too thick, add a splash of hot water or a squeeze of lemon. When all the butter is added, season with salt and white pepper and the remaining lemon juice. Place in a warm spot until ready to use.

Melt the butter in a saucepan over high heat. Add the watercress or spinach and cook for 2 minutes, or until it wilts. Remove from the heat and season with salt and pepper. If you are using spinach, squeeze the leaves once cooked to remove any excess moisture. Arrange the toasted baguette slices on warm plates, set the smoked ocean trout and eggs on top. Lay a good portion of watercress or spinach over each egg and spoon a generous dollop of hollandaise on top, to serve.

VARIATIONS: Instead of the smoked ocean trout you could use smoked salmon, smoked ham or some sliced smoked pork loin. Cut some thick slices of eggplant and fry them to use as a base instead of the bread.

SCRAMBLED EGGS WITH TRUFFLE AND MUSHROOM

Oeufs brouillés à la truffe et aux champignons   Serves 4

This is a special occasion dish that I make each year for family birthdays. I either try to get truffles from France in the summer months for my wife's birthday, or fresh black truffles from Australia for my birthday in July. The secret to this dish is patience — you have to infuse the eggs for four days in a sealed jar with the whole truffle to allow the flavour and aroma to impart, but it is well worth the wait.

4 large field mushrooms

125 ml (½ cup) olive oil

60 g butter, diced and
softened

8 free-range eggs

50 ml pouring cream

1 fresh black truffle,
thinly sliced into
rounds

Preheat the oven to 180°C.

Put the mushrooms on a baking tray with the oil and roast in the oven for 20 minutes, or until cooked and tender. Keep warm.

Use a little bit of the butter to grease a heavy-based saucepan. Whisk the truffle-infused eggs in a bowl with the remaining butter until well combined. Season with salt and pepper.

Pour the eggs into the prepared pan and set over a saucepan of hot water (just below boiling point). Stir the eggs continuously in a slow movement, making sure you scrape the bottom and sides of the pan to avoid the eggs overcooking. Continue stirring until the eggs are creamy and cooked. Remove the pan from the heat. Add the cream and stir until well incorporated.

To serve, place the mushrooms on four warm serving plates and spoon the scrambled eggs over the top. Scatter the sliced truffle over the eggs.

VARIATIONS: Blanched sliced asparagus or sautéed diced tomatoes with basil can also be served with the truffled eggs. A little shaved parmesan also makes a nice addition.

BAKED EGGS IN CRUSTY BREAD WITH PANCETTA

Oeuf en croûte de pain

Every member of the family will love these crusty rolls. They are filling and great for breakfast on a winter's day before venturing out for a game of soccer or a walk in the park.

8 slices stringy pancetta
   or thin bacon

4 crusty bread rolls
   (rosetta rolls are ideal)

125 g butter

8 free-range eggs

Preheat the oven to 160°C.

Place the sliced pancetta or bacon on a baking tray lined with baking paper. Roast in the oven for 15–20 minutes, until crispy, making sure to check the slices regularly to prevent them from burning. Keep warm.

Cut the tops off the rolls and scoop out most of the soft bread. Melt half of the butter and brush the inside of the rolls. Set the rolls on a baking tray and crack two eggs into the hole in each roll. Slice a thin piece of the remaining butter and set on top of each egg to prevent them from overcooking. Bake for about 10 minutes, or until the white of the egg is firm.

Serve the rolls in flat bowls with the pancetta and season with salt and pepper.

VARIATIONS: After you have brushed the rolls with melted butter you can line them with slices of ham or Gruyère cheese, or fill the bottom of the roll with sautéed spinach or garlic mushrooms.

PEACH CAKE

Gâteau aux pêches

Serves 8

This is a great cake to serve sliced for breakfast or for school lunches. It is an alternative to banana bread. You could use nectarines, apricots, pears or apples in the wintertime.

1 kg ripe peaches

350 g butter, softened

2 tablespoons honey

250 g (1¼ cups) caster sugar

4 free-range eggs

250 g (2 cups) self-raising flour

1 pinch of salt

2 pinches of ground ginger

Preheat the oven to 160°C. Lightly grease a 22 cm round cake tin with oil spray, then dust with flour and refrigerate until ready to use.

Blanch the peaches briefly in boiling water, then remove the skin. Cut the peaches into wedges, discarding the stones. In a large frying pan, melt 100 g of the butter and add the peaches. Cook over medium heat for 3–4 minutes to soften, then add the honey and cook for 2 minutes, or until the peaches have caramelised. Remove from the heat and set aside.

Cream the sugar and remaining butter in the bowl of an electric mixer fitted with a whisk attachment on high speed for 5 minutes, or until the sugar has dissolved and the mixture is light and fluffy. Add the eggs, one at a time, and mix on low speed for 3–4 minutes until combined. Add the flour, salt and ground ginger and mix well.

Line the bottom of the cake tin with a layer of caramelised peaches. Dice any leftover peaches and add them, with any cooking juices, to the cake batter, folding well to combine. Pour into the tin and bake in the oven for 90 minutes. Check to ensure the centre is cooked by testing with a wooden skewer — if it comes out clean the cake is done. If it is still wet, cook for a further 10 minutes. Allow to cool for 10–15 minutes in the tin before turning out onto a wire rack to cool completely.

VARIATIONS: You could make this cake in a bread tin, serve it for dessert with chantilly cream or serve it with ice cream.

BAKED CHEESE CUSTARD

Ramequin de Beaufort à la crème

These smooth custards are delicious for a weekend breakfast. They can be made ahead of time, even the day before you are going to eat them. Serve them in individual dishes or turn out of their moulds and serve with toast fingers.

250 ml (1 cup)
    full-cream milk

30 g butter

40 g (⅓ cup) plain flour

1 pinch of nutmeg

100 g (¾ cup) grated
    Beaufort or Gruyère
    cheese

3 free-range egg yolks

2 free-range egg whites

300 ml pouring cream

Preheat the oven to 180°C. Lightly grease six 8 x 4 cm (or 2/3 cup) ramekins with oil spray. Lightly grease a baking dish with oil spray.

Put the milk in a saucepan over medium heat and bring to the boil. Once boiling, remove from the heat and set aside.

Melt the butter in a separate saucepan over low heat. Add the flour and stir for 2 minutes with a wooden spoon. Add the milk and whisk, to remove any lumps, until thick and smooth. Season with the nutmeg, salt and pepper, and lastly add two-thirds of the cheese and the egg yolks, mixing well to combine. Remove from the heat and allow to cool. Whisk the egg whites to stiff peaks and fold into the custard.

Spoon the custard into the ramekins until about two-thirds full. Sit the ramekins in a deep roasting tray and pour in enough boiling water to come halfway up the side of the ramekins. Cook in the oven for 20 minutes, or until set. Remove from the oven and allow to cool.

Gently turn the custards out of the ramekins and sit them in the prepared baking dish. Sprinkle the remaining cheese over the custards, pour the cream over the top and bake in the oven for 15 minutes, or until the cheese is gratinée or browned.

Serve in the baking dish at the table with some toasted sourdough bread.

VARIATIONS: This custard could be served with a fresh tomato sauce (see page 172) instead of the cream. You could also serve the custard in the ramekins, with sautéed mushrooms or spinach on the side, or bake the custard in small individual gratin dishes.

MUSHROOM TARTLET WITH GREEN VEGETABLES

Tartelette de légumes verts à la duxelle

Serves 4

This is a beautiful looking breakfast tart filled with mushroom duxelles and served with a healthy dose of fresh green vegetables. Sometimes I leave out the mushrooms and simply fill the tart shells with the vegetables and serve them with a hollandaise sauce (see page 32) — this creates a richer flavour and makes a great alternative to eggs Benedict.

2 sheets puff pastry

8 field mushrooms, peeled, stems removed and roughly chopped

50 ml olive oil

150 g butter, diced

2 French shallots, finely chopped

1 garlic clove, finely chopped

1 large handful (200 g) mixed green vegetables, such as asparagus, snow peas, green beans, broccoli and sugar snap peas, trimmed, prepared, blanched and refreshed

4 free-range eggs, poached (see page 31)

1 handful snow pea leaves (optional), to serve

Preheat the oven to 100°C. Lightly grease four 10 cm round tart tins, about 3 cm deep, with oil spray.

Roll out the pastry on a lightly floured surface to about 3 mm thick. Cut the pastry into four equal portions, then into 14 cm rounds. Press into the tart tins making sure you leave no air pockets around the base. Trim the edges and refrigerate for 30 minutes.

Line the tart shells with baking paper and pour in enough uncooked rice or baking beads to fill. Bake in the oven for 15–20 minutes, or until golden and crisp. Remove from the oven, discard the rice and baking paper and allow to cool.

To make the mushroom duxelles, put the mushrooms in a food processor and process until finely chopped. Heat the oil and 50 g of the butter in a frying pan over high heat. Add the shallots and garlic and cook for 1 minute, without colouring. Add the mushrooms and cook for approximately 30 minutes, or until most of the moisture has evaporated. Season well with salt and pepper, then stir in 50 g more of butter.

Re-heat the tart shells in the oven.

In a large saucepan, melt the remaining butter over low heat. Add the blanched vegetables and sauté them for 2 minutes to warm through. Season with salt and pepper.

Spoon the mushrooms into the warm tart shells, top with the vegetables, the poached eggs and some snow pea leaves.

VARIATIONS: Add smoked salmon, sliced ham or roasted cherry tomatoes instead of or with the poached egg.

BAKED SALMON WITH LEEKS, POTATOES AND CREAM

Saumon à la crème de poireaux

This is a rich breakfast dish that is ideal for Sunday brunches. Instead of the salmon you can use ocean trout or even poached smoked fish. The leek and potatoes can be pre-cooked and the dish baked just before serving.

1 tablespoon butter

2 large potatoes, peeled and cut into small chunks

1 leek, white part only, rinsed and finely chopped

1 garlic clove, sliced

300 ml pouring cream

4 x 80 g salmon fillets

½ tablespoon chopped flat-leaf parsley

Preheat the oven to 160°C. Lightly grease four 10 cm round baking dishes, about 6 cm deep, or one 24 cm long baking dish, with butter.

Put the potatoes, leek, garlic and cream in a small casserole dish over medium heat and cook for about 15 minutes, or until the potatoes are tender. Strain the vegetables, and return the cream to the dish over medium heat and continue to cook until the liquid reduces by one-third.

Season the salmon with salt and pepper and place in the centre of each dish. Spread the leek and potato around the salmon and pour the reduced cream over the top. Sit the dishes in a deep roasting tin and bake in the oven for 10 minutes. Garnish with parsley before serving.

VARIATIONS: To create a vegetarian version of this dish, simply replace the salmon fillets with chopped, roasted field mushrooms (see page 33) or steamed green beans. Serve with toasted sourdough bread or with a poached egg for a rich winter breakfast.

TOULOUSE SAUSAGE WITH ROAST TRELLIS TOMATOES

Saucisse de Toulouse aux tomates rôties

Serves 4

Toulouse sausages are a classic French sausage made with diced pork and garlic and often sold in a coil or spiral. They are used in cassoulet or other dishes that need a robust sausage. Your butcher will be able to make one for you held together with bamboo skewers or you could use any pre-made coiled sausage.

125 ml (½ cup) vegetable oil

1 kg pork sausage with garlic or any other fresh coil sausage

400 g trellis tomatoes

50 g butter

2 large potatoes, boiled in the skin, peeled and grated

Preheat the oven to 150°C.

Heat 1½ tablespoons of the oil in a frying pan over medium heat. Sear the sausage for about 5 minutes, until you have achieved good colour, then turn and cook for a further 2 minutes. Arrange the sausage in a roasting tray and place in the warm oven — it will finish cooking slowly and stay warm while you prepare the tomatoes.

Wipe the pan clean with paper towels. Heat another 1½ tablespoons of the oil in the pan over high heat. Add the tomatoes, in a bunch, and sear well on both sides. Transfer to the tray, with the sausage, in the oven. Some tomatoes might fall off but just put them with the sausage.

Wipe the pan clean with paper towels. Add another 1½ tablespoons of the oil to the pan with half of the butter over medium heat. Add the potato and spread out to make a large pancake. Season with salt and pepper and cook for 10–15 minutes, or until the potato is crispy and golden. Place a large plate over the potato in the pan and carefully flip over the pan to remove the potato cake.

Clean the pan with paper towels, add the remaining oil and butter and return the potato cake to the pan to cook the other side for 10 minutes — a nice crust should form. Season again.

To serve, arrange the sausage, tomato and potato on a warm platter for your guests to help themselves.

VARIATIONS: Skewer regular pork sausages together to form a large sausage flan if you cannot source a single long sausage from your butcher. Roma tomatoes, cut into halves, can replace trellis tomatoes.

BLACK PUDDING WITH ROAST PEAR AND SAUTÉED POTATOES

Boudin noir aux poires   Serves 4

Black or blood pudding is a unique food delicacy that may not appeal to everyone but which I learnt to love at a young age. My grandfather was a butcher and you could see the coiled sausages hanging from the hooks in his shopfront window. My father was the one who prepared this dish at home. Since coming to Australia I have added pear to his recipe, which gives a contrast in flavour.

3 tablespoons vegetable oil

4 small onions, halved

100 g butter

2 pears, cored and halved

500 g black pudding, cut into small pieces

2 large Dutch Cream or kipfler potatoes, boiled with skin on and sliced

1 teaspoon chopped flat-leaf parsley

Preheat the oven to 160°C.

Heat 1 tablespoon of the oil in a cast-iron frying pan (if you have one) over medium heat. Add the onion, cut side down, and cook for 10 minutes, or until the onion is a nice dark brown colour, and turn over. Season with salt and pepper.

Add one-third of the butter to the pan and place the pears in the pan, cut side down. Cover with a sheet of foil and cook in the oven for 20 minutes, or until the pears and onion are tender. Remove from the pan and set aside on a plate.

In the same pan, heat half of the remaining butter and 1 tablespoon of the oil over medium heat. Add the black pudding and cook for 10 minutes — a few well-cooked edges will only add to the taste of the dish. Once cooked, remove the black pudding to a plate and set aside.

Add the remaining butter and oil to the pan over high heat. Add the potatoes and cook for 10 minutes on all sides, or until a nice golden colour. Season with salt and pepper, then add the chopped parsley. Return the black pudding, pears and onions to the pan and transfer to the oven for 10 minutes to heat through before serving.

VARIATIONS: If you can't find blood pudding for this dish, try using cervelat or kransky sausages instead. For a savoury version you can roast tomatoes instead of pears.

BEEF HASH

Hachis parmentier

Serves 4

This dish is more North American in style than French, but I learnt to prepare it when I started to cook in hotels and I have cooked it at home and on the farm for a hearty breakfast.

400 g cooked corned beef

4 potatoes, boiled with skins on and cooled

I tablespoon vegetable oil

I small onion, finely chopped

50 g butter

I tablespoon tomato paste

I tablespoon chopped flat-leaf parsley

Dice the corned beef into small cubes. Peel the potatoes and dice to the same size as the corned beef.

Heat the oil in a large nonstick frying pan over medium heat. Add the onion and cook for 2 minutes, or until it has softened but not browned. Increase the heat and add the potato and butter; season with salt and pepper. Sauté for 10 minutes, or until the potato starts to form a crust.

Add the beef, tomato paste and parsley to the pan and mix well. Cook for 10 minutes, turning gently to crust up on all sides, being careful not to stir too much to avoid crushing the mixture. Serve on warm plates.

VARIATIONS: This dish is a great way to use up leftover roast or boiled meats — lamb and beef are both good alternatives. I often serve this hash with a fried or poached egg, which makes it a complete breakfast.

I love the seasonal,
regional and unusual;
pomegranate is such
an evocative fruit –
mysterious, gorgeous
and delicious.

LUNCH

Lunch

For me, lunch is a salad with a crispy vegetable tart or simple smoked trout, or in the winter a warm soup. In France, a simple baguette with pâté, often homemade, or a soupe au pistou is enough to replenish. I love the seasons and the produce that comes and goes – fennel paired with anchovy or a stunning heirloom tomato salad with sea salt and tasty feta are two of my ideal summer lunches.

ONION SOUP
Soupe à l'onion gratinée

This is a classic French soup that is very satisfying and easy to make as it contains very few ingredients and can be made with water if you don't have any stock. Just take into account that you might need more seasoning if you do not use stock.

2 tablespoons vegetable oil

8 large brown onions, thinly sliced

3 litres (12 cups) vegetable, chicken or beef stock (see pages 61–62) or water

500 ml (2 cups) white wine (optional), or extra water

4 bay leaves

2 thyme sprigs

4 slices sourdough bread, toasted, to serve

200 g Gruyère or Emmental cheese, grated, to serve

Heat the oil in a very large saucepan or stockpot over high heat. Add the onion and cook for 5 minutes, stirring well to coat in the oil. Reduce the heat to low and sweat the onion for about 20 minutes — they will give up plenty of steam and reduce in volume, slowly acquiring some colour; stir from time to time until the onion is golden. Add the stock or water, wine, bay leaves and thyme and season with salt and pepper. Bring to the boil, then reduce the heat and simmer for 40–60 minutes, or until the onion is tender. Discard the thyme and bay leaves.

Preheat the grill to high. When ready to serve, fill ovenproof serving bowls two-thirds full of hot soup. Break some of the toasted sourdough over the top of each bowl and sprinkle the cheese over the bread. Grill until you have a nice crust.

NOTE: This soup can be stored in an airtight container in the refrigerator for up to 4 days.

PEA SOUP WITH GARDEN GREENS

Soupe de pois frais aux herbes du jardin

Serves 8

I have always enjoyed making pea soup. I started to make this soup the way my father used to, with dried split green peas, but now I use fresh if I can get them, or sometimes frozen peas, which produce a vibrant and light pea soup.

2 litres (8 cups) vegetable stock (see page 61)

1 small potato, peeled and diced

1 garlic clove, finely chopped

500 g (3¼ cups) fresh or frozen peas

100 g butter

8 free range eggs, poached (optional) (see page 31)

½ iceberg lettuce, diced

1 bunch chives, cut into short sticks

1 bunch chervil, leaves picked

¼ bunch flat-leaf parsley, finely chopped

1 tablespoon mint leaves, finely chopped

Put the vegetable stock, potato and garlic in a large saucepan or stockpot over medium heat. Cook for 10 minutes, or until the potato is tender. Add the peas and bring to the boil. As soon as the water boils, remove from the heat and strain the vegetables, reserving the liquid.

Put the peas and potato in a deep pot and start blending with a stick blender, adding spoonfuls of the stock as needed to reach a smooth consistency. Add the butter and blend until smooth; adjusting the seasoning to taste. You could also make this in small batches in a blender or food processor.

Sit the warm poached eggs in serving bowls over the iceberg lettuce and top with the herbs. Pour the soup into bowls at the table to serve.

VEGETABLE AND PESTO SOUP

Soupe au pistou

This soup has everything going for it, including the fact that the whole family will love it too! Flavour, colour, substance and easy to put together — it doesn't get much better than this.

150 g (¾ cup) white
    cannellini beans,
    soaked in cold water
    for 4 hours

2 carrots, diced

1 onion, diced

1 small leek, white part
    only, rinsed and diced

1 large potato, peeled
    and diced

2 zucchini, partly peeled
    and diced

100 g green beans,
    trimmed and cut into
    short lengths

4 bay leaves

2 thyme sprigs

Pesto

2 tomatoes, halved

4 garlic cloves

1 bunch basil

125 ml (½ cup) olive oil

Drain the cannellini beans and rinse under cold running water, then drain again. Put the beans in a large saucepan or stockpot with 2 litres (8 cups) water. Bring to the boil, then reduce the heat and simmer for 1 hour, or until they start to split.

Meanwhile, make the pesto. Preheat the oven to 160°C. Put the tomatoes and garlic on a baking tray and roast in the oven for 15 minutes, or until the garlic is soft. Peel the tomato skins and place the flesh in a blender or food processor with the garlic, basil and olive oil. Process for a few seconds to create a coarse paste.

Drain the beans and return to the clean pan over medium heat. Add the carrots, onion, leek, potato, zucchini, green beans and herbs and cover with 3 litres (12 cups) water. Season with salt and simmer for 1 hour, or until the cannellini beans are soft but not mashed. Check the seasoning, to taste.

Ladle the soup into serving bowls and serve with a tablespoon of the pesto in each bowl.

VARIATIONS: For a winter meal, cook a veal shank in water seasoned with salt until tender, skimming as often as necessary to remove any scum. Serve the shank with the bone in a large serving bowl, or when the shank has cooled a little, shred the meat off the bone and divide between the serving bowls, then ladle the soup over the top.

NOTE: Any leftover pesto can be stored in an airtight container in the refrigerator for up to 5 days.

CAULIFLOWER SOUP

Soupe de choux-fleur

This is another easy soup to make at home; in general I do not use stock to make it unless I have some homemade vegetable stock on hand. You can use the same method to make carrot or potato and leek soup. I use butter to enrich the soup, but you can also add a touch of cream.

1 kg cauliflower

100 g butter

1 French baguette, cut
    into thick slices,
    to serve

Clean the cauliflower of any green leaves. Cut into quarters and remove the hard core. Cut the remaining cauliflower into small florets.

Put the cauliflower and 2 litres (8 cups) water in a large saucepan or stockpot over high heat. Season with salt and pepper, then cook for 15 minutes, or until the cauliflower is tender. Strain the cauliflower, reserving the liquid.

Return the cauliflower to the pan and top with half of the cooking liquid and all of the butter. Start blending with a stick blender until you have a smooth, creamy texture — you may need to add extra cooking liquid to reach the right consistency. Adjust the seasoning to taste. You could also make this in small batches in a blender or food processor.

Ladle the soup into bowls and serve with crusty bread.

VARIATIONS: I often use carrot to make a similar soup, or leek and potato. Simply replace the cauliflower with the same quantity of carrot or other vegetable and adjust the thickness by adding more or cooking liquid.

LENTIL SOUP WITH HAM HOCK
Soupe de lentille au jarret de jambon

Not everyone at home likes my lentil soup but for a soup that uses winter leek I think it's pretty good. If you refrigerate the soup you will need to add some water to bring it back to a runny consistency.

1 smoked ham hock, about 750 g

1 tablespoon vegetable oil

1 onion, diced

1 garlic clove, chopped

200 g brown lentils, washed

1 large leek, white part only, rinsed and sliced

100 g butter

1 tablespoon chopped flat-leaf parsley, to serve

Wash the ham hock under cold running water, then place in a large saucepan and pour in just enough water to cover. Bring to a simmer over medium heat and cook for 5 minutes to purify the ham hock. Discard the water and rinse the hock.

Heat the oil in a large saucepan or stockpot over medium heat. Add the onion and cook for 3 minutes, or until softened. Add the garlic and cook for 1 minute. Add the lentils and leek and stir for 1 minute, then add the ham hock and 2 litres (8 cups) water. Bring to the boil, then reduce the heat to low and simmer for 1 hour, skimming to reduce any scum that rises to the surface.

Remove the hock and set aside. Strain the lentils, reserving the cooking liquid. Return three-quarters of the lentils to a clean saucepan with half of the cooking liquid and all of the butter. Blend with a stick blender to break up the lentils and make a coarse soup. You could also make this in small batches in a blender or food processor.

Add the balance of the lentils back to the pan and check the seasoning. Break the hock apart to separate the meat from the bone, fat and skin. Shred the meat with your fingers and return to the soup. Reheat the soup if needed and stir through the parsley just before serving.

MUSSEL SOUP WITH FENNEL, POTATO AND SAFFRON

Soupe aux moules

Serves 8

This is a hearty soup that works well as a main meal. The soup will have a beautiful golden colour due to the addition of saffron — a perfect marriage of flavour with the mussels.

I kg black mussels, scrubbed and de-bearded

100 ml white wine or water

I large fennel bulb, trimmed and diced

2 potatoes, peeled and diced

I celery stalk, chopped

I leek, white part only, rinsed and diced

I carrot, diced

I litre (4 cups) vegetable stock (see page 61)

300 ml pouring cream

2 pinches of saffron threads

I French baguette, sliced, to serve

Check all the mussels. If there are any broken or open ones, discard them. Rinse the rest under cold water and drain.

Heat a large saucepan over high heat. When the pan is hot, toss in the mussels, then add the wine or water, cover and cook for 3 minutes, until the mussels open. Strain the liquid into a large bowl. Set the mussels aside and keep warm.

Strain the mussel stock through a fine strainer back into the pan over high heat. Add the fennel, potatoes, celery, leek, carrot and the vegetable stock. Bring to the boil, then reduce the heat to a simmer and cook for 20 minutes, or until the vegetables are soft. Strain the vegetables and set aside, returning the stock to the pan. Add the cream and saffron threads and season with salt and pepper. Simmer the broth for 20 minutes, skimming any scum that rises to the surface.

Remove most of the mussels from the shells, retaining some with shells to serve. When the soup is cooked, return the vegetables to the soup to heat through, then lastly add the mussels. Spoon into warm serving bowls and serve with crusty baguette on the side.

A Family Lunch

Vegetable and pesto soup

Onion, tomato and olive flan

Open sandwiches

Shredded chicken salad

Orange cakes

CHESTNUT SOUP
Soupe aux marrons

This is a signature soup that I make in autumn when chestnuts are in season. It requires no cream and could be made with water in place of stock. It has a beautiful, rustic flavour that makes me think of the forests of France.

500 g chestnuts

2 tablespoons olive oil

100 g butter, diced

5 shallots, chopped

2 garlic cloves, peeled

3 litres (12 cups) vegetable or chicken stock (see pages 61–62)

Preheat the oven to 220°C.

Score the base of the chestnuts with a sharp paring knife. Set on a baking tray and roast in the oven for about 5–8 minutes, or until they start to open. Remove them from the oven. Lower the oven temperature to 150°C.

While the chestnuts are still warm, the hard husk away with a clean tea towel. Return the chestnuts to the tray and to the oven for 5 minutes to crisp the inner husk. Remove from the oven and rub the husks again with a clean tea towel. Remove the skin embedded in the groove of the chestnuts with a paring knife, then roughly chop.

Heat half the olive oil in a large saucepan or stockpot over medium heat. Add 1 tablespoon of the butter, the shallots and garlic, and sweat for 3 minutes, or until the shallots are soft and translucent. Remove to a plate.

Add the remaining oil to the pan and cook the chestnuts for 10 minutes, or until their edges start to brown slightly. Return the shallots and garlic to the pan. Add the stock and bring to the boil, then reduce the heat and simmer for 45 minutes, or until the chestnuts are tender.

Strain the chestnuts and vegetables and reserve the cooking liquid. Put the cooked chestnuts and vegetables in a blender or food processor and process to make a smooth purée, adding extra cooking liquid to the soup until smooth and creamy. Taste the soup, adjust the seasoning and add the remaining butter, blending well to combine. There should be no need to strain the soup, but if you prefer a fine result you could pass the soup through a fine sieve. Reserve any leftover cooking liquid to thin the soup later, which will thicken as it cools down.

Reheat the soup to serve. It is great served with cooked lentils, or with shredded duck confit (see page 205) as a main course.

VEGETABLE STOCK

Fumet de légumes

Makes 4–6 cups

2 carrots, peeled

¼ bunch celery

2 leeks, washed

1 large white onion,
    peeled

1 handful flat-leaf parsley

2 sprigs thyme

2 garlic cloves, peeled
    and chopped

½ teaspoon black
    peppercorns

fine salt

Chop all the vegetables into small pieces. Place the vegetables in a medium-size pot, add 2 litres (8 cups) water, the herbs, garlic and peppercorns and a little salt. Bring to the boil, then simmer for 30 minutes. Cool, strain and discard the sediment before storing in the refrigerator until needed (up to 5 days) or in the freezer (up to 2 months).

FISH STOCK

Fumet de poisson

Makes 4–6 cups

head and bones of
    2 snapper or other
    white fish

1 medium carrot, peeled
    and chopped

1 celery stalk, chopped

1 small leek, washed and
    chopped

1 medium onion, peeled
    and chopped

1 bay leaf

1 handful flat-leaf parsley

150 ml white wine

Place all the ingredients with 2 litres (8 cups) water in a stockpot. Bring to the boil, then simmer for 20 minutes, skimming frequently. Strain through damp muslin (cheesecloth) that is sitting over a large bowl. Allow the stock to cool. Pour into a storage container and discard the sediment at the bottom of the bowl. Store in the refrigerator until needed (up to 2 days) or in the freezer (up to 2 months).

CHICKEN STOCK
Fond blanc de volaille

Makes 4–6 cups

1 whole free-range chicken or 1 kg chicken bones

1 carrot, peeled

2 celery stalks

1 leek, washed

1 large white onion, peeled

2 bay leaves

1 handful flat-leaf parsley

1 sprig thyme

1 garlic clove, peeled and crushed

½ teaspoon black peppercorns

fine salt

Wash the chicken under cold water and put into a narrow but tall pot. Chop all the vegetables into small pieces and place in the pot. Add 2 litres (8 cups) water, the herbs, garlic and peppercorns and a little salt. Bring to the boil, then simmer gently for 30 minutes. Remove the whole chicken to use for another recipe, such as artichoke, chicken, bean and parsley salad (see page 68), and cook the stock for another hour. Cool. Strain before use and discard the sediment. Store in the refrigerator until needed (up to 5 days) or in the freezer (up to 2 months).

BEEF STOCK
Fond blanc de veau

Makes 4–6 cups

1.5 kg veal bones

1 medium carrot, peeled

1 celery stalk, chopped

1 small leek, washed and chopped

1 medium onion, peeled

1 handful flat-leaf parsley stalks

½ teaspoon whole black peppercorns

1 teaspoon salt

1 bay leaf

Place the veal bones and 2 litres (8 cups) cold water in a narrow but tall pot. Bring to the boil for 5 minutes, then drain, discarding water. Wash the bones under cold water, then return to the pot with 2 litres (8 cups) fresh water, or enough to cover the bones. Add all the remaining ingredients. Simmer slowly for 4 hours without any heavy bubbling, skimming regularly. Strain, cool, store in the refrigerator until needed (up to 3 days) or in the freezer (up to 2 months).

NOTE: to make a dark beef stock, roast the bones in a preheated 200°C oven for 30 minutes or until the bones are browned. Place the bones into a large pot, add 2 tablespoons tomato paste and 2 tablespoons plain flour. Pour cold water into the baking dish to scrape up all the flavours, then transfer to the pot. Pour in enough water to cover, then add the remaining ingredients and continue with method as above.

SIMON'S FENNEL AND ANCHOVY SALAD

Salade de fenouil aux anchois

Serves 8

This recipe was introduced to me by my friend Simon Johnson. Simon imports anchovies from Spain and used them in a salad that was served at one of my birthdays and was a highlight of the meal.

4 fennel bulbs, trimmed

125 ml (½ cup) extra
  virgin lemon oil

juice of 1 lemon

16 Spanish anchovy fillets

Use a mandoline to thinly shave the fennel into a bowl. Add the lemon oil, lemon juice and anchovies and season well with salt and pepper. Toss to combine and coat the fennel in the oil and juice, then set aside for 30 minutes before serving to allow the flavours to develop.

This salad is quite versatile and can be served as a simple entrée or with grilled fish or any grilled meat, such as lamb cutlets or veal cutlets, or with smoked or marinated salmon.

FENNEL SALAD WITH WALNUTS, APPLES AND BEANS

Salade de fenouil aux noix

Serves 4

12 walnuts

1 large fennel bulb,
  trimmed and finely
  sliced

1 apple, peeled, cored and
  cut into thin wedges

juice of 1 lemon

100 ml sour cream

50 ml apple cider vinegar

½ teaspoon finely
  chopped parsley

½ teaspoon finely
  snipped chives

16 large red grapes,
  halved and seeded

100 g green beans,
  blanched and halved
  lengthways

Preheat the oven to 160°C. Place the walnuts on a baking tray and roast for about 10 minutes. Remove from the oven, lay them on a clean tea towel and rub over to remove any loose skin.

Put the fennel and apple in a bowl and pour over half of the lemon juice, mixing well to combine.

Prepare the salad dressing by mixing together the sour cream, vinegar, parsley, chives and remaining lemon juice. Season with salt and pepper and adjust the texture by adding a touch of hot water to make a runny dressing.

Mix the grapes and beans in a serving bowl with the walnuts, fennel and apple, then drizzle over the dressing, to taste.

TOMATO SALAD WITH FRESH CURD CHEESE AND CUCUMBER

Salade de tomate fermière

If you don't have a garden to grow your own tomatoes but you do have friends who grow them and they are in season, beg for them. There is nothing more refreshing in summer than a tomato salad served with crusty bread. It does not matter what variety you use for this recipe, but if you can, use ones that have ripened on the vine. Tomatoes should never be refrigerated.

1 kg tomatoes, heirloom and any other varieties

1 cucumber, peeled

250 g fresh curd cheese (see page 4) or Australian marinated feta

65 ml (¼ cup) extra virgin olive oil

Wash the tomatoes and pat dry with paper towels. Remove the core of any large tomatoes but leave the cores in the smaller ones. Cut each tomato in different ways, some quartered, others in halves and some sliced, then arrange them in an even layer on a serving plate just large enough to contain them.

Slice the cucumber lengthways into thin ribbons using a vegetable peeler and arrange on top of the tomatoes. Top with the curd cheese or feta, season with salt and pepper and drizzle with olive oil or some of the oil from the marinated feta.

Serve with grilled lamb or chicken, or country-style sausages.

WITLOF, APPLE, CELERY, WALNUT AND WATERCRESS SALAD

Salade d'hiver   Serves 4

**I like having a salad to start dinner and this one is perfect served on a winter's night.
The apples are in season and if you can find local walnuts they should be fresh from
the end of their growing season.**

100 g (1 cup) walnuts

2 heads witlof, trimmed

4 celery stalks, trimmed
and peeled

2 large pink lady apples

juice of 1 lemon

125 g (½ cup)
mayonnaise

60 ml (¼ cup) crème
fraîche or sour cream

1½ teaspoons apple cider
vinegar

1 pinch of celery salt
(optional)

1 bunch watercress,
trimmed

Preheat the oven to 160°C.

Place the walnuts on a baking tray and roast for about 10 minutes.
Remove from the oven, lay them on a clean tea towel and rub over to
remove any loose skin.

Remove the leaves from the witlof, cutting the stem as you detach them.
Cut the celery first into 5 cm lengths and then slice into matchsticks.
Cut the apple into matchsticks. Fill a bowl with cold water and add half
the lemon juice to make acidulated water, then immerse the apple in the
water to prevent it from browning.

Mix together the mayonnaise, crème fraîche, vinegar and remaining
lemon juice in a separate bowl. Add a touch of celery salt and pepper,
to taste.

Just before serving, toss together the drained apple, the walnuts, witlof,
celery and watercress in a bowl. Pour over the dressing and toss well
to coat.

VARIATIONS: Instead of using mayonnaise you can dress this salad lightly
by simply stirring the apple cider with a touch of walnut oil and vegetable
oil. If you have pear or nashi, you can substitute them for the apple.
For a more refined taste you can blanch the walnuts for 10 minutes in
500 ml (2 cups) full-cream milk, drain, and then peel with a small
paring knife before roasting them.

NOTE: You can find celery salt in the spice section at most grocery
shops. I use this salt to season stuffing, roasts and salads when I wish to
have a more intense celery flavour.

ARTICHOKE, CHICKEN, BEAN AND PARSLEY SALAD

Salade de poulet aux artichauts

Serves 4–8

I think it is important to try different ingredients, especially when they are in season. Ideally you would use fresh artichokes in this salad, which pair perfectly with green beans, but no matter what vegetables you use the chicken is best shredded for texture.

1 whole free-range chicken, boiled (see page 62)

8 large fresh artichokes or 8 artichoke hearts in oil

juice of 1 lemon

250 g (1⅔ cups) fresh or frozen broad beans

250 g green beans, trimmed

½ bunch flat-leaf parsley

125 g (½ cup) mayonnaise

60 ml (¼ cup) verjuice

1½ tablespoons extra virgin olive oil

Boil the chicken as directed on page 62. Remove the legs and wings and use them in another recipe. Once the chicken has cooled, pull the breast away from the bone, discard the skin and bones and remove the flesh in long strands.

For fresh artichokes, trim the stems quite short then peel the leaves until you expose the artichoke. Cut the heads so you only end up with the bases. Fill a bowl with cold water and add half the lemon juice. Use a spoon to remove the soft hearts of the artichokes and immerse them in the water as you go to prevent them from browning. Drain well, then cook in a saucepan of salted boiling water for 10 minutes, or until tender. Drain hearts on paper towels and cut into quarters. For bottled artichokes, simply cut them into quarters.

Blanch the fresh broad beans in a saucepan of salted boiling water for 2 minutes, refresh under cold water, then peel the skins so you end up with the bright green flesh only. If you are using frozen broad beans, simply defrost and peel off the skins. Blanch the green beans in salted boiling water, strain and refresh by plunging under cold running water to preserve their colour. Blanch the parsley in salted boiling water for about 8 seconds, then drain and plunge immediately into cold water to refresh. This is best done with the bunch still attached by the stem. Drain well and pat dry on a clean tea towel. Roughly chop the leaves.

To make the dressing, combine the mayonnaise, verjuice and the remaining lemon juice in a bowl and season with salt and pepper. Toss the broad beans, green beans and parsley in the olive oil with a touch of salt and pepper. Arrange the chicken, artichokes, broad beans, parsley and green beans on a serving plate and drizzle over the dressing.

GRILLED CAPSICUM SALAD WITH MARINATED GARFISH AND ANCHOVY DRESSING

Salade de poivron et poisson mariné, sauce au anchois Serves 4

There are many brands of anchovies available in most supermarkets but I always prefer to use Spanish anchovies as they are less salty, more fleshy and are easy to love, especially paired with grilled capsicum. As part of this dressing the anchovies go well with the garfish. These days you can find boned and butterflied garfish at fish markets which are perfect for this salad.

4 whole garfish, butterflied

1 red onion, finely sliced

250 ml (1 cup) olive oil, plus extra for drizzling

2 garlic cloves, crushed

2 bay leaves

2 thyme sprigs

1 handful basil, leaves picked and finely chopped, stalks reserved

120 g tinned Spanish anchovies, drained

juice of 1 lemon

2 red capsicums, roasted and peeled (see opposite page)

2 green capsicums, roasted and peeled (see opposite page)

Remove the heads and tails of the garfish and discard. Lay the fish in a shallow baking dish just large enough to fit them.

Blanch the onion in a saucepan of salted boiling water for 1 minute. Drain and lay the onion over the garfish.

Put the oil in a small saucepan over low heat and add the garlic, bay leaves, thyme and the reserved basil stalks. Heat up to a warm temperature, but not sizzling hot — the idea is to infuse the oil with the flavour of the herbs; you should still be able to put your finger into the oil and feel that it is hot without burning. Try to maintain this for 30 minutes. You will need to keep checking and might need to turn the heat off at some point.

Strain the oil over the onion and garfish to barely cover them. Leave to marinate at room temperature for 1 hour (any longer and it should be refrigerated).

This dish is best served at room temperature, so make sure the garfish is taken out of the refrigerator at least 1 hour before you wish to serve.

To make the anchovy dressing, put the drained anchovies into a mortar and pestle or use a food processor to pulp the anchovies, then add the lemon juice to create a coarse dressing. Season with pepper.

Remove the onion from the marinated fish and set aside in a small bowl. Put the garfish on a chopping board and trim to make eight whole fillets.

Discard the marinade. Arrange the onion in a layer on the bottom of each serving plate and alternately layer the garfish and capsicum over the top to highlight the varying colours. Drizzle over a little anchovy dressing. Scatter the basil leaves over the fish and serve.

VARIATIONS: You can omit the garfish from this recipe if you prefer and serve a vegetarian version by roasting 2 sweet yellow capsicums instead.

Roasting and peeling capsicums

To roast and peel capsicums, preheat the oven to 200°C. Drizzle a touch of olive oil in a baking tray and add the whole capsicums. Roast for 20 minutes until blistered and blackened all over, turning the capsicums several times so they cook evenly. Remove from the oven, place them in a bowl and cover with plastic wrap. Set aside to sweat for 15 minutes — this will make them soften and easier to peel.

When ready to use, cut the capsicums in half, remove juices, seeds and membranes, then using a small knife, separate the skin from the flesh and peel away the rest of the skin with your fingers. Trim the halves to neaten and use as directed.

Once roasted, the capsicums can be stored in an airtight container for up to 3 days.

CELERIAC SALAD WITH SMOKED OCEAN TROUT

Rémoulade de céleri-rave à la truite fumé

Serves 4

I find it surprising how many people do not use celeriac at mealtimes. Granted it is an odd-looking vegetable, but once peeled it is so easy to handle and tastes particularly delicious. I love the refined taste of smoked ocean trout and the slight aniseed flavour of the celeriac marries perfectly with the trout.

1 large celeriac, trimmed and peeled

50 ml white wine vinegar

2 French shallots, finely diced

125 g (½ cup) mayonnaise

1 tablespoon mixed chopped herbs, such as parsley, tarragon or chives

½ tablespoon wholegrain mustard

400 g smoked ocean trout, sliced

1 tablespoon extra virgin olive oil

2 lemons, cut into wedges, to serve

Cut the celeriac in half and use a mandoline to slice it thinly, then use a sharp knife to julienne. Blanch the celeriac in a saucepan of salted boiling water for 1 minute. Drain and squeeze out any excess water, then pat dry with paper towels.

Put the vinegar and shallots in a saucepan over high heat and cook for 2 minutes, or until the vinegar has nearly evaporated. Remove from the heat, allow to cool, then stir through the mayonnaise, mixed herbs and mustard.

In a bowl, mix together the celeriac with a spoonful of dressing at a time, and keep adding the dressing to taste.

Lay the smoked trout on a serving plate, pile plenty of celeriac in the centre and drizzle over the oil. Season with pepper and serve with the lemon wedges on the side for squeezing over.

VARIATIONS: Cooked fennel and boiled potatoes could be used instead of the celeriac, or you could try the smoked trout with fresh uncooked endive or cucumber.

BABY BEETROOT SALAD WITH BROAD BEANS
Salade de bette à l'huile de noix

This is a simple salad that requires some preparation beforehand. It is a marvellous dish, especially if you are able to get sweet yellow beetroot and some walnut oil for the dressing. The beetroot needs to be cooked separately to avoid the red beetroot bleeding into the water and staining the yellow beetroot.

12 small yellow beetroot, scrubbed clean

125 ml (½ cup) white wine vinegar

12 small red beetroot, scrubbed clean

150 g (1 cup) fresh or frozen broad beans

4 French shallots, sliced

60 ml (¼ cup) red wine vinegar

60 ml (¼ cup) walnut oil

Put the yellow beetroot in a saucepan. Add the white wine vinegar and 500 ml (2 cups) water or enough to cover. Season with salt and bring to a simmer over medium heat. Cook the beetroot until you are able to easily pierce them with the point of a knife. Remove the beetroot with a slotted spoon and set aside to cool.

Add the red beetroot to the same cooking liquid, topping with more water to cover if necessary, and cook until tender. Drain the liquid and allow the beetroot to cool.

Using disposable gloves to avoid staining your hands, first peel the yellow beetroot and then the red, reserving them in separate bowls at room temperature.

Blanch the broad beans in a saucepan of salted boiling water for 2 minutes. Drain and immediately plunge into a bowl of iced water to refresh, then peel off the outer husk.

Put the shallots in a small saucepan with the red wine vinegar, season with salt and pepper, and cook for about 3 minutes. Remove from the heat and allow to cool, then gently stir through the walnut oil to make a dressing.

Place the beetroot in a large serving bowl, some of the larger beetroot could be cut in two, and scatter the broad beans on top. Drizzle with the dressing and serve.

VARIATION: You can use hazelnut oil instead of walnut oil if you prefer. Use green beans if they are in season instead of broad beans.

BASIC VINAIGRETTE

Vinaigrette   Makes 330 ml (1⅓ cups)

This is a basic vinaigrette, good for using on soft leaves. For a stronger taste, or to
use with a vegetable salad, substitute the white wine vinegar for red wine vinegar. For
a salad to be served with grilled fowl, such as quail, duck or chicken, you could use a
fruit vinegar, such as raspberry, or verjuice.

250 ml (1 cup) vegetable, grapeseed or peanut oil

80 ml (⅓ cup) white wine vinegar

white pepper

Combine the oil and vinegar in a jar with a lid and season with salt and
white pepper, to taste. Shake well to combine.

CREAMY VINAIGRETTE

Vinaigrette à la crème   Makes 375 ml (1½ cups)

This is a dressing that will cling to lettuce leaves and is perfect for butter lettuce, oak
leaves or crisp cos or iceberg lettuce.

2 free-range egg yolks

½ teaspoon sugar

1 teaspoon Dijon mustard

white pepper

250 ml (1 cup) vegetable oil

80 ml (⅓ cup) white wine vinegar

2 tablespoons cream or milk

In a bowl, combine the egg yolks, sugar, mustard and white pepper, to
taste. While stirring, slowly add the vegetable oil, white wine vinegar and
cream or milk in small quantities to prevent the dressing from splitting
(or separating). Stir until well combined and season with salt, to taste.

MUSTARD SEED DRESSING

Vinaigrette à la moutarde de grain

Makes 330 ml (1⅓ cups)

This dressing is perfect for drizzling over large leafy greens, such as butter or cos lettuce leaves. It is a rustic vinaigrette, great for a salad to accompany any red meat dish.

1 free-range egg yolk

1 teaspoon wholegrain mustard

250 ml (1 cup) vegetable oil

80 ml (⅓ cup) white wine vinegar

1 teaspoon honey

white pepper

Whisk together the egg yolk and mustard until well combined. Continue whisking while adding the oil, a little at a time, and when it starts to look too thick, add some of the vinegar alternately with the oil until you have an emulsified dressing. Stir through the honey and season with salt and white pepper, to taste.

CHAMPAGNE VINAIGRETTE

Vinaigrette au vinaigre de champagne

Makes 500 ml (2 cups)

This refined vinaigrette goes perfectly with light salads or delicate herb salads.

½ tablespoon Dijon mustard

½ tablespoon honey

125 ml (½ cup) champagne vinegar

125 ml (½ cup) vegetable oil

125 ml (½ cup) extra virgin olive oil

125 ml (½ cup) sparkling wine

white pepper

Blend all of the ingredients, except pepper, in a blender or whisk together by hand until well combined. Season with salt and white pepper, to taste.

FRENCH DRESSING

Vinaigrette Française

Makes 500 ml (2 cups)

This is a strongly flavoured dressing with plenty of onion and is the vinaigrette most used in restaurants in France to dress green leafy salads.

1 small brown onion
1 garlic clove, crushed
1 teaspoon Dijon mustard
100 ml white wine vinegar or tarragon vinegar
150 ml vegetable oil
150 ml extra virgin olive oil
1 teaspoon honey
1 tablespoon finely chopped parsley
1 tablespoon finely snipped chives
white pepper

Peel the onion and grate over a bowl to extract as much onion juice as possible. Add the onion juice to a blender with the garlic, mustard, vinegar, oils and honey. Process until well combined, or whisk together by hand. Season with salt and white pepper, to taste, then whisk in the parsley and chives just before serving.

WALNUT OIL DRESSING

Vinaigrette à l'huile de noix

Makes 300 ml (1¼ cups)

This vinaigrette uses the best vinegar and oil and is expensive to make but is simply stunning on salad leaves or vegetable salads, such as green beans, artichokes and endive.

50 ml aged red wine vinegar
50 ml sherry vinegar
100 ml walnut oil
100 ml grapeseed oil
white pepper

Stir all of the ingredients together in a bowl and season with salt and white pepper, to taste.

TOMATO AND BACON SANDWICH

Sandwich à la tomate

I have to admit that a tomato sandwich is my stand-by snack as it is always easy to rustle up at home. Despite the fact that I own a restaurant, when I come home from work late I am always happy to eat one of these sandwiches and that's not just because it is quick and simple to prepare!

1 head baby cos lettuce, trimmed and shredded

2 tablespoons mayonnaise

1 tablespoon butter, softened

8 slices dense country-style rye bread, toasted

2 vine-ripened tomatoes, sliced

8 slices bacon, crisply cooked

4 slices Cantal, Beaufort or cheddar cheese

Put the shredded lettuce in a bowl with 1 tablespoon of the mayonnaise and stir to combine, then season with salt and pepper.

Spread the butter on four pieces of the toast. Pile plenty of lettuce on the buttered toast, then add the tomato slices on top and season to taste. Top with the bacon and cheese.

Spread the remaining mayonnaise over the rest of the toast and lay it on top to make four sandwiches. Press well and cut in half diagonally with a serrated knife. Serve as it is.

VARIATIONS: You can add slices of grilled or baked chicken instead of bacon or try it with both. Vary the type of bread you use, but always use the ripest best-quality tomatoes you can find.

PRESSED GOAT'S CHEESE, CAPSICUM AND ANCHOVY BAGUETTE

Pan–bagnat provençal

Serves 4

The traditional French pan bagnat is a round bread loaf filled with onions, capsicum, olives and anchovies, pressed and then cut into wedges like a tart, but there is no limit to the number of flavour combinations you can come up with. Having said that, the one constant is that it be drizzled with plenty of olive oil. It could be made with a full loaf of bread or a sourdough baguette as I've done here. A baguette makes the perfect worker's sandwich — it is pressed to make it easier to eat and to save space.

1 crusty sourdough
  baguette

60 ml (¼ cup) extra
  virgin olive oil

2 large red capsicums,
  roasted and peeled
  (see page 71)

100 g tinned Spanish
  anchovies, drained

200 g goat's cheese

1 handful basil leaves

Cut the baguette lengthways leaving one long edge joined and press open so you are able to stack the filling. Drizzle the bread with the olive oil, set a layer of capsicum on the base of the baguette. Season with pepper, then lay the anchovies at regular intervals along the length of the roll.

Cut the goat's cheese into slices (use a knife dipped in hot water) and lay the cheese over the anchovies and capsicum. Tear the basil and sprinkle over the top. Close the baguette, place on a baking tray and press with another board or tray on top to weigh the baguette down — the bread could be pressed for a couple of hours. When ready to serve, trim the ends and cut the baguette into small portions.

VARIATIONS: Instead of using goat's cheese in this sandwich, use a cow's milk cheese such as camembert, or try olive tapenade or even some marinated artichoke hearts or grilled eggplant.

MUSHROOMS IN CRUSTY BREAD

Croûtes de champignon

These little bread croustades make a nice change from a regular sandwich and are much more satisfying than mushrooms on toast. Select soft, small white bread rolls that are available in most bakeries.

4 small white bread rolls

100 g butter, melted, plus extra for brushing

80 ml (⅓ cup) olive oil

4 French shallots, finely chopped

500 g white mushrooms, sliced

2 garlic cloves, finely chopped

300 ml pouring cream

1 bunch chives, snipped

100 g thinly sliced ham, cut into small strips

Preheat the oven to 200°C.

Cut the bread rolls in half and scoop out some of the soft centre to create a hollow for the filling. Brush a little of the extra melted butter around the interior and edge of each roll. Place the rolls on a baking tray and bake for 5–10 minutes, or until they are lightly toasted and crisp. Set aside.

Heat half of the oil in a frying pan over medium heat. Add half of the shallots and cook for 2 minutes, or until softened. Add half of the mushrooms, half of the garlic and half of the butter and cook over high heat for 5 minutes, or until all the water has evaporated and the mushrooms are cooked. Remove to a plate, wipe the pan clean with paper towels and repeat with the remaining oil, shallots, garlic, mushrooms and butter until all are cooked. Return all of the mushrooms back to the pan and add the cream. Bring to the boil and cook until the mushrooms form a thick compote. Add the chives, check the seasoning, then remove from the heat. Stir through the ham to combine.

Spoon the mushroom filling into each bread roll and return to the oven for 5–10 minutes to heat through before serving.

VARIATIONS: If you wish to turn this recipe into a more serious meal you could add a finely sliced chicken breast to the mushrooms and cook in the cream, or add small cooked and peeled prawns at the end with the chives.

ROAST BABY EGGPLANT WITH GOAT'S CHEESE CRUST

Aubergine à la croûte de fromage de chèvre

Serves 4

At the markets you often see large glossy eggplants but you can also buy the very beautiful baby variety. These do not need to be peeled like the large ones do and they provide a wonderfully sweet flavour which is perfect in this dish balanced with the goat's cheese.

8 baby eggplants

100 ml extra virgin olive oil

4 garlic cloves, sliced

4 shallots, sliced

finely grated zest and juice of 1 lemon

1 tablespoon chopped flat-leaf parsley

1 tablespoon chopped oregano

1 red onion, sliced

100 g dried olives or black olives

1½ tablespoons red wine vinegar

200 g matured goat's cheese

4 slices sourdough bread

Preheat the oven to 200°C.

Prick the eggplants all over with the tip of a knife to prevent them from splitting during cooking. In a bowl, toss the eggplants with half of the olive oil, the garlic, shallot, lemon zest, lemon juice and herbs. Season well with salt and pepper, then place in the base of a roasting tin and cook for 20 minutes, or until soft when pressed with your fingers. In the last few minutes of cooking, add the onion, olives and red wine vinegar. Remove from the heat and remove the eggplant to a plate. Keep warm.

Stir the remaining oil into the tin with all of the cooking juices, herbs and onions and season well — this will be used as a dressing.

Slice the goat's cheese and lay on the sourdough slices. Place under a hot grill and cook until the bread browns at the edges.

To serve, place a slice of bread on each plate, put two of the eggplants on each slice and drizzle the dressing over and around the plate.

VARIATIONS: You can use haloumi cheese instead of goat's cheese or even use fresh mozzarella if you prefer.

ROSEMARY FOUGASSE WITH ASPARAGUS, ARTICHOKE AND HAM

Fougasse aux asperges, artichaut et au jambon de bayonne   Serves 4

Fougasse are from the south of France. They are traditionally flat, often unleavened bread, with long slits in them, which are cooked directly on the stone base of a bread oven. The origin of this bread goes back to Roman times.

2 teaspoons (7 g) dried yeast

2 tablespoons olive oil, plus extra for greasing

350 g (2⅓ cups) plain flour, sifted, plus extra for dusting

1 pinch of salt

½ tablespoon sugar

1 tablespoon rosemary or thyme leaves

sea salt flakes

8–12 asparagus spears, peeled, trimmed and blanched, to serve

4 marinated artichoke hearts or use freshly cooked (see page 68), to serve

1 tablespoon extra virgin olive oil, to serve

8 slices Bayonne ham or prosciutto, to serve

To make the fougasse, put the yeast in a bowl with 60 ml (¼ cup) warm water, stirring to combine. Set aside for 20 minutes in a warm place — it should develop a foam. In a separate bowl, mix together the olive oil and 125 ml (½ cup) lukewarm water, then add to the yeast mixture.

Put the flour in a large bowl with the salt and sugar, make a well in the centre and add the yeast mixture, mixing slowly by combining a little flour at a time until incorporated. Form a ball and knead firstly in the bowl and then on a lightly floured work surface to develop a good elastic dough.

Brush a large bowl with the extra olive oil. Place the dough inside and smear the top with a touch more oil. Cover with plastic wrap and a clean tea towel to ensure the dough does not lose heat too rapidly — by keeping the dough in a warmish place it will double in size over the next hour.

Cut the dough into four portions and, working on a lightly floured surface, press the dough flat with your hand to create a piece the size of your hand. Cut four slits in the top, brush with olive oil, sprinkle over the rosemary and some sea salt. Set aside for 15 minutes to rise.

Preheat the oven to 200°C. Bake the fougasse for about 20 minutes, or until crisp. Remove from the heat and set aside to cool.

Serve the fougasse topped with the asparagus and artichokes dipped in a little extra virgin olive oil. Lay the ham on top, drizzle with more oil and season with pepper.

VARIATIONS: Try grilled eggplant, semi-dried tomatoes, pitted olives, goat's cheese or fresh ham with your favourite cheese.

HAM AND CHEESE TOASTED SANDWICHES
Croque monsieur

Most croque monsieurs are made with white sliced bread but I find them more enjoyable if you use hand-sliced sourdough bread or country-style bread. For the best results use ham that has been freshly carved from the bone.

400 g Gruyère cheese

8 slices sourdough or rye bread

400 g ham, sliced from the bone

1 tablespoon butter

2 tablespoons plain flour

250 ml (1 cup) full-cream milk

1 pinch of nutmeg

Slice half the Gruyère cheese thinly with a sharp knife and grate the other half. Lay half the cheese slices over four slices of the bread and top with the ham. Place another layer of cheese slices over the ham. Cover with the remaining slices of bread and wrap each one in plastic wrap. Place on a small tray with another tray on top and weigh them down for 1 hour in the refrigerator while you are preparing the sauce.

Melt the butter in a small saucepan over medium heat and add the flour, stirring to make a roux — add a touch more butter if the mix is too dry. Cook for 1–2 minutes, then stir in the milk until well combined — the sauce should be thick or have the consistency of a béchamel. Add the nutmeg and season with salt and pepper, to taste. Remove from the heat and allow to cool.

Preheat the oven to 180°C.

Use a spatula to spread 2 tablespoons of the sauce over the top of each sandwich. Sprinkle over the grated Gruyère cheese. Set the croque monsieurs on the middle shelf of the oven for 10 minutes — if the cheese needs more colour transfer to the top shelf for a minute or so, or until golden. Cool for a few minutes and cut into fingers to serve.

VARIATIONS: For a quick and easy version of this recipe simply butter two slices of bread per person. Sit one slice over a sheet of baking paper and top with a slice of Gruyère cheese, slices of ham and another slice of Gruyère. Top with the remaining bread slices, butter side up, and pan-fry over medium heat until the cheese has melted and the bread is golden. Rest for a minute or two before serving.

HAM, CHEESE AND ROCKET SANDWICH WITH HONEY FIGS

Tartine au jambon et aux figues au miel   Serves 4

I like tartines, the French version of an open-faced sandwich, because they can become anything that takes your fancy. The toppings can be as varied as your imagination allows. The bread can be toasted or left fresh if it is a heavier bread, such as sourdough. I particularly like this version as it makes for a complete meal and the saltiness of the ham and the sweetness of the fig work very well together.

4 figs

2 tablespoons honey

1 tablespoon butter, softened

4 slices Swiss or country-style bread, toasted

100 g sheep's milk or cheddar cheese, sliced or grated

200 g ham, sliced from the bone (or use prosciutto)

1 handful rocket leaves

½ tablespoon extra virgin olive oil

Preheat the oven to 220°C.

Cut the figs in half and place on a small baking tray. Drizzle the honey over the top and cook in the oven for 5 minutes. Set aside.

Spread the butter generously over the bread slices. Arrange slices of the cheese and ham on top. Toss the rocket with the oil and a touch of salt and pepper and put a small mound in the centre of each tartine over the ham. Add two fig halves on each and drizzle with some of the hot honey to serve.

VARIATIONS: You can use blue cheese instead of hard cheese to go with the figs for a richer flavour.

PICKLED VEGETABLES

Légumes à la grecque

I am a big fan of preparing dishes that can be stored in the fridge and used up over the following days as an easy snack. Pickled vegetables fall into this category and are a great way to use up leftover produce in your fridge. Best of all, they are the perfect accompaniment to dry saucisson, a type of French sausage, or boiled ham and make a wonderful addition to any sandwich or even a nibblies platter.

250 ml (1 cup) white wine vinegar

250 ml (1 cup) white wine (optional)

80 ml (⅓ cup) extra virgin olive oil

1 tablespoon pickling spices, wrapped in a piece of muslin

2 bay leaves

1 tablespoon salt

250 g button mushrooms, stems trimmed

8–12 small pickling onions

½ small cauliflower, cut into small florets

2 carrots, cut into matchsticks

1 small fennel bulb, trimmed, cut into eighths

2 celery stalks, cut into matchsticks

juice of 1 lemon

Put the vinegar, wine, oil and 1 litre (4 cups) water in a saucepan over high heat. Add the pickling spices, bay leaves and salt and bring to the boil. Boil for 10 minutes. Add the mushrooms and cook for 10 minutes, or until cooked through, then remove from the stock with a slotted spoon. Drain and set the mushrooms aside on a plate.

Blanch all of the vegetables separately, starting with onions, then cauliflower, carrot, fennel and celery, cooking one batch completely before adding the next. All the vegetables should be drained and then combined before transferring to sterilised airtight jars to cool.

When all the vegetables are done, continue to cook the poaching liquid until reduced by half, then add the lemon juice. Strain over the vegetables in the jars. Seal the jars and allow to cool in the refrigerator for a few hours before using. The pickles can be stored for up to 5 days in the refrigerator.

When ready to use, drain the quantity required and bring to room temperature. Serve as an accompaniment to sandwiches or with cold meats.

VARIATION: You can vary the vegetables you use in this dish. Try adding some sliced red capsicum, artichoke hearts, baby leek or baby cucumber cut into small pieces.

BEETROOT TAPENADE

Tapenade de betteraves

This tapenade is a great condiment to serve on sandwiches, with cold meats, or to spoon over grilled duck breast, quail or even lamb cutlets.

4 large beetroot, scrubbed clean

4 French shallots or I onion, finely chopped

I garlic clove, finely chopped

125 ml (½ cup) aged red wine vinegar

2 tablespoons salted capers, rinsed, drained and chopped

120 g tinned Spanish anchovies, drained and chopped

I tablespoon chopped flat-leaf parsley

finely grated zest of I lemon

125 ml (½ cup) extra virgin olive oil

Preheat the oven to 180°C.

Place the beetroot on a small roasting tray and roast for 90 minutes, or until tender — check them after I hour. When done you should be able to easily pierce the beetroot with the point of a knife. Remove from the oven, allow to cool, then use disposable gloves to peel off the skins.

Put the shallots and garlic in a small saucepan over high heat. Add the vinegar and cook for 2 minutes, or until the shallots are soft and the vinegar has reduced by half. Remove from the heat and allow to cool.

Roughly chop the beetroot — you may want to cut the beetroot over a sheet of baking paper to prevent staining the work surface. Put the beetroot in a food processor and process until you have a coarse mixture, using a spatula to scrape the sides to ensure you have a uniform mix. Transfer to a large mixing bowl.

Add the capers and anchovies to the beetroot and stir to combine. Add the shallot mixture, parsley, lemon zest and olive oil, season with salt and pepper, and mix gently to combine. Cover with plastic wrap and set aside for 4 hours to allow the flavours to develop, then refrigerate until ready to serve.

VARIATIONS: If you prefer to omit the anchovies from the tapenade you can simply double the amount of capers instead. You can also add I tablespoon wholegrain mustard for a more complex flavour.

OPEN-FACED SANDWICHES

Sandwiches à la danoise

In summer I like improvising and creating sandwiches with many ingredients, like leftover roast meats, smoked salmon, eggs, tomato, tuna and cheese. Use any condiments or lettuce you have in the refrigerator. I have suggested some possible flavour combinations below but with open-faced sandwiches the guiding principle is be creative with the ingredients. You have the option of toasting or not toasting the bread. If you do toast the bread, keep the slices warm in a low oven and assemble all the other ingredients on a serving platter for your guests to help themselves.

2 loaves sourdough or crusty bread, sliced

200 g marinated feta cheese

4 vine-ripened tomatoes, sliced

120 g tinned Spanish anchovies, drained

1 punnet micro herbs

2 tablespoons wholegrain mustard

100 g onion or tomato jam

200 g sliced ham

100 g Beaufort or Gruyère cheese, sliced

1 cup prawns, cooked, peeled and deveined

1 fennel, shaved

2 tablespoons mayonnaise

1 tablespoon dill

1 tablespoon lemon juice

For the anchovy, spread the marinated feta over 8 slices of bread, top with 2 pieces of tomato and a Spanish anchovy. Garnish with the micro herbs.

For the ham, spread a little mustard over 8 slices of bread, then some onion or tomato jam. Top with slices of ham and the Beaufort or Gruyère cheese.

For the prawns, shaved fennel tossed in the mayonnaise spiked with a touch of chopped dill and lemon juice would be good. Put some lettuce on the bread first and then top with the other ingredients.

VARIATIONS: Other great sandwiches can be made with smoked salmon and cream cheese, county-style pâté with beetroot tapenade (see page 87), hard-boiled eggs and diced cucumber, or roast beef and horseradish cream.

In summer I like improvising
and creating sandwiches with
many different fresh ingredients

ONION, TOMATO AND OLIVE FLAN
Pissaladière

Pissaladière had its origins near Genoa in Italy as a form of pizza, then made its way to Provence where these days puff pastry is used to make most versions of this flat crust. It makes a wonderful light summer brunch and by using pre-bought puff pastry it is also an easy meal to prepare. The onion can also be cooked the day before so you can assemble everything at the last minute.

60 ml (¼ cup) extra virgin olive oil

4 onions, sliced

2 sheets butter puff pastry

1 free-range egg, well beaten, for egg wash

250 g cherry tomatoes, halved

250 g teardrop tomatoes, halved

120 g tinned Spanish anchovies, drained

155 g (1 cup) pitted kalamata olives

2 handfuls watercress, rocket or nasturtium leaves, to serve

Preheat the oven to 220°C. Lightly grease a baking tray with oil spray.

Heat half of the oil in a large saucepan over medium heat. Add the onions, season with salt and pepper, and cook for 5 minutes, or until nearly dry. Reduce the heat to low and continue cooking for 15 minutes, or until the onions are lightly caramelised. Remove from the heat and set aside to cool.

Cut each pastry sheet in half to create four rectangles. Cut two 1½ cm wide strips from the long side of each rectangle. Brush the long edges of each of the larger rectangles with the egg wash and press the thinner strips on top to create a raised edge. Place on the prepared trays.

Spoon the onion mixture in the centre of each pastry base, spreading all the way to the raised edges. Arrange the tomatoes artistically on top (not a geometrical and predictable pattern). Top with the anchovies and olives and season with salt and pepper. Drizzle over the remaining oil and bake for 15 minutes, or until the pastry is golden. Turn the oven off and briefly open the oven door to remove any moisture and excess heat for a minute, then close the oven door and let the pastry crisp up in the oven for a few more minutes.

When you are ready to serve, cut each pissaladière in half or into large strips and serve on a platter with the watercress, rocket or nasturtium leaves as a garnish.

VARIATIONS: Pissaladière can be made with pizza dough (see page 116). Add goat's cheese or use sardines instead or anchovies for an equally delicious result.

BEETROOT TART TATIN WITH MACHE AND WALNUTS

Tarte tatin à la betterave

250 g (¾ cup) rock salt

4 large beetroot, scrubbed clean

50 g (½ cup) walnuts

2 tablespoons sugar

100 g butter

12 French shallots, peeled

120 g (⅔ cup) light brown sugar

80 ml (⅓ cup) good-quality red wine vinegar

1 head witlof

1 handful mache lettuce, rocket or baby leaves

vinaigrette or dressing of your choice (see pages 75–77)

4 sheets butter puff pastry

Preheat the oven to 180°C. Sprinkle the rock salt in the base of a large roasting tin and place the beetroot on top (try not to cut into the flesh of the beetroot). Roast in the oven for 90 minutes, or until tender — check them after 1 hour — you should be able to easily pierce the beetroot with the point of a knife. Remove from the oven, allow to cool, then use disposable gloves to peel off the skins. Cut the beetroot into even-sized wedges.

Blanch the walnuts in a saucepan of boiling water for 2 minutes. Drain well. Heat the sugar in a saucepan over low heat. When it starts to melt and turn golden, toss in the walnuts and gently stir until the walnuts are evenly coated. Remove from the heat and set aside on a tray to cool.

Heat 50 g of the butter in a frying pan over medium heat. Add the shallots and cook for 5 minutes, or until golden. Add 2 tablespoons water, cover with a lid and cook gently for 10 minutes, or until all of the moisture has evaporated. Remove from the heat and set aside.

Reduce the oven temperature to 170°C. Put four 15 cm round pie dishes in the oven to heat up. Once warm, divide the remaining butter between the four dishes. Add some salt and 1 tablespoon each of brown sugar and vinegar to the dishes. Fill with the beetroot and shallots.

Remove the core of the witlof and wash and dry the leaves. Toss the witlof and mache or rocket leaves with the walnuts and drizzle with just enough of the salad dressing to moisten. Set aside until ready to serve.

Cut a 15 cm round from each sheet of pastry and dock them with a fork to stop them from rising as they cook. Cover each dish with a round of pastry and tuck in the edges. Bake for 10–15 minutes, or until the pastry is crisp and golden. Remove from the heat and allow to cool just enough to handle. Run a knife around the edges of the pie dish to free the pastry.

To serve, invert the dish onto a serving plate so the pastry is at the bottom. Drizzle any excess cooking liquid around the plate and top each tatin with a handful of the salad and a good grind of pepper.

CARAMELISED TOMATO AND SPRING ONION TART TATIN

Tarte tatin à la tomate

8 roma tomatoes, halved

4 bulb spring onions, halved

4 garlic cloves, sliced

4 thyme sprigs, leaves picked

2 tablespoons olive oil

200 g (1 cup) caster sugar

3 tablespoons sherry vinegar

200 g savoury shortcrust pastry (see page 95)

Preheat the oven to 250°C.

Put the tomatoes, spring onions, garlic, thyme and olive oil in a bowl. Season with salt and pepper and toss well to combine. Arrange in a roasting tray, making sure the tomatoes are placed cut side down, and roast in the oven for 10 minutes. Remove from the oven. Reduce the oven temperature to 120°C. Peel the skin from the tomatoes and return them to the tray, cut side down, then continue cooking for about 4 hours, turning them halfway through cooking, until the tomatoes have acquired an intense red colour and lost most of their moisture. Increase the oven temperature to 180°C.

Meanwhile, make the caramel syrup. Put the sugar and 1 tablespoon water in a small saucepan over low heat and cook, stirring, until the sugar dissolves. Continue cooking until the syrup caramelises, stirring regularly to avoid burning — if the side of the pan starts burning, clean it with a pastry brush dipped in cold water. Once the caramel darkens (this might take 10 minutes), remove from the heat and add the sherry vinegar to stop the cooking process — be careful as the caramel will be extremely hot. Pour enough caramel syrup into the base of four 8–10 cm round ceramic or metal pie dishes to make a layer about 5 mm deep.

Lay the tomato and spring onions over the caramel in each dish, cutting them into smaller pieces to fit if needed. Roll out the pastry on a lightly floured work surface to 3 mm thick. Use a pastry cutter to make four 12 cm rounds. Lay a pastry round over each dish and tuck in the edges. Sit the dishes on a baking tray and bake for 20 minutes, or until the pastry is golden and crisp. Remove from the oven and set aside to rest for 5 minutes before inverting onto individual serving plates.

Serve with a fresh spinach or rocket salad with blanched cold asparagus or a salad of green leaves.

VARIATIONS: You can use French shallots instead of spring onions and add pitted olives to the tart before cooking.

VEGETABLE AND GOAT'S CHEESE GÂTEAU

Gâteau de légumes au fromage de chèvre

This is a light terrine or gâteau with plenty of flavour, crunch and colour. Adding sour cream to the goat's cheese and setting with gelatine gives it a lighter taste, but I also used to make this with a goat's cheese and butter mix for a somewhat richer gâteau.

1 large red capsicum, seeded and halved

1 carrot, cut into matchsticks

12 asparagus spears, trimmed and lightly peeled

100 g green beans, trimmed

100 g yellow beans, trimmed

100 g snow peas, trimmed

12 x 5 g gelatine sheets

1 kg fresh goat's cheese, at room temperature

250 g (1 cup) sour cream

60 ml (¼ cup) boiling water

2 tablespoons black olive tapenade

2 tablespoons pesto

60 ml (¼ cup) extra virgin olive oil

1 French baguette, sliced, to serve

Line a 24 cm round springform cake tin or a 30 x 8 x 8 cm classic terrine tin with plastic wrap.

Peel as much of the capsicum skin off as you can and cut into strips. Bring a saucepan of water to the boil and blanch the capsicum, carrot, asparagus, beans and snow peas in separate batches. Drain each batch and plunge immediately into a bowl of iced water to refresh.

Soak the gelatine sheets in a bowl of cold water to soften.

Crumble the goat's cheese into the bowl of an electric mixer fitted with a paddle attachment. Add the sour cream and mix gently on low speed to combine. Squeeze the excess water from the gelatine sheets and add to the cheese mixture with the boiling water and continue mixing until well combined; season with salt and pepper.

Spoon one-third of the goat's cheese mixture into the base of the prepared tin and scatter over half of the vegetables. Spoon the tapenade evenly over the top and spread with another one-third of the goat's cheese, then the remaining vegetables. Spoon the pesto evenly on top and finish with the remaining goat's cheese mixture. Cover with plastic wrap and refrigerate for at least 4 hours to firm up.

When ready to serve, slide the gâteau onto a serving plate. Discard plastic wrap. Dip a serrated knife in hot water and slice into wedges. Drizzle with extra virgin olive oil, season with cracked pepper and serve with the bread.

VARIATIONS: Substitute the sour cream, gelatine and water with 200 g of butter, diced and at room temperature. Mix with the goat's cheese in an electric mixer until combined. Then continue with the layering of the cheese mixture and vegetables.

COUNTRY-STYLE PORK AND WALNUT TERRINE

Terrine de porc aux noix en tartine du pays

Serves 10

When I lived in Montréal I made countless terrines, never really worrying about the correct proportion of fat to meat or what ingredients I was using. The overall principle is that they include plenty of fatty pork, some minced or diced rabbit, chicken, duck or pheasant, generally with walnuts or pistachios added, so feel free to experiment with this recipe to find the terrine that best suits you. Ask your butcher to mince the pork and back fat with a coarse blade to ensure the meat is at its freshest. You will need to make the terrine one to two days before you wish to serve it to allow the flavours to mature and develop.

500 g coarse minced pork

500 g coarse minced pork back fat

200 g chicken livers, trimmed of fat

60 ml cognac, muscat or Madeira

1½ teaspoons vegetable oil

12 chicken tenderloins

400 g minced veal or chicken

50 g (½ cup) walnuts

2 garlic cloves, finely chopped

1 teaspoon salt

1 teaspoon thyme leaves

⅛ teaspoon allspice

12 slices rindless full-length bacon

toasted sourdough bread, sliced, to serve

Combine both of the minced porks in one bowl and place the chicken livers in another. Pour half of the cognac into each bowl and marinate for about 2 hours in the refrigerator.

Meanwhile, heat the oil in a frying pan over medium heat. Add the chicken and cook for 1 minute, turning to cook evenly on all sides without much colour. Or poach the chicken for 2 minutes in simmering salted water. Remove from the heat and allow to cool, then place in the refrigerator until needed.

Preheat the oven to 180°C. Lightly grease a 30 x 8 x 8 cm terrine or loaf tin with oil spray and line with baking paper, leaving an overhang of 6 cm on each side.

To make the terrine, put the marinated chicken livers and one-quarter of the minced pork into a food processor and blend until fairly smooth.

Transfer to a large bowl and combine with all of the remaining ingredients, except the chicken and bacon. Mix well by hand and allow to stand for 15 minutes.

Line the terrine tin with the bacon slices so they are slightly overlapping and let the excess hang over the sides of the tin. Put one-third of the mince mixture in the bottom of the tin over the bacon. Arrange six chicken tenderloins in an even layer over the mince, then top with half

of the remaining mince. Continue layering with another six chicken tenderloins and cover with the remaining mince. The mixture will shrink during cooking so make sure you fill the terrine tin to the very top. Flatten the top of the terrine and fold over the overhanging bacon — try to tuck the bacon into the sides of the terrine to hold it in place during cooking. Fold the baking paper over the top of the terrine.

Place the terrine tin in a deep roasting tin and pour in enough boiling water to come two-thirds up the sides of the terrine. Bake for 10 minutes, then reduce the oven temperature to 150°C and cook for a further 45 minutes, or until the juices run clear when pierced with a skewer.

To press the terrine, I cut a piece of cardboard the size of the terrine and wrap the cardboard in foil and set over the top of the terrine. Use a couple of weights (soups tins are good) to weigh down the terrine. Some excess cooking liquid will come over the sides so sit it back in the empty roasting tin to catch them. Refrigerate for about 4 hours, at which point you could remove the weights and aluminium board. Use a spatula to slide the terrine from the tin, remove the baking paper and wrap it in plastic wrap. Refrigerate for a day or two before serving.

When ready to serve, slice the terrine and serve with toasted sourdough bread and a little wholegrain mustard or onion jam. It also goes well with cornichons, olives, caperberries, pickled vegetables or leek vinaigrette.

VARIATIONS: You can be flexible about what you add to this terrine. Don't be afraid to introduce some rabbit, pheasant or even turkey instead of or as well as the chicken. The most important thing is to retain the proportion of fat to lean meat.

I love serving
a well-chilled
French Champagne
to start — it
creates a sense
of occasion

BAKED GRUYÈRE CHEESE SOUFFLÉS

Soufflé au gruyère

Serves 6

I have included this recipe from the menu at Bathers' Pavilion Café because I know how many people will ask for it if I don't. It is great served for breakfast or lunch, but the best thing about it is the rich Gruyère cheese flavour. This dish is best made a few hours ahead of time as it just improves once warmed up. Serve them warm with a salad or bake them again placed in an ovenproof dish filled with a ragoût of creamy mushrooms.

55 g butter

60 g (½ cup) plain flour

450 ml full-cream milk, warmed

4 free-range egg yolks

160 g (1¼ cups) grated Gruyère cheese, plus extra to serve

2 pinches of salt

2 pinches of cayenne pepper

2 tablespoon snipped chives

6 egg whites

Preheat the oven to 210°C. Lightly grease six 200 ml ramekins or six 6 cm wide x 8 cm deep metal timbales or similar moulds with oil spray.

Melt the butter in a large saucepan over low heat. Add the flour and stir for 1–2 minutes until well combined and smooth. Remove from the heat and gradually add the warm milk, a little at a time, mixing well after each addition, until all the milk is incorporated and the mixture is smooth. Add the egg yolks and return to medium heat. Bring to the boil and cook for 1 minute, then add the cheese, salt, cayenne pepper and chives and stir until the cheese is melted. Remove from the heat and set aside.

Whip the egg whites until soft peaks form. Fold a third of the egg whites through the cheese mixture until well combined, then gently fold through the remaining egg whites.

Pour the mixture into the prepared ramekins so they are three-quarters full. Bake for 20 minutes, or until puffed and no longer wet in the middle. Serve immediately.

VARIATIONS: Use blue cheese instead of Gruyère, or even cheddar cheese, and add some freshly chopped herbs, such as chives or parsley. You could also double cook the soufflés — to do this, remove the soufflés from the ramekins when they are cool enough to handle and place them on a baking tray. Sprinkle with more Gruyère cheese and bake at 220°C for 5 minutes. Serve with a mushroom ragoût.

COOKING FOR KIDS

I have been blessed with two gorgeous children – Celéste and Sasha – and they fill our house with joy and also some challenges with the many birthday parties, get-togethers with friends and weekend sports. We are still at a stage where our children like simple sandwiches, pies and crispy meat croissants, but I like planning a few surprises like rolled ham sandwiches, fresh fruit juice icy poles or fruit jelly, although it seems there is always an eager wait for the sweet finish.

HAM MOUSSE ROLLS
Rouleaux à la mousse de jambon

I have fond memories of my mother making us little rolled sandwiches when I was a child. Sometimes she made them with salmon mousse or with plain cream cheese with cherries, but it always seemed very special. These rolls are a great way of turning an everyday snack into a real treat.

400 g ham, sliced from the bone

100 g butter or cream cheese, softened

1 tablespoon mild mustard

1 loaf brown or white bread, sliced lengthways by your baker

250 g jar sweet cornichons (small gherkins), ends trimmed

Put the ham in a food processor with half of the butter or cream cheese and a touch of pepper and process until it resembles a fine mousse.

Add the mustard to the remaining butter or cream cheese and mix well by hand with a spoon.

Discard the top and bottom crust ends of the loaf, then remove all of the crusts with a serrated knife. Roll out the bread, one slice at a time, with a rolling pin on a clean work surface to flatten them. Cover the bread with a damp cloth to prevent it from drying out.

Take one slice of bread at a time and spread over the mustard butter, top with the ham mousse to about 5 mm thick, spreading all the way to the corners. Take three or four cornichons and lay them in a line along the shortest edge of the bread. Roll it into a neat log, then wrap immediately in plastic wrap to keep it in shape. Repeat with the remaining bread pieces until they are all individually wrapped. Refrigerate for about 2 hours.

When ready to serve, unwrap each bread roll and cut into slices about as thick as your finger. Serve on a large platter for the kids to help themselves.

VARIATIONS: You can make a smoked salmon mousse, a chicken mousse with mayonnaise or even use tuna instead of ham. Instead of rolling the sandwich into a log you can spread the mousse over each slice of bread, cover with a layer of cream cheese and garnish with shredded lettuce and herbs.

ROLLED CREAM CHEESE PINWHEELS WITH SMOKED SALMON

Rouleaux de saumon au fromage blanc

These pinwheels make decorative little sandwiches for special occasions, such as birthdays. Use fresh bread and prepare them ahead of time to leave you free to enjoy the festivities. If you prepare them a day in advance all you will need to do is unwrap them and slice them before serving — easy!

½ bunch flat-leaf parsley

250 g (1 cup) light cream cheese, softened

juice of 1 lemon

1 loaf brown or white bread, sliced lengthways by your baker

400 g smoked salmon, sliced

Put the parsley in a food processor and process until it is very finely chopped. Add the cream cheese and continue to process to make a herb spread, adding a little lemon juice and salt and pepper to season.

Discard the top and bottom crust ends of the loaf, then remove all of the crusts with a serrated knife. Cover the bread with a damp cloth to prevent it from drying out.

Take one slice of bread at a time and spread with a thin layer of the herb spread, then top with a slice of smoked salmon and add a touch of pepper. Roll into a neat log, then wrap immediately in plastic wrap to keep it in shape. Repeat with the remaining bread pieces until they are all individually wrapped. Refrigerate for about 2 hours.

When ready to serve, unwrap the bread and cut each roll into slices about as thick as your finger. Serve on a large platter for the kids to help themselves.

VARIATIONS: Add some spring onions with the parsley for a different flavour or use ham, smoked turkey or mortadella instead of the smoked salmon.

TURKEY, WATERCRESS AND CRANBERRY SANDWICHES

Sandwiches à la dinde et canneberge   Serves 12

I like making these turkey and cranberry sandwiches as they looks quite distinctive
and add a little touch of sophistication to special occasions. They can be made in
advance and cut when you need them. For success with this recipe, you need two types
of similar density bread. Once refrigerated the loaves are easy to trim and slice.

1 bunch watercress, stalks
    trimmed

125 g butter, room
    temperature

1 loaf of dense brown
    bread, sliced

1 loaf of dense rye bread,
    sliced

400 g sliced turkey

100 g cranberry sauce

100 g soft butter, for
    spreading

Wash the watercress and spin dry in a salad spinner. Put the watercress
in a food processor and process until finely chopped. Add the butter,
season with salt and pepper and process until smooth.

Spread the butter mixture over 8 slices of brown bread. Cover with a
slice of turkey and top with the cranberry sauce making sure the surface
is well covered and fairly flat. Top with a buttered slice of rye bread.
Repeat until you have two layers of turkey and cranberry.

Spread the avocado on the two dark rye slices and top with a slice of
buttered light rye. Cover with a slice of turkey and top with the cranberry
sauce making sure the surface is well covered and fairly flat. Repeat until
you have a manageable height. Wrap in plastic wrap and refrigerate for
two hours.

When ready to serve, unwrap the sandwiches and with a serrated knife,
remove the crusts and form an equal side cube. Slice across in finger
thick slabs for perfect layered sandwiches.

MINI CHICKEN SANDWICHES

Rondelles de poulet au céleri

Round chicken sandwiches are another favourite for children and this is a recipe that is quite easy and fun to make as each sandwich uses one slice of white and one slice of brown bread. These sandwiches are great for kids' parties and can be kept in the refrigerator for a whole day. If you wish to avoid wastage, make them with sandwich bread and simply remove the crust before cutting them into four squares, triangles or fingers.

1 loaf country-style rye or brown bread, sliced

1 loaf country-style white bread, sliced

150 g butter, softened

1 whole roast or boiled chicken

2 celery stalks, trimmed and lightly peeled

125 g (½ cup) mayonnaise

Spread all of the bread slices from each loaf with butter, discarding all four crusty ends. Fit together one white and one dark slice, effectively making butter sandwiches. Use a pastry cutter with a 5 cm diameter to cut rounds from each sandwich. Place them under a damp tea towel. Discard the off-cuts. (You could use the crusts to make a bread and butter pudding or breadcrumbs if you like).

Pull apart the chicken and remove the meat, discarding the bones, fat and skin. Dice the chicken and place in a large bowl. Chop the celery into very small dice and add to the chicken. Season with salt and pepper, then add the mayonnaise a little at a time to just moisten the chicken.

Take one little sandwich at a time, open them up and spoon a small amount of chicken salad between each slice, then close again. Place back under the damp tea towel and continue until all are done. Refrigerate. When the kids are ready to enjoy them, or the party is about to start, set the little round sandwiches on a platter and serve.

VARIATIONS: You can just as easily replace the chicken with tuna salad, ham and cheese, or cream cheese with smoked salmon.

CHICKEN PICCATAS WITH FRESH TOMATO SAUCE

Escalopes de volaille, sauce tomate

Serves 12

Piccatas are little medallions or escalopes of meat. In this recipe I have used thinly sliced chicken breast but you could also use veal fillet or the boned leg of veal. I dip them in egg before frying, which gives them a nice coating that will not stick to the pan. The kids love them!

4 chicken breast fillets

60 g (½ cup) plain flour

I free-range egg, well beaten

I tablespoon chopped flat-leaf parsley

60 ml (¼ cup) olive oil

50 g butter

50 g (½ cup) finely grated parmesan cheese (optional)

500 g (2 cups) fresh tomato sauce (see page 172) or tomato passata, warmed, to serve

Using a sharp knife, cut the chicken breast into piccatas by cutting through the thickest part of the breast to remove the first slice. Then cut the remaining breast in two at a flat angle to produce two thin pieces. Each breast should give you three piccatas of roughly the same thickness.

Dust the piccatas first in the flour, turning to coat on all sides, then dip into a bowl of the combined egg and parsley, shaking to remove any excess.

Heat a little oil and butter in a large frying pan over medium heat. Add the piccatas, a few at a time. Season the uncooked side with salt and pepper, then turn after 3 minutes to cook the other side. Season again and remove to a plate and keep warm in a low oven. Repeat with the remaining oil, butter and piccatas until all are cooked.

When you are ready to serve, sprinkle the parmesan, if using, over the piccatas and then serve them on a platter with the tomato sauce on the side.

VARIATIONS: You can use fresh turkey fillet instead of the chicken and serve the piccatas with steamed brown rice or fried polenta.

MINI CHICKEN AND LEEK PIES

Tartelettes au poulet et aux poireaux

Makes 24

1.2 kg free-range chicken

2 leeks, white part only, rinsed and halved

1 large carrot, chopped

2 brown onions, peeled

200 g button mushrooms

2 bay leaves

2 thyme sprigs

white pepper

60 g butter

80 g (⅔ cup) plain flour

1 kg shortcrust pastry (see page 95)

1 free-range egg, well beaten, for egg wash

To make the chicken and leek filling, rinse the chicken under cold water and put it in a large, deep saucepan. Add the leek, carrot, onions and mushrooms. Season with salt and white pepper, add the bay leaves and thyme, and pour in just enough water to cover. Bring to a gentle simmer and cook for 10 minutes, then turn the heat off and allow the chicken to cool in the stock for 1 hour. Strain all the ingredients, reserving the stock. Remove the skin and bones from the chicken and dice the meat. Dice the vegetables and place in a large bowl with the chicken.

Return the stock to a clean saucepan and boil until the liquid has reduced to about 500 ml (2 cups). Melt the butter in a small saucepan and add the flour, stirring to make a roux. Cook for 3–4 minutes over low heat, then add the reduced chicken stock in small quantities, whisking to make a thick sauce. Continue cooking for 5 minutes, then season with salt and pepper. Add the sauce to the chicken and leek mixture and gently fold through. Refrigerate for 2 hours.

Preheat the oven to 220°C.

Lightly grease 24 small aluminium pie plates and line with shortcrust pastry cut into circles about 8 cm in diameter or big enough to fit the pie mould. Fill with the chicken mix. Brush the edge of the pastry with egg wash and top with a shortcrust pastry round cut to about 6 cm in diameter, or big enough to cover. Pinch the edges to seal. Refrigerate for 10 minutes, then egg wash the tops.

Cook in the oven for 5 minutes, then reduce the heat to 180°C and cook for a further 15 minutes. Cool for 5 minutes before serving.

VARIATIONS: You can make more adult-style pies by using rabbit instead of chicken, or boiled diced veal (see old-fashioned veal blanquette, page 224). You can even use minced beef cooked with a touch of water and some very finely diced potato to thicken the mix.

PIZZA DOUGH

Pâte à pizza

This pizza dough is slightly sweet, yeasty and crisp once cooked. It is a good one to make at home as it can be prepared ahead of time and keeps well for a day or two in the refrigerator. Children also enjoy helping you make it — they can learn all about yeast as they watch it come to life!

14 g (2 x 7 g sachets) dried yeast

2 tablespoons honey

400 ml lukewarm water

80 ml (⅓ cup) olive oil

800 g plain flour, sifted

2 teaspoons salt

Put the yeast, honey and 60 ml (¼ cup) of the lukewarm water in a bowl and set aside for 15 minutes, or until the yeast starts foaming.

Add the remaining water and olive oil to the yeast mixture, stirring to combine.

Put the flour in a large bowl with the salt and make a well in the centre. Add the yeast mixture and start mixing with a spoon. When the dough comes together, start mixing with your fingers. If the dough is too sticky, add a touch more flour. Turn the dough out onto a lightly floured work surface and knead until it becomes quite stretchy, about 5–8 minutes.

Put a touch of the oil in a bowl and place the dough inside and smear with the oil. Cover with plastic wrap and then a warm damp tea towel and set the bowl in a warmish place for 2 hours. After this time, the dough will be ready to use, although you could easily put it in the refrigerator and store it for up to 2 days wrapped in plastic film. When you are ready to use the dough, just knock it back to remove the air and roll out the dough on a lightly floured work surface as directed.

HOMEMADE PIZZAS

La pizza des enfants

Makes 8 pizzas

Making your own pizza is a very rewarding experience, it might be a challenge at first, but you will have gained new cooking skills and probably a few friends at home if you persist. The dough will easily keep for a couple of days in the fridge, so get ready to involve the kids who are always keen to come up with their own ideas for toppings. For best results it is preferable to use a little domestic pizza oven. If you have one, put it outside when you are having a party so the children can see you cooking the pizzas.

1.2 kg pizza dough
(see previous page)

2 tablespoons plain flour
or semolina flour

720 g tomato passata

500 g (4 cups) grated
cheddar or mozzarella
cheese

200 g ham, finely sliced

200 g salami, finely
sliced

2 tablespoons chopped
herbs, such as parsley,
basil and oregano

Divide the dough into eight even-sized portions and roll each portion out on a lightly floured work surface into a circle with a 24 cm diameter, about 3 mm thick. Place on a plate lined with baking paper, dusted with plain flour or semolina flour. Top with another sheet of baking paper and continue to roll the bases out and pile over each other until all are done. Refrigerate until needed.

Preheat the oven to 250°C. Prepare all of the toppings in advance and place them in small bowls to make it easier for children to work with.

Working with one pizza base at a time, slide it onto a tray with the paper underneath. Spread on the tomato passata, then garnish with the cheese, meat and herbs. Cook for 3–5 minutes, or until the cheese is melted and bubbling and the base is crisp. Remove from the oven, place on a cutting board and cut into slices to serve.

VARIATIONS: Tempt the children with different cheeses, such as goat's cheese, parmesan or manchego. Almost any vegetable toppings are likely to be popular — choose beans, beetroot or mushrooms — and try olives, anchovies and even pineapple.

Birthday Party

Smoked salmon pinwheels

Mini meat croissants

Mini chicken and leek pies

Jelly with soft cream

Strawberry jam biscuits

Pineapple, cranberry and
honeydew icy poles

Chocolate cake with
ganache icing

MINI MEAT CROISSANTS
Croissants à la viande

Makes 36

These will be a hit with the kids as they are small, crispy and delicious. They are great served with fresh tomato sauce (see page 172).

2 tablespoons vegetable oil

1 small onion, finely chopped

400 g minced beef

100 g (1 cup) dry breadcrumbs

1 tablespoon chopped flat-leaf parsley

100 ml full-cream milk

1 free-range egg, lightly beaten

2 sheets butter puff pastry

plain flour, for dusting

1 free-range egg, well beaten, for egg wash

Heat 1 tablespoon of the oil in a frying pan over medium heat. Add the onion and cook for 5 minutes, or until soft and golden. Season with salt and pepper, then transfer to a large bowl.

Wipe the frying pan clean with paper towels and heat the remaining oil over high heat. Add the beef and cook for 5 minutes, or until dry and browned. If the beef contains too much water, drain it in a strainer and return to the pan. Once cooked, transfer to the bowl with the onion, and add the breadcrumbs, parsley, milk and egg, stirring well to combine — you should have a firm mix. If it is sloppy, add more breadcrumbs. Season well.

Preheat the oven to 200°C. Lightly grease a baking tray with oil spray.

Lay the pastry on a lightly floured work surface. Cut the pastry into three even-sized strips, about 8 cm wide. Cut little triangles down the length of each strip to make 36 triangles in total.

Place a heaped teaspoon of the filling in the centre of each triangle and roll from the base to the tip to make small croissants. Place them on the prepared tray and refrigerate for 10 minutes to firm up.

Glaze the croissants with the egg wash and cook in the oven for 15 minutes, or until crisp and golden. Allow to cool for 5 minutes before serving.

VEAL AND BREAD MEATBALLS

Boulettes de viande

Easy to make, easy to love and easy to serve, these classic meatballs taste great with a fresh tomato sauce on the side, or you can cook the meatballs in the sauce in a 180°C oven for 20 minutes.

250 g minced beef

250 g minced veal

200 g (2 cups) dry
   breadcrumbs

2 free-range eggs

1 onion, grated

250 ml (1 cup)
   full-cream milk

60 g (½ cup) plain flour

2 tablespoons olive oil

1 tablespoon butter

fresh tomato sauce
   (see page 172) or
   tomato passata,
   warmed, to serve

Mix the beef and veal mince together in a large bowl, add the breadcrumbs, eggs, onion and milk and stir well to combine. Season with salt and pepper, then refrigerate for about 20 minutes to firm up the meat.

Sift the flour onto a tray. Use slightly wet hands to roll the meat mixture into small, neat balls. Roll in the flour to coat, then transfer to a plate. Repeat until all the mince is used.

Preheat the oven to 180°C. Heat the oil and butter in a frying pan over medium heat. Cook the meatballs, in batches, for 5 minutes, turning them regularly to give them colour on all sides. Remove to a baking tray and repeat with the remaining meatballs until all are seared.

Continue to cook the meatballs in the oven for 15 minutes, or until cooked through. Remove from the oven, cover with foil, and allow to cool for 10 minutes before serving. To serve, spike them with little wooden forks and have the tomato sauce on the side for dipping.

VARIATION: You can use minced pork instead of the beef if you prefer.

VEAL AND ONION SAUSAGES

Friands au veau

Serves 12

These friands are a great alternative to sausage rolls. I often add a grating of carrot and a couple of stalks of celery, finely chopped, to make the mix healthier. They taste great with green tomato relish, fresh tomato sauce (see page 172) or a sweet homemade plum sauce.

2 tablespoons olive oil

2 onions, finely chopped

250 g minced pork

250 g minced veal

4 free-range eggs, hard-boiled and finely chopped

100 g (1 cup) dry breadcrumbs

1 tablespoon chopped flat-leaf parsley

4 sheets shortcrust pastry (see page 95)

1 egg, well beaten, for egg wash

Heat the oil in a heavy-based frying pan over medium heat. Add the onions and cook for 5 minutes, or until soft, but without much colour. Add the pork and veal mince and cook over high heat for 15 minutes, or until all the water has evaporated. Stir in the egg, then add the breadcrumbs and parsley; season well with salt and pepper — you may need to adjust the texture by adding more breadcrumbs if it is too wet or even a touch of milk if it is too dry. Transfer to a large bowl and refrigerate to cool completely.

Roll out the pastry on a lightly floured work surface to 3 mm thick. Cut out four long rectangles, about 30 x 15 cm each. Spoon the mince mixture lengthways down the centre of the pastry in a line. Brush both sides of the pastry with the egg wash and roll the pastry over to enclose and make a sausage roll. Pinch the ends to seal, then invert each roll so they are seam side down on a baking tray lined with baking paper. Refrigerate for 15 minutes to firm up.

Remove from the refrigerator, and cut a deep slit at a slight angle at regular intervals in each roll — the cut should go almost, but not completely through the pastry and filling. Brush with the egg wash and refrigerate again for 10 minutes.

Preheat the oven to 220°C. Bake the sausage rolls for 5 minutes, then reduce the oven temperature to 180°C and continue to bake for 40 minutes or until the pastry is crisp and golden. Remove from the oven and allow to cool for 10 minutes before serving. Arrange the long rolls on a cutting board for children to tear off pieces themselves.

MINI BEEF BURGERS
Brioche burgers

If you know your baker well then perhaps you can ask them to cook you some miniature buns made out of brioche dough. They look great and have a touch of sweetness with a great yeasty aroma that makes a nice change from ordinary white bread rolls. Or you could use sweet rolls often found in bakeries. Either way, most children are bound to enjoy these bite-sized beef burgers, which are excellent for outdoor entertaining and great for the barbecue!

500 g minced beef

12 small brioche or sweet bread rolls

100 g butter, softened

2 tablespoons vegetable oil

3 slices cheddar cheese, cut into quarters

4 cos lettuce leaves, shredded

3 roma tomatoes, sliced

mustard, pickles or sauce, to serve

Form the mince into 12 small beef patties, place on a plate, cover with plastic wrap and refrigerate until needed.

Cut the rolls in half and butter them well, then set aside until needed.

Heat a barbecue flat plate to high and the grill to low, if you have both — it is good to heat the bread rolls over the grill while the meat is cooking, although this is not essential. Season the meat with salt and pepper, brush the barbecue plate with oil and cook the burgers, in batches, for 1–2 minutes each, or until brown on one side. Turn the burgers over to cook the other side, for 1–2 minutes, and place a slice of cheese on the cooked side. Meanwhile, heat the rolls on the grill, if you like.

When the bread is hot and slightly toasted, put all the bases on a platter, put a touch of shredded lettuce and a slice of tomato on top, then add the cooked patty with the cheese. Top with the other half of the bun and serve with mustard, pickles or your favourite sauce.

VARIATIONS: You can make an equally delicious burger using minced chicken or use small fish fillets and serve them with tartare sauce.

STRAWBERRY JAM BISCUITS

Biscuits à la confiture

These little round biscuits are a favourite with children because they have sweet jam in their middle. In France there are called cyclops or one-eyed monsters. If you can spare the time and effort, these biscuits taste even better using homemade jam.

250 g butter, diced

125 g (⅔ cup) caster sugar

350 g plain flour, sifted, plus extra for dusting

2 tablespoons icing sugar

100 g (⅓ cup) strawberry or raspberry jam

Put the butter and sugar in the bowl of an electric mixer fitted with a paddle attachment. Mix on high speed for 3 minutes until pale and creamy. Gradually add the flour to make a smooth dough, but do not overmix — you will need to scrape the side of the bowl from time to time to make sure it is all incorporated. Gather the dough into a ball, wrap in plastic wrap and refrigerate for 1 hour.

Preheat the oven to 150°C. Line two baking trays with baking paper.

Roll out the dough on a lightly floured work surface to form a rectangle, about 3 mm thick. Use a 5 cm round pastry cutter to press out as many biscuits as you can. Re-roll any scraps of dough, refrigerate for 5 minutes to firm up and continue pressing out biscuits until all of the dough is used — you should make about 60 rounds in total. Use a 2 cm round pastry cutter to press out a smaller circle in the centre of half of the biscuits. Set the hollowed out rounds on top of the biscuit bases and press very lightly. Arrange the biscuits on the prepared trays and refrigerate again for 20 minutes so the biscuits hold their shape during cooking.

Bake the biscuits in the oven for 15–20 minutes. Allow to cool on the trays for 10 minutes, before transferring to wire racks to cool completely. Before serving, dust the biscuits with icing sugar. Put the jam in a piping bag fitted with a plain nozzle and use it to fill the centre of each biscuit.

Strawberry jam biscuits can be stored in an airtight container for 7 days.

VARIATIONS: You could remove 2 tablespoons of flour from the dough mixture and add 2 tablespoons of cocoa in its place to make chocolate cyclops, then fill them with chocolate ganache (see page 138). You could also use Nutella or caramel in place of the jam.

PINEAPPLE, CRANBERRY AND HONEYDEW ICY POLES

Barres glacées aux jus de fruits

These icy treats are great for kids on a hot day. Use the fruit juice of your choice, but using a variety will create better flavours and colours. You could make them in large ice-cube trays or in flexible ice-cube moulds of different shapes, but I like using little shot glasses that have a nice smooth shape — you will need about 30 in total. You will also need wooden icy pole sticks for easier handling.

250 g (1¼ cups) caster
    sugar

½ honeydew melon

300 ml pineapple juice

300 ml cranberry juice

First, make a sugar syrup. Put the sugar and 250 ml (1 cup) water into a saucepan and bring to the boil. Once the sugar has dissolved, remove from the heat and set aside to cool.

To make honeydew icy poles, remove the skin from the honeydew melon, discard the seeds and chop the flesh into chunks. Place in a food processor or blender and process to make a smooth purée — you should end up with about 300 ml.

Combine the honeydew purée with 50 ml of the sugar syrup and 100ml water and mix well to combine. Pour this mixture into 10 shot glasses or similar moulds and freeze for 30 minutes, or until they start to set. At this stage you will need to add icy pole sticks to the glasses. Freeze for a further 2 hours, or until the icy poles are completely frozen.

To make pineapple icy poles, mix the pineapple juice with 50 ml of the sugar syrup and 100 ml water, pour into shot glasses and freeze as above.

To make cranberry icy poles, mix the cranberry juice with 50 ml of the sugar syrup and 100 ml water, pour into shot glasses and freeze as above.

When ready to serve, remove the icy poles from the freezer and wait for a few minutes so they easily come out of their moulds. Another method is to dip the base of the glass in hot water for a few seconds. Serve the icy poles immediately on crushed ice.

VARIATIONS: You can use the purée or juice of strawberries, passionfruit, mangoes, lychees or even try rhubarb cooked in the syrup — it will be fun to ask the children to try to guess the flavours.

You don't need to overdo it to make a great party – simple things done well can be best.

JELLY WITH SOFT CREAM

Gelée à la crème

Little fruit jellies are always a popular item for children and set in small glasses they look beautiful. These days you are able to find plain setting jelly that will set fresh fruit juice. It is a great option instead of using commercial crystals to avoid food colouring and artificial flavours. I like serving the jelly with softly whipped cream, but when I was young my mother used to serve them with a little jug of milk and a dusting of fruit sugar.

2 x 170 g packets plain fruit setting jelly crystals

500 ml (2 cups) boiling water

400 ml orange, pink grapefruit or cranberry juice

125 ml (½ cup) pouring cream

1 tablespoon caster sugar

Put the jelly crystals in a mixing bowl and add the boiling water. Stir until the jelly crystals have dissolved. Add the fruit juice and mix well. Refrigerate for at least 4 hours to set. You could do this the day before to ensure they are completely set.

To serve, whip the cream and sugar until light and fluffy, but still a little runny. Remove the jelly from the refrigerator and spoon into small glasses until half full. Add a spoonful of the whipped cream on top.

VARIATIONS: You can make this jelly using any leftover poaching syrup from various fruits, such as rhubarb, pears, quinces (see page 307) or peaches (see page 315).

Luscious summer berries, thick egg and vanilla custard and crunchy sablé biscuits make a special combination of contrasting but complementary ingredients that just captures the essence of great summer desserts.

SABLÉ BISCUITS WITH FRESH BERRIES AND SOFT CREAM

Sablé aux fruits rouges

Serves 10

120 g butter, softened

60 g (½ cup) icing sugar, plus extra for dusting

180 g plain flour, plus extra for dusting

1 free-range egg, well beaten with a touch of milk, for egg wash

½ teaspoon natural vanilla extract

vanilla custard (see page 352)

4 punnets mixed berries, such as strawberries, raspberries, blackberries and red currants

berry coulis (see page 315)

Put the butter and icing sugar in the bowl of an electric mixer with a paddle attachment and mix on medium speed for 5 minutes. While mixing, add the egg and mix on low speed to combine. Stop the mixer, add the flour and vanilla, then mix on low speed until well combined. Gather into a ball, wrap in plastic wrap and refrigerate overnight.

Preheat the oven to 180°C. Line a baking tray with baking paper.

Roll out the biscuit dough on a lightly floured work surface to about 3 mm thick all over. Cut the dough with a daisy shape cutter. Put the biscuits on the prepared tray and brush the egg wash over the top of each. Bake in the oven for 10–15 minutes, or until golden. Remove from the oven and allow to cool.

Meanwhile, prepare a half-quantity of the vanilla custard as per page 352.

When ready to serve, rinse the berries. Place one sablé biscuit in the centre of a plate and pipe a small amount of custard on top. Place some mixed berries on top of the custard and drizzle with a touch of berry coulis. Put a second sablé biscuit which has been dusted with icing sugar on top. Garnish with more berries and set a spoon of soft whipped cream on top.

VARIATIONS: Add 2 tablespoons roasted pistachios, 2 tablespoons candied ginger, 2 tablespoons chocolate chips or 2 tablespoons espresso coffee to the biscuit dough.

CHOCOLATE CAKE WITH GANACHE ICING
Gâteau au chocolat

This chocolate cake is what chocolate lovers would wish to have for their birthday. It is covered with rich chocolate ganache and can be easily prepared at home with the children. Just watch for those wandering fingers.

Chocolate ganache

500 ml (2 cups) pouring cream

500 g (3⅓ cups) chopped good-quality dark chocolate

50 g butter, diced and softened

Chocolate cake

335 g plain flour

500 g (2¼ cups) sugar

185 g (1½ cups) cocoa powder

2 teaspoons baking powder

2 teaspoons bicarbonate of soda

1 teaspoon salt

2 teaspoons natural vanilla extract

2 free-range eggs

250 ml (1 cup) full-cream milk

125 ml (½ cup) vegetable oil

250 ml (1 cup) boiling water

Preheat the oven to 180°C. Lightly grease a 26 cm round cake tin with butter and line the base and side with baking paper.

To make the chocolate ganache, put the cream in a saucepan and bring to the boil. Put the chocolate in a bowl and pour on the cream in three stages, mixing well between each addition. Allow to cool slightly, about 5–10 minutes, then gradually add the butter, stirring continuously until well combined. Refrigerate for about 10 minutes, until semi-firm — it should be maleable and easy to spread like soft butter.

To make the chocolate cake, sift the flour, sugar, cocoa, baking powder, bicarbonate of soda and salt into a large mixing bowl. In a separate bowl, use a hand-held whisk to combine the vanilla, eggs and milk. Pour over the dry ingredients and stir well to combine, scraping down the side of the bowl as you go and making sure there are no lumps. Add the oil and mix well, then stir in the boiling water until well combined.

Pour into the prepared tin and bake for 25–30 minutes, or until a cake skewer comes out clean. Remove from the oven and allow to cool in the tin for 10 minutes, before turning out onto a wire rack to cool completely.

When the cake is cool, cut the top dome off the cake to create a flat surface. Slice the cake horizontally in half to make two layers. Spread the ganache over one half, top with the other cake layer. Using a spatula or knife, spread the ganache on the top and sides of the cake. Then use the tip of the spatula to create a great messed-up look. Serve with ice cream.

VARIATIONS: Add some chopped roasted hazelnuts to the cake mixture before baking, or even a layer of raspberry jam between the two cakes.

Fish

Chicken and Game

Veal

Pork

Lamb

Beef

Dinner

FISH

We are blessed with an amazing variety of fresh fish and shellfish in Australia. Their availability and affordability gives us plenty of reasons to marinate, grill, bake or pan fry this stunning produce. Simplicity in cooking is the key to enjoying fish — a dill butter, a fresh herb crust or a flavoursome ragoût of fennel, tomato, capers and lemon is enough to enhance any fish dish.

FRESH SARDINES WITH NIÇOISE SALAD

Sardines niçoise, vinaigrette d'onion

Serves 4

These days you can almost always find sardine fillets at the fish market that have already been cleaned and are often already split, or butterflied. It is best to look for sardines in winter when they are at their freshest.

12 sardine fillets, butterflied (ask your fishmonger to do this)

80 ml (⅓ cup) red wine vinegar

1 teaspoon sugar

1 garlic clove, chopped

1 red onion, diced

185 ml (¾ cup) extra virgin olive oil

1 large waxy potato, boiled and diced

2 large tomatoes, blanched, peeled and diced

1 zucchini, peeled, diced and blanched

12 green beans, trimmed, blanched and sliced

24 ligurian olives

½ bunch basil, thinly sliced

2 free-range eggs, hard-boiled and halved

Rinse the sardines, pat dry with paper towels and remove the small pin bones with tweezers. Refrigerate until ready to use.

To make the niçoise dressing, put the red wine vinegar, sugar, garlic and onion and a touch of salt in a saucepan and bring to the boil. Cook for 5 minutes, or until all the liquid has been absorbed and the onion is soft, then remove from the heat and allow to cool. Add 60 ml (¼ cup) of the olive oil and stir through to combine, then set aside until needed.

Combine the potato, tomatoes, zucchini, green beans and olives in a large bowl. Add the basil and season with salt and pepper. Add 60 ml (¼ cup) of the olive oil and toss to coat. Set aside until needed.

Heat the remaining oil in a frying pan over medium heat. Season the flesh side of the sardines with salt and pepper and place them in the pan, skin side down, pressing down with a spatula to flatten them completely. Cook for about 10 seconds, then turn over and cook the other side for about 10 seconds, or until cooked through. Season the skin side and remove from the heat. You could also grill the sardines on the barbecue if you wish.

Divide the vegetables among serving plates and arrange the sardines and egg halves over the top. Just before serving, spoon some of the dressing over and around the salad.

VARIATIONS: Adding diced anchovies to the salad makes for an additional layer of flavour and texture. You could also use mullet (*rouget*) fillets or red mullet (*barbounia*) instead of sardines.

MARINATED SARDINES

Escabèche de sardines

Serves 4

Fresh sardines are great in season and arguably at their best cooked in olive oil and marinated with cucumber and tomato as they do in the south of France and Spain. The fish will keep for three days in the refrigerator. Prepare a day in advance.

800 g sardine fillets

plain flour, for dusting

250 ml (1 cup) olive oil

4 garlic cloves, crushed, plus 1 extra, halved

4 bay leaves

8 thyme sprigs

2 red onions, sliced

100 ml white wine

1 cucumber, peeled and sliced lengthways

2 tomatoes, sliced

4 slices crusty bread

2 tablespoons extra virgin olive oil

Rinse the sardines and pat dry with paper towels. Remove the small pin bones with tweezers. Toss the sardines in the flour to coat.

Heat the olive oil in a large frying pan over medium heat. Add the garlic and cook for 3–4 minutes to flavour the oil. Carefully strain the oil and return to the pan and start frying the sardines for about 1 minute on each side, or until they are golden all over. Remove from the heat and transfer the sardines to a large, deep baking dish. Strain almost all of the oil from the pan and reserve. Season the sardines with salt and pepper, then arrange the bay leaves and thyme on top.

Return the pan to medium heat and cook the onions for about 8 minutes, or until soft, but without much colour. Add the wine and season and continue cooking until the liquid has been absorbed. Arrange the onions over the sardines in the dish, followed by the cucumber and then the tomatoes. Pour the still hot reserved oil over the top and refrigerate overnight.

Preheat the oven to 180°C. Rub one side of the bread with the halved garlic clove and brush with the extra virgin olive oil. Roast for 4 minutes, or until crisp. Bring the sardines to room temperature before serving. Remove the cucumber and the tomato to a bowl, discard the bay leaves and the thyme. Place the bread on individual plates and sit the sardines on top, then add some of the tomato and cucumber. Drizzle with the oil marinade and serve.

VARIATIONS: You can use tuna, swordfish or kingfish fillets, small fish such as red mullet (*barbounia*) or even baby snapper. Add a slice of chilli to the oil or a teaspoon of smoked paprika for added spice.

CURED SALMON WITH RIESLING AND DILL

Saumon mariné à l'aneth et au vin blanc   Serves 8–12

This is a very simple recipe that makes a marvellous entrée. The only thing it needs is plenty of time to cure and slowly marinate — leave at least one whole day and night. Serve it with warm toast, crème fraîche or just on its own with a touch of marinade or with lemon cheeks. It would go perfectly with a cucumber salad (see page 175) and seaweed bread (see page 148).

1 fillet, about 1 kg, of salmon or ocean trout, skin on

500 g (1⅔ cups) rock salt

375 ml (1½ cups) Riesling

125 ml (½ cup) extra virgin olive oil

4 French shallots, finely chopped

1 handful mixed herbs, such as parsley, rosemary or dill, chopped

2 tablespoons fennel seeds, crushed

1 tablespoon white peppercorns, crushed

4 lemons (optional)

Trim the fish well so you have a smooth fillet. Remove any small pin bones using tweezers (you could ask your fishmonger to do this). Put the fish, skin side down, on a large tray. Spread the rock salt over the flesh, then cover with plastic wrap. Refrigerate for 8 hours.

Wipe off the salt using paper towels and dry the fish, discarding the salt and residual liquid. Clean the tray and place the salmon skin side down.

Put the wine, oil, shallots, herbs and spices in a bowl and stir well to combine. Spoon the marinade over the fish, turning to coat both sides and refrigerate for a further 24 hours.

Remove the fish from the tray, straining the marinade into a separate bowl, and season with salt and pepper. Wipe the excess marinade off the salmon, discarding the herbs, and pat dry with paper towels. Wrap in plastic wrap until ready to use.

When ready to serve, use a sharp knife to thinly slice strips of the fish, starting at the tail end. Place three or four slices on each plate and drizzle with a little marinade or serve with lemon cheeks on the side for squeezing over if you prefer.

VARIATIONS: Serve with a celeriac salad (see page 73) and toasted spiced bread (see page 213).

SEAWEED BREAD

Pain aux algues

This recipe makes two small loaves of bread that are laced with seaweed — perfect for serving in slices with cured salmon with Riesling and dill (see page 146) or with fresh oysters or any other raw seafood really.

1 kg plain flour

1 teaspoon salt

2 teaspoons (7 g) dried yeast

100 ml olive oil, plus 2 tablespoons extra

30 g mixed dry seaweed, such as nori, hijiki or kombu, finely chopped

Put the flour, salt, yeast, olive oil and seaweed in the bowl of an electric mixer fitted with a dough hook attachment. Add 600 ml warm water and mix on medium speed for about 10 minutes, or until a smooth dough forms. Transfer to a bowl, cover with plastic wrap and refrigerate for 2 hours.

Turn the dough out onto a lightly floured work surface. Divide into two even-sized portions and shape each into two loaves. Place the loaves on a baking tray that has been lightly greased with oil spray. Brush the extra olive oil over the top of the loaves and set aside to prove in a warmish place for 30–40 minutes, or until doubled in size.

Preheat the oven to 230°C. Bake the loaves for 30 minutes, or until the bread is cooked through. Check by tapping on the base of each loaf — if it sounds and feels hollow, it is ready. Allow to cool on a wire rack.

When you are ready to serve, slice the bread with a serrated knife and grill on a barbecue or toast lightly. Any leftover bread can be wrapped in plastic wrap and frozen for up to 1 month.

SMOKED RAINBOW TROUT WITH FENNEL AND DILL MAYONNAISE

Truite fumé, salade de fenouil

Serves 4

Ocean trout is so much more popular than old-fashioned hot-smoked rainbow trout but I still find it works best for this recipe. They have a wonderful flavour that works perfectly with the fennel and dill mayonnaise.

1 fennel bulb, trimmed, halved and thinly sliced

1 handful dill, chopped

125 g (½ cup) mayonnaise

juice of 1 lemon

2 smoked rainbow trout about 200 g each, skin off

2 tablespoons extra virgin olive oil

Blanch the fennel in a saucepan of salted boiling water for 1 minute. Plunge immediately into iced water to refresh, then drain well and pat dry with paper towels. Put the fennel in a bowl with the dill and toss to combine. Add half the mayonnaise and toss with the lemon juice, to taste. Add more mayonnaise as required, seasoning with salt and pepper, to taste.

Remove the head and tail of the trout and discard. Carefully lift the fillets from each side of the trout. Clean off any small bones left on the flesh and remove the skin so you have two perfect trout fillets per fish.

Lay a trout fillet on each plate and top with a good spoonful of fennel and dill mayonnaise, then drizzle with some olive oil, to serve.

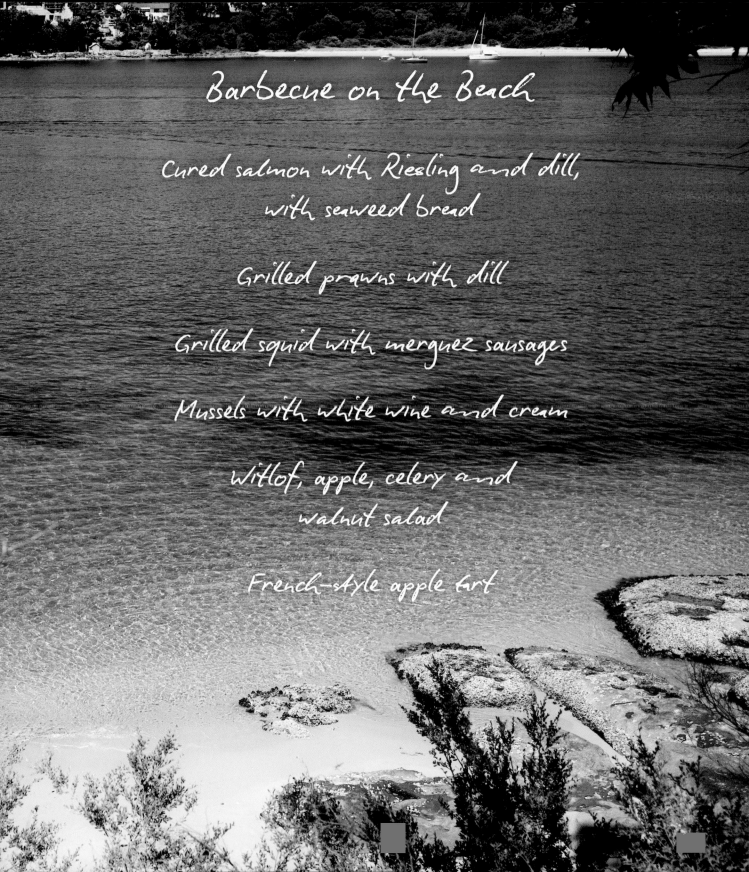

Barbecue on the Beach

Cured salmon with Riesling and dill,
with seaweed bread

Grilled prawns with dill

Grilled squid with merguez sausages

Mussels with white wine and cream

Witlof, apple, celery and
walnut salad

French-style apple tart

SPLIT PRAWNS WITH SHALLOT BUTTER

Crevettes au beurre blanc à l'échalote verte

If you are able to source large king prawns this is a great recipe for them, as they are cooked whole in their shell, although they are first split and butterflied. When you eat them use a fork to just pull out the flesh — delicious!

16 extra large raw king prawns

125 ml (½ cup) white wine

125 ml (½ cup) vermouth or Champagne

1 tablespoon white wine vinegar

6 French shallots, finely chopped

200 g butter, diced, plus 50 g extra

1 tablespoon olive oil

Remove and discard the prawn heads, rinse the bodies and pat dry with paper towels. With a sharp serrated knife, make a cut down the back of each prawn, making sure you don't cut all the way through, then split the prawns open so they are butterflied. Place them on a tray, remove the dirt sacs, and lay a piece of baking paper over the top. Place another tray over the top and use a weight, such as tinned food, to press the prawns flat. Refrigerate until ready to cook.

Put the wine, vermouth or Champagne, vinegar, salt and pepper in a small saucepan and bring to the boil. Continue to boil until the liquid reduces by about one-third. Add the shallots and stir through, then remove from the heat and start adding the butter, one piece at a time, until all the butter has melted and the sauce is smooth. Adjust the seasoning, to taste. Set aside and keep warm.

Heat the oil and extra butter in a large frying pan over high heat. Remove the weights from the prawns, season the cut side, then turn over and cook the prawns, cut side down, for 1 minute, pressing down with a spatula to flatten them while cooking. Turn over and cook for 1 minute to scorch the shells. Remove to a serving platter and serve immediately with the shallot butter drizzled over the prawns.

VARIATIONS: For a milder butter, finely chop 4 French shallots and cook them in the wine, adding 1 tablespoon of chopped parsley at the end. You could also use scampi or even small marron tails if they are available.

PRAWNS WITH CHAMPAGNE AND CELERY

Crevettes au Champagne et au céleri   **Serves 4**

Prawns are a real treat so it is important not to waste them by overcooking. There are two vegetables that go very well with seafood, but are rarely used together — celery and cucumber. This recipe uses both and with a few glasses of Champagne it makes for a very good meal.

20 large raw prawns

2 large celery stalks, trimmed, peeled and cut into 5 cm sticks

1 English cucumber, peeled, seeds removed and cut into 5 cm sticks

4 slices white bread

2 tablespoons olive oil

375 ml (1½ cups) Champagne or Riesling

4 shallots, finely chopped

2 garlic cloves, finely chopped

300 ml pouring cream

celery salt or sea salt (see Note page 66)

50 g butter

1 handful celery leaves, rinsed

Peel and devein the prawns, then using a small sharp knife, make a shallow cut along the back of each prawn, following the line of the vein, and set aside.

Blanch the celery in a saucepan of salted boiling water for 2 minutes, then rinse immediately under cold water, drain and reserve.

Blanch the cucumber in a saucepan of salted boiling water for 1 minute, then rinse immediately under cold water, drain and reserve.

Preheat the oven to 160°C. Cut the crusts off the bread and discard. Brush the bread with the olive oil. Cut each slice into small triangles and set them on an oven tray. Roast the bread until crisp. Set aside.

Put the Champagne or Riesling, shallots and garlic in a small saucepan over high heat. Bring to a simmer and reduce the liquid by two-thirds. Add the cream and continue to simmer until reduced by half, skimming the surface regularly. Season with the celery salt or sea salt and pepper. Remove from the heat, strain into a clean bowl and set aside.

Heat the butter in a nonstick frying pan over high heat. Add the prawns and sauté for 2 minutes, or until seared. Add the celery, cucumber and cream sauce and simmer until the prawns have opened and are cooked. Add the celery leaves to the pan and toss. Serve immediately with the crispy bread croutons as a garnish.

VARIATIONS: Use yabbies instead of the prawns, although you will need to poach them gently first. Balmain bug tail meat or scallops also work well. You can add oysters to the sauce or poach some large pacific oysters and serve them separately with the sauce and the croutons.

GRILLED PRAWNS WITH DILL

Crevettes grillé à l'aneth

Over the years brochettes, or skewered meat or fish, have lost some of their appeal, as they were often served overcooked. If you use care and a deft touch when you cook them they are a great way to enjoy some beautiful produce, like these prawns. The dill combines beautifully with the garlic and lime to add plenty of fresh flavours. For best results cook them on a barbecue plate.

20 large raw king prawns, peeled and deveined, tails left intact

80 ml (⅓ cup) olive oil

2 tablespoons Pernod, gin or brandy (optional)

4 French shallots, finely chopped

1 handful dill, finely chopped

125 g butter, diced, softened

1 garlic clove, finely chopped

juice of 1 lime

2 tablespoons vegetable oil

1 lime, cut into wedges, to serve

Soak 20 bamboo skewers in water for 1 hour to prevent them from burning during cooking.

Thread a prawn onto each skewer, piercing through the tail and head, and place in a large dish.

Combine the olive oil, Pernod, gin or brandy, half of the shallots, and one-third of the dill in a bowl. Season with salt and pepper, then pour over the prawns and marinate for at least 1 hour in the refrigerator.

Put the butter, garlic, remaining shallots and dill and the lime juice in a food processor. Season with salt and pepper and start mixing on low speed, then increase the speed to produce an evenly mixed butter. Set aside at room temperature to prevent the butter from hardening.

Heat a barbecue plate to high. Drizzle half the vegetable oil on the barbecue and cook half of the prawns for 2 minutes, turning over once, until they have acquired some colour. Remove to a platter and repeat with the remaining oil and prawns.

To serve, spoon over plenty of dill butter and put the lime wedges on the side for squeezing.

VARIATIONS: You can use the marinade with butterflied bug tails or scampi — both taste terrific served with the dill butter. You could also just roast some Tasmanian scallops with a small slice of bacon on top before spooning over the butter.

MUSSELS WITH WHITE WINE AND CREAM
Moules à la crème   Serves 4

These days you are able to purchase perfectly cleaned and prepared mussels. No longer do you need to spend time scrubbing the mussels of barnacles and pulling out the beards. The only thing you need to remember is to discard any open mussels *before* you cook them. While many people think that any mussels that are still closed after cooking should be discarded it is actually the opposite. Indeed, some mussels are so fresh that they stay sealed; just pry them open with a knife before you serve them.

3 kg mussels, scrubbed and de-bearded

250 ml (1 cup) dry white wine

2 garlic cloves, sliced

300 ml pouring cream

2 tablespoons chopped flat-leaf parsley

1 French baguette, torn, to serve

Check all the mussels to see if there are any broken or open ones and discard them. Rinse the mussels under cold water and drain. Heat a large saucepan over high heat and toss in the mussels. Add the wine and the garlic, cover, and steam for 3–4 minutes until the mussels open. Strain the cooking liquid into a large bowl. Set the mussels aside.

Return the mussel stock to the pan over high heat. Add the cream and boil for 5 minutes, or until the stock has reduced by one-third. Add the mussels, season with salt and pepper and cook for a few minutes to warm through, then add the parsley and divide between four serving bowls. Serve with crusty baguette.

VARIATIONS: You can use fresh tomato sauce (see page 172) instead of the cream if you prefer, or omit the cream altogether and serve in a clear broth. You could cool the mussels and discard the top shells to serve them open with the meat in their shells — take 100 g (1 cup) dried breadcrumbs and mix with finely chopped garlic cloves, some chopped parsley and moisten with olive oil, then spoon over the mussels in their shell before grilling in a very hot oven for 10 minutes.

CRUMBED GARFISH WITH CELERIAC REMOULADE
Petit poisson panée, rémoulade de céleri-rave

Garfish and celeriac are ingredients that are often overlooked, which is a shame as garfish has a wonderfully refined taste. Celeriac is quite easy to clean and prepare and with its apple and celery taste makes this a delicious starter.

1 celeriac, trimmed and peeled

1 small onion, diced

50 ml white wine vinegar

4 cornichons, or small gherkins, chopped

1 tablespoon salted capers, rinsed and chopped

1 tablespoon mixed chopped herbs, such as parsley, chives, tarragon or chervil

1 tablespoon Dijon mustard

250 g (1 cup) mayonnaise

juice of ½ lemon

8 whole garfish, about 120 g each, butterflied

2 tablespoons plain flour

1 free-range egg, well beaten with a little milk, for egg wash

100 g (1 cup) dry breadcrumbs

125 ml (½ cup) olive oil

1 head cos lettuce, trimmed and quartered, to serve

1 lemon, cut into wedges, to serve

Cut the celeriac in half. Use a mandoline to slice it thinly, then use a sharp knife to julienne. Blanch the celeriac in a saucepan of salted boiling water for 1 minute. Drain well, squeeze out any excess water, then pat dry with paper towels.

Put the onion and vinegar in a frying pan over medium heat and cook for 10 minutes, or until almost all the liquid has been absorbed. Remove from the heat and transfer to a bowl with the celeriac, cornichons, capers, mixed herbs, mustard and just enough of the mayonnaise to moisten the salad, stirring well to combine. Add the lemon juice, season with salt and pepper and mix well. The salad will keep for up to 2 days, so you can prepare it in advance.

Make sure the garfish is cleaned of any small pin bones, if not, remove them with tweezers. Dust the garfish first in the flour, then dip in the egg wash and finally in the breadcrumbs to evenly coat all over. Press the crumbs firmly on the fish to ensure they stick during cooking.

Heat the oil in a large frying pan and cook the fish, skin side down, for 2 minutes, then turn and cook the other side for 2 minutes, or until golden and crisp. Remove from the pan and drain on paper towels.

Serve the fish on serving plates with the cos lettuce and top with the celeriac salad and a lemon wedge for squeezing.

VARIATIONS: You could replace the garfish with any fish really — try whiting or bream fillets. The celeriac is unique but you could use a combination of shaved celery and apples for a variation of flavour, or add some cooked diced potatoes or even chopped anchovy for more substance.

GLAZED SCALLOPS WITH MUSHROOM AND SHALLOT PURÉE

Pétoncles aux champignons et à l'échalotte

Serves 4

If you can find fresh scallops in their shells this is a great way to cook them, otherwise buy some large scallops from your fishmonger and prepare this recipe in gratin dishes.

20 scallops, in the shell

12 French shallots, peeled

2 thyme sprigs

2 bay leaves

250 ml (1 cup) vegetable stock (see page 61) or water

2 tablespoons vegetable oil

200 g button mushrooms, sliced

150 g enoki mushrooms, trimmed

1 garlic clove, finely chopped

1 tablespoon finely chopped flat-leaf parsley

2 tablespoons butter

250 ml (1 cup) hollandaise sauce (see page 32)

1 French baguette, sliced, to serve

Remove the scallops from their shells. Clean the scallops to remove the grit bag. Clean the shells and set aside. Set the scallops on a tray lined with paper towels to drain any moisture and refrigerate while making the sauce.

Put the shallots in a small saucepan over low heat. Add the thyme, bay leaves, a touch of salt and just enough stock or water to cover, then cook for 10 minutes, or until nearly dry. Remove the herbs, strain and reserve the stock.

Put the shallots in a food processor and process to make a smooth purée, adding a touch of the cooking stock if needed.

Heat 1 tablespoon of the oil in a frying pan over high heat and cook the mushrooms for 10 minutes, or until seared and dry. Add the garlic and season with salt and pepper. Remove from the heat, stir through the parsley and set aside.

Heat the remaining oil in the same pan over high heat. Season the scallops and cook for 30 seconds to achieve a nice golden colour, adding the butter to caramelise. Turn and cook the other side for 30 seconds. Make sure you do not overcook them. Remove the scallops to a tray lined with paper towels to drain.

Preheat the grill to high. Put a good spoonful of warm shallot purée into half of the cleaned scallop shells, then sit a scallop inside. Top with some warm mushrooms, spoon on a touch of hollandaise and grill to give colour to the sauce. Serve immediately with slices of crusty bread on the side.

VARIATIONS: Use raw prawns that have been peeled and deveined instead of the scallops, making sure they are lightly sealed and cooked through before serving. Served with steamed asparagus on the side, it makes a wonderful main meal.

ROASTED SCALLOPS WITH LEEK AND BACON

Saint-Jacques rôties au poireau et au porc salé

From time to time a box of live scallops in their shells appears at the fish markets and it is always exciting to see. You can source saucer scallops from the warmer waters of Australia, such as Hervey Bay and Shark Bay. They are easy to recognise as they have a flat shell, but they do not possess the colourful roe of the Tasmanian variety. Either type of scallop can be used, but the saucer scallop will cook faster.

20 scallops, in the shell

8 slices streaky pancetta or bacon

100 g butter, diced

1 leek, white part only, rinsed, halved lengthways and thinly sliced

1 tablespoon chopped flat-leaf parsley

1 tablespoon snipped chives

2 handfuls wild rocket

1 tablespoon extra virgin olive oil

2 lemons, cut into cheeks, to serve

Remove the scallops from their shells and clean them to remove the grit bag. Clean the shells and set aside. Set the scallops on a tray lined with paper towels to drain any moisture and refrigerate until needed.

Finely chop four of the pancetta slices and cut the remaining pancetta into strips about 2 cm wide. Set aside until needed.

Heat half of the butter in a frying pan over low heat. Add the leek, season with salt and pepper, and cook for about 10 minutes, or until the leek is tender. Add the chopped pancetta to the pan and continue cooking for 5 minutes, or until cooked. Remove from the heat.

Put the remaining butter in a small bowl, add the herbs and a touch of salt and pepper and stir well to combine.

Preheat the oven to 240°C.

Lay half of the cleaned scallop shells on a baking tray. Place a spoonful of the leek mixture in the base of each shell, and top with a scallop. Arrange the pancetta strips over the top and spoon over a little herb butter to finish. Roast the scallops in the oven for 10 minutes.

Meanwhile, toss the rocket with the olive oil and season with salt and pepper. Serve the scallops in the shell with the rocket and a lemon cheek on the side for squeezing.

GRILLED SQUID WITH MERGUEZ SAUSAGES

Calmar aux saucisses de merguez

Serves 4

This flavour combination is popular in the south of France but also in the Basque region of Spain. It is fairly common as a snack before lunch or dinner during the summer months, especially if you are serving a chilled glass of rosé. Any spicy sausages will work well in this dish, but use mild ones for the children.

8–12 small merguez or chilli sausages

60 ml (¼ cup) extra virgin olive oil

12 small squid, cleaned (see Note)

2 lemons, cut into cheeks, to serve

1 tablespoon chopped parsley, to serve

Take the sausages out of the refrigerator at least 30 minutes before you wish to start cooking.

Heat a barbecue grill plate or a grill pan to high. Brush with a touch of the oil and cook the sausages until they just start to colour, then reduce the heat to medium and continue cooking for 2 minutes, turning halfway, until they are cooked through. Remove to a plate, cover and keep warm while you cook the squid.

Brush the grill to clean and wipe with paper towels soaked in a touch of olive oil. Season the squid with salt and pepper. Set the squid on the hot grill and cook for 1–2 minutes, turning only once. The head and tentacles will cook first and when they have a nice colour remove them to a plate. Put the lemon cheeks on the grill, cut side down, while the squid tubes finish cooking, it should take about 1 minute more.

Arrange the sausages and squid on a plate and serve with the char-grilled lemon cheeks on the side for squeezing. Drizzle the remaining olive oil over the top, season and sprinkle with chopped parsley. Serve immediately.

NOTE: If you are preparing the squid from scratch, grasp the body in one hand and the head and tentacles in the other; pull firmly to separate. Pull the cartilage from inside the body and discard. Remove and discard any white membrane. Rinse the body under cold running water and pull away the skin. Rinse the head and trim the long tentacles. Rinse again and pat dry with paper towels, then set aside until ready to cook. You can prepare the squid several hours in advance and refrigerate until you are ready to use it.

GROPER WITH ANCHOVY AND PARSLEY PASTE

Fillet de poisson au anchois

Serves 4

Anchovy and parsley paste has a strong robust flavour that is ideal to smear over thick fish fillets. If you really like anchovies, keep some of the oil from the tin and drizzle a little into the paste when you make it.

2 garlic cloves, crushed

4 French shallots, roughly chopped

1 small red chilli, seeded

1 handful flat-leaf parsley

100 g tinned Spanish anchovies, drained

finely grated zest of 1 lemon

4 x 180 g skinless groper, blue eye or bar cod fillets

2 tablespoons olive oil

2 lemons, cut into wedges, to serve

The ideal way to make the anchovy paste is to use a mortar and pestle. First crush the garlic, shallots and chilli to make a paste. Add the parsley leaves and continue to pound to combine. Add the anchovies and lemon zest and continue to pound until you have a rough paste; season with salt and pepper.

Put the fish on a roasting tray and spread the anchovy paste evenly over all sides, then refrigerate for at least 2 hours to allow the flavours to infuse. Take the fish out of the refrigerator at least 15 minutes before you wish to start cooking.

Heat the oil in a large frying pan over medium heat. Add the fish and cook for 2 minutes. Turn the fish and cook for a further 2 minutes — some of the paste will fall off but the flavours will remain.

Serve the fish immediately with lemon wedges on the side for squeezing. The groper will taste terrific served with blanched and sautéed green beans, sugar snap peas or a mixture of green vegetables with a serve or small roasted or boiled new potatoes.

VARIATIONS: You can use this paste on a whole snapper — cut some deep slits in the flesh on each side of the fish and smear the anchovy paste all around. Roast in a 160°C oven for 30 minutes, or until cooked through.

PINK SNAPPER WITH FENNEL AND PERNOD

Dorade au fenouil et Pernod

I find the combination of fish, fennel and Pernod pretty irresistible. You can use any firm fish for this recipe, such as leather jacket or flathead, and either fillets or well trimmed whole fish.

125 ml (½ cup) olive oil, plus 4 tablespoons extra for cooking fish

1 large fennel bulb, trimmed and diced

2 celery stalks, peeled, cut into short lengths and blanched

½ handful dill, chopped

4 x 160 g pink snapper fillets or 1 kg small whole snapper

2 tablespoons plain flour

30 ml Pernod

juice of 1 lemon

saffron potatoes (see page 166), to serve

Heat the olive oil in a small saucepan over low heat. Add the fennel and cook for 10 minutes, or until tender but without colour. Add the celery and dill, season with salt and pepper and toss to combine. Remove from the heat and keep warm.

Season the fish fillets with salt and pepper on both sides and dust with the flour, shaking off any excess. Heat the extra olive oil in a large frying pan over medium heat. Add the fish and cook for 3 minutes on the skin side, then turn and cook on the other side for 2 minutes. If you are using whole fish you will need to increase the cooking time slightly. Add the Pernod and flambé the fish.

Re-heat the fennel if required and squeeze in the lemon juice just before serving. Serve the fish fillets with the fennel spooned over the top and the saffron potatoes on the side.

VARIATIONS: You could blanch 400 g spinach, roughly chop it and add it to the fennel for a very healthy dish.

SAFFRON POTATOES
Pomme safranée   Serves 4–6

Saffron used to be an extremely rare spice, hard to source even for us chefs. These days good-quality saffron is still expensive but you are able to find it in most good food stores. I like the way the potatoes acquire the flavour and colour of the saffron — a little touch goes a long way. These potatoes work particularly well with Pink snapper with fennel and Pernod on page 165.

500 ml (2 cups) vegetable stock (see page 61)

1 pinch of saffron threads

2 pinches of salt

6 large desiree or Dutch Cream potatoes

Preheat the oven to 180°C.

Put the vegetable stock, saffron and salt in a saucepan over high heat. Bring to the boil and cook for 5 minutes, or until the saffron has infused the stock.

Peel the potatoes and slice them into 5 mm thick rounds. Lay them in a baking dish and pour over the saffron stock. If there is not enough stock to cover the potato add a touch of water. Cover with baking paper and bake for 20 minutes, or until cooked but still firm. Drain the liquid and reserve for another dish. Transfer the potatoes to a serving dish and serve warm.

VARIATIONS: You can cook fennel in the same way as these potatoes. The leftover stock could be used to make a mussel soup or a leek and potato soup, or could be added to any fish stock.

MARINATED KINGFISH WITH TOMATO SALAD AND GREEN TOMATO DRESSING

Carpaccio de poisson blanc à la vinaigrette de tomate verte

Serves 4

Sashimi, carpaccio, ceviche, tartare — nearly every country eats a variation of fish served raw. Use Hiramasa kingfish if you can get it as it is farmed and has a more predictable freshness. To eat raw fish does not require much: a touch of salt, soy sauce, pickles, lemon or lime, or a dressing that has plenty of acidity. This green tomato dressing is a variation of one of my mother's favourites. She used to make a green tomato ketchup with some of the unique tomatoes growing in our garden, and this dressing is in keeping with my childhood memories of her ketchup.

800 g skinless Hiramasa kingfish fillets

2 vine-ripened, heirloom or Black Russian tomatoes, sliced

60 g (¼ cup) black olive tapenade

1 handful flat-leaf parsley

12 white anchovies, to serve (optional)

grissini to serve (optional)

Green tomato dressing

1 green tomato, chopped

1 shallot, chopped

1 tablespoon verjuice or white balsamic vinegar

60 ml (¼ cup) extra virgin olive oil

Use a very sharp knife to slice the fish into thin strips, about 3 mm wide, avoiding the bloodline, or dark part of the flesh. Set the fish strips on a plate lined with baking paper. Cover in plastic wrap and refrigerate until needed.

To make the green tomato dressing, put the tomato, shallot and verjuice or vinegar in a food processor and process to combine. Add the oil and continue to process to make a dressing with a runny consistency. Season with salt and pepper and set aside.

Divide the kingfish between four serving plates. Top with slices of tomato and drizzle on some of the dressing. With a teaspoon dipped in hot water, scoop about 3 teaspoons of the tapenade over the fish. Garnish with parsley and a few white anchovies if using, and serve with the grissini on the side if desired.

VARIATIONS: You can use whiting fillets, scallops or ocean trout instead of the kingfish if you like, or use roasted and peeled yellow capsicums for a vegetarian option. The dressing will also go very well with blanched asparagus or even slices of goat's cheese.

CONFIT SNAPPER, FENNEL AND CITRUS SALAD

Confit de poisson aux agrumes

Serves 4

This recipe can be made ahead of time as the fish will be cooked and will keep easily for hours at room temperature. The fish absorbs the fragrance and fruitiness of the olive oil, which is a perfect balance to its natural saltiness.

200 g (1½ cups) salt

4 x 150 g boneless snapper fillets

250 ml (1 cup) olive oil

100 g (⅔ cup) blanched almonds

1 tablespoon shelled pistachios

1 orange, peeled and divided into segments

1 pink grapefruit, peeled and divided into segments

1 tangelo or mandarin, peeled and divided into segments

1 lime, peeled and divided into segments

1 fennel bulb, trimmed

1 tablespoon mixed tarragon and chervil

125 ml (½ cup) extra virgin lemon oil or extra virgin olive oil

Spread the salt on a tray, place the fish fillets on the salt and roll to coat them. Refrigerate for at least 2 hours.

Preheat the oven to 120°C.

Wipe the salt off the fish and pat dry with paper towels. Place the fish fillets in a single layer in the base of an ovenproof saucepan. Add enough olive oil to cover the fish (you might need more depending on the size of your saucepan). Put the pan in the oven and cook for 2 hours. Remove from the oven and allow the fish to cool in the oil.

Increase the oven temperature to 180°C.

Put the almonds and pistachios on a baking tray and cook for 5 minutes, or until lightly roasted. Remove from the oven.

Trim the segments out of all the citrus, removing any noticeable pips, and place in a large bowl. Trim the outer leaves of the fennel, cut in half and thinly shave and add to the citrus. Add the nuts, tarragon, chervil and lemon or olive oil and mix well. Season with salt and set aside to marinate for 15 minutes.

When ready to serve put a generous portion of citrus and fennel salad in the centre of each plate and top with the lukewarm fish.

VARIATIONS: Use any firm white fish fillets for this recipe. You can try radish instead of fennel or substitute the citrus for a variety of tomatoes instead.

KINGFISH FILLETS WITH HERB CRUST AND FRESH TOMATO SAUCE

Filet de poisson à la croûte verte, sauce à la tomate fraîche

Serves 4

This recipe can be prepared ahead of time, which makes it handy for entertaining. The crust contains parmesan cheese and herbs but I have also cooked it using olives and mushrooms. The fish is cooked on a piece of baking paper to prevent the parmesan sticking to the pan.

I small handful flat-leaf parsley, roughly chopped

I small handful chervil, roughly chopped

100 g (I cup) dry breadcrumbs

I garlic clove, finely chopped

finely grated zest of I lemon

50 g (½ cup) freshly grated parmesan cheese

125 g butter, diced, at room temperature

4 x 180 g skinless, boneless kingfish fillets

I tablespoon olive oil

fresh tomato sauce (see page 172) or tomato passata, warmed, to serve

Put the parsley and chervil in a food processor or blender and process until crushed and combined. Add the breadcrumbs and blend until you have a smooth green paste. Add the garlic, lemon zest, parmesan and butter and pulse until well incorporated. Scrape onto a large piece of baking paper, cover with another sheet of paper and roll out to make a thin dough, about 3 mm thick. Refrigerate until needed.

Preheat the oven to 200°C.

Wipe the fish fillets with paper towels to remove any moisture. Take the herb dough from the refrigerator and sit it in the paper on a clean work surface. Peel off the top layer of paper and place one piece of fish at a time onto the dough. Use a sharp knife to cut the dough and paper around the contour of each fish.

Heat the oil in a large ovenproof frying pan over medium heat. Gently transfer the fish to the pan, paper side down. Cook for 3 minutes, or until you achieve some colour on the crust. Turn over and cook for a few minutes in the oven.

Remove from the oven and serve immediately on warm plates with the fresh tomato sauce on the bottom. This dish goes well with a simple salad or steamed greens.

VARIATIONS: Jewfish, snapper or swordfish could all be used. I keep a few bottles of good-quality tomato passata or smooth tomato sauce in my pantry and if you need to make a quick meal substitute this for the homemade one.

Fresh tomato sauce   **Makes 500 g (2 cups)**

2 garlic cloves, peeled

2 thyme sprigs

2 oregano sprigs

I handful basil leaves

I tablespoon olive oil

8 roma tomatoes, halved

Preheat the oven to 160°C.

In a baking tray, scatter over the garlic, thyme, oregano and basil. Drizzle on the olive oil and season with salt and pepper. Put the tomatoes, cut side down, on top of the herbs. Roast in the oven for 30 minutes. Remove from the oven and allow to cool slightly, then peel off the skins. Reserve the garlic and discard the herbs.

Reduce the oven temperature to 140°C, return the tomatoes to the baking tray and roast for I hour. Remove from the oven and allow to cool slightly before using a stick blender to purée into a smooth sauce. Alternatively you could do this in a food processor. Strain to remove the seeds. Mash the garlic and add to the sauce. Pour the sauce into a saucepan over low heat and cook for 30 minutes, or until it thickens. Adjust the seasoning and reserve until ready to use.

The sauce can be stored in an airtight container in the refrigerator for up to 4 days. Gently reheat the sauce, adjusting the seasoning with salt and pepper, before using.

WHITING WITH SCORCHED TOMATOES AND BASIL

Fillet de poisson aux tomates et basilic

Serves 4

This is one of my simplest and most loved fish recipes. People often have problems with fish sticking to their pan or are unsure what temperature to cook the fish. This recipe makes everything simple by first dipping the fish in eggwash.

12 x 60 g fillets red spotted whiting

1 egg, well beaten, for egg wash

100 ml extra virgin olive oil

100 g cherry tomatoes, halved

100 g yellow teardrop tomatoes, halved

2 shallots, finely chopped (optional)

1 garlic clove, chopped (optional)

1 handful basil, leaves picked, large leaves torn

50 ml good-quality red wine vinegar, verjuice or balsamic vinegar

Preheat the oven to 120°C.

Dip the fish fillets in the egg wash to coat all over.

Heat half of the oil in a frying pan over medium heat and gently cook the fish for 3 minutes. Season with salt and pepper, turn the fish over, season again and cook for a further 3 minutes, or until cooked through. Transfer the fish to an ovenproof dish in the oven to keep warm.

Clean the frying pan and heat the remaining oil over high heat. Add the cherry and teardrop tomatoes and scorch them for 2 minutes until the skin blisters. Remove the tomatoes and set aside. Add the shallots, garlic, basil and vinegar to the pan and mix together. Cook for 1 minute then turn the heat off. Return the tomatoes to the pan, season with salt and pepper.

To serve, divide the fish among serving plates and spoon over the scorched tomatoes and oil.

SKATE WINGS WITH BURNT LEMON BUTTER

Filet de raie au beurre noisette

Serves 4

These days people are so much more adventurous and eager to broaden their food repertoire. When I first put skate on the menu at the Bathers' Pavilion Café I was sceptical and thought that people wouldn't go for it. I was wrong. Skate is a beautiful fish with a very different structure to most fish. Ask your fishmonger for small and thin wings as these are best. Once you have tasted it and understand its texture, it will become something you look for to cook at home.

1 teaspoon ground paprika

2 tablespoons plain flour

4 x 180 g skate wings

50 ml olive oil

150 g butter, diced

1 tablespoon chopped flat-leaf parsley

juice of 1 lemon

Preheat the oven to 160°C.

Mix the paprika and flour in a bowl and season with salt and pepper. Pat the fish dry with paper towels, then dust evenly in the flour to coat.

Heat the oil and 1 tablespoon of the butter in an ovenproof frying pan over medium heat. Add the fish and cook for about 2 minutes on each side, or until you have a nice brown colour. Transfer the pan to the oven to keep warm.

Heat the remaining butter in a separate frying pan over medium heat and stir with a spatula or simply move the pan in a circular motion. As soon as it starts to foam and change colour, add the parsley and lemon juice, then quickly transfer to a small bowl before the butter burns.

To serve, divide the fish among serving plates and spoon the warm butter over the top.

VARIATIONS: You can add capers or diced tomato to the herb butter with the parsley. One tablespoon of mashed anchovy combined with the butter would also add another layer of complexity.

SALMON STEAKS WITH CUCUMBER, GRAPE AND DATE SALAD

Darne de saumon, salade de concombre aux dates

I will always remember seeing the farmed salmon in Tasmania when the fish farming industry first started. Today the salmon and ocean trout products available in Australia are without question an essential part of any restaurant menu and make ideal, practical and delicious fish to cook at home.

2 French shallots, sliced

I handful dill, roughly chopped

I cucumber, peeled, seeded and chopped

4 dates, seeded and chopped

juice of I lime

200 g red grapes

100 ml extra virgin lemon oil or extra virgin olive oil

4 x 200 g thick salmon steaks

I French baguette, sliced, to serve

Put the shallots, dill and salt in a mortar and pestle and pound to crush them together. Add the cucumber and pound again to make a rough salad. Add the dates and lime juice and crush to combine the flavours. Add the grapes, toss to combine, and then add 80 ml (⅓ cup) of the oil, mixing well. Set aside.

Preheat the oven to 180°C. Pat the fish dry with paper towels and cut the end of the belly or flap of each salmon to end up mostly with the core. If you have kitchen string, tie a length around the width of each piece of salmon to form a compact steak.

Heat the remaining oil in an ovenproof frying pan over medium heat. Add the salmon, season the top with salt and pepper and cook for 2 minutes, or until the underside of the fish has good colour. Turn the steaks over, season again, then transfer to the oven to cook for a further 5 minutes. Remove from the oven, cut the kitchen string and discard.

Serve the salmon with the cucumber, date and grape salad on top and slices of crusty bread on the side.

VARIATIONS: You can replace the salmon steaks with ocean trout. Some walnuts or toasted pecans added to the salad give it a delicious crunch. You could also toast a couple of slices of sourdough, break them up into small pieces and mix into the salad just before serving.

BAKED SNAPPER WITH FENNEL

Poisson entier en papillote

Cooking a whole fish can be daunting but really it is very simple. The cooking time is less of an issue as the fish will remain moist once baked in the papillote, or wrapping of baking paper and foil which acts like a sealed cooking bag.

2–3 kg whole snapper, gutted and scaled

1 large fennel bulb, trimmed and sliced, top fronds reserved

125 ml (½ cup) extra virgin lemon oil or extra virgin olive oil

1 onion, sliced

2 lemons, sliced

60 ml white wine

8 thyme sprigs

4 garlic cloves, sliced

100 g butter, diced

Preheat the oven to 180°C.

Wash the fish inside and out under cold water. Pat dry with paper towels and remove the dorsal and side fins with kitchen scissors. Place the reserved fennel fronds inside the fish.

Put the oil, fennel, onion and lemons in a bowl. Season with salt and pepper and toss well to combine. Roll out two sheets of foil and lay them side by side on a clean work surface. Place another sheet in the middle to overlap with the first two. Repeat with baking paper. Lay one-third of the fennel mixture in the middle of the paper to create a nest for the fish to sit on. Lay the fish on top, put some fennel mixture in the fish cavity with some extra salt, and finish with the remaining fennel on top of the fish. Drizzle on the white wine, add the thyme and garlic and scatter the butter all over the fish. Wrap carefully to seal the fish, but do not make it too tight — it is better to create a bit of space around the fish so it is able to steam inside the papillote. Seal the foil securely and place in a baking tray.

Bake the fish in the oven for 20 minutes, then leave to rest in the papillote for 10 minutes.

To serve, open the papillote carefully and spoon the flesh and fennel onto serving plates. Once one side of the fish is served, break the central spine near the head and pull the whole rib cage or the bone structure out. Clean the flesh of any visible bones and portion out the rest of the fish, including the juice.

VARIATIONS: You can use small snapper fillets if you prefer — they will only take about 5 minutes to bake in the oven.

JOHN DORY WITH FENNEL, TOMATO AND CAPERS

Saint Pierre au fenouil, tomate et capres

Serves 4

John Dory, also known as Saint Pierre in France, is a stunning fish. Make sure you purchase it with the skin on and look for the distinctive black thumb mark on the skin that guarantees you are purchasing the real thing and not an inferior relative. I find fennel and fish an ideal pairing. You can prepare the fennel relish ahead of time and warm it up just before you cook the fish.

2 vine-ripened tomatoes

1 large fennel bulb, trimmed and diced

250 ml (1 cup) extra virgin lemon oil or extra virgin olive oil

4 handfuls wild rocket

2 tablespoons salted capers, rinsed and drained

1 lemon, peeled, seeded and diced

4 x 160 g boneless John Dory fillets, skin on

Make a cross in the top of each tomato and plunge into a saucepan of boiling water for about 10 seconds, then immerse in cold water until cool enough to peel. If the skin is not coming off easily, blanch for a bit longer but always refresh the tomatoes in the cold water. Cut in half, remove the seeds and dice the flesh. Set aside.

Place the diced fennel in a small saucepan and pour in just enough oil to cover. Season with salt and cook over low heat for about 15 minutes. Do not boil, just use enough heat to soften the fennel. Add the rocket and stir until it wilts. Stir through the tomato, capers and lemon to combine, season with salt and pepper, then remove from the heat and set aside.

Season the fish fillets with salt and pepper. Heat 2 tablespoons of the oil in a nonstick frying pan over medium heat. Lay the fish fillets in the pan, skin side down — the fillets will curl and you will need to press them down with a spatula for a few seconds to flatten them. Cook for about 2 minutes, then turn over and cook for a further 2 minutes, or until cooked through. I often cook the fish on a piece of baking paper in a slightly oily pan, as this helps the fish retain a nice unbroken skin.

Divide the fish among serving plates and spoon over the fennel, tomato and caper relish to serve.

BALLOTINE OF TROUT WITH SALT COD BRANDADE

Ballotine de truite de mer à la brandade   Serves 4–6

Do not be daunted by this recipe. The brandade is very easy to make if you remember it is simply puréed potato with flaked salted cod, garlic and olive oil. If you like it creamy, add a touch of hot cream. It also works perfectly spread over croutons for a canapé or on its own without the trout. You will need to start preparing the cod a day in advance.

400 g salted cod

1 skinless ocean trout
　fillet, about 1 kg

4 large handfuls spinach
　or rocket, blanched
　and squeezed dry

4 potatoes, peeled and
　diced

2 garlic cloves

60 ml (¼ cup) extra
　virgin olive oil

125 ml (½ cup) cream
　(optional)

juice of 1 lemon

Cut the cod in half and place in a saucepan, cover with water and set aside for a couple of hours to soak, changing the water several times. After you have done this a few times to wash most of the salt away, top up with fresh water and leave to soak overnight.

Lay the trout on a clean work surface and trim off all the brown fatty tissue on the skin side (or you could ask your fishmonger to do this). Trim the tail away and keep it for a single meal portion to use at another time. Season both sides of the trout with salt and pepper and arrange the spinach in the centre of the trout, pressing and rolling to make a large sausage shape. Wrap the trout in several layers of plastic wrap. Cut the fish into four even-sized pieces and wrap again, this time twisting the ends on each side to seal — you should have four little trout ballotines. Refrigerate until the brandade is ready.

Drain the cod and return to the saucepan with enough fresh water to cover. Bring to a bare simmer over medium heat, then remove from the heat and leave the cod in the water for 20 minutes. Drain again, then break the fish apart, discarding the skin, bones and fatty tissue. Use your fingers to break the cod flesh into small even-sized pieces.

Put the potato, garlic and a pinch of salt in a saucepan with enough water to cover. Bring to the boil over high heat and cook for 10 minutes, or until the potatoes have softened. Allow to cool slightly, drain well, then force the garlic and potatoes through a kitchen sieve into a clean saucepan. Put the saucepan over low heat, add half of the olive oil and half of the cod and mix well to combine. If you are using the cream, heat it up and add half to the potato mixture, stirring well to combine. Repeat with the remaining oil, cod and cream in small amounts, continually stirring with a wooden spoon until you have a firm but creamy brandade. Season with salt, pepper and lemon juice, to taste. Set aside.

Run hot water from the sink tap and adjust it so that it is warm — we call it blood temperature. Put the trout in a small saucepan and cover with plenty of warm water and place over low heat — the idea is to maintain a warm temperature for the next 30 minutes — you will need to test the temperature regularly and if the water gets too hot turn it off. The idea is to not cook the protein in the fish, which you can see when a white substance leaches out of the cooked fish.

Remove the trout from the water and take off the plastic wrap. Trim the ends with a sharp knife. Gently reheat the brandade and spoon onto serving plates. Set the trout on the brandade and season with salt. Serve with sautéed spinach.

VARIATIONS: Only trout achieves the great texture of these ballotines when cooked, but you could vary the brandade composition by adding crabmeat, smoked trout broken with your fingers or even roasted and chopped parsnip.

CHICKEN & GAME

The versatility of chicken, the unique flavour of duck and the gaminess of venison all have their place for beautiful dinners at home. But I also enjoy cooking rustic dishes with big flavour, especially if I am in the country. A silky duck pâté is delicious and I love the pairing of roast partridge with a walnut stuffing or roast pheasant with a crispy straw potato cake or slow-cooked cabbage compote spiked with a sweet aged red wine vinegar.

BASQUE-STYLE CHICKEN

Poulet Basquaise

There are as many Basque-style chicken recipes as they are Basque cooks, but most use the same ingredients — capsicum, onion, garlic and their famous local chilli, the Espelette pepper. But for me, a classic poulet Basquaise will also use some Bayonne ham.

100 ml olive oil

1 large onion, cut into large dice

2 garlic cloves, sliced

1.8 kg free-range chicken, cut into 8 portions

2 tablespoons plain flour

250 ml (1 cup) white wine

150 g Bayonne ham or prosciutto, diced

1 red capsicum, seeded and cut into large dice

1 green capsicum, seeded and cut into large dice

8 tomatoes, blanched, peeled, seeded and quartered

1 small red chilli, seeded and chopped (or use 1 pinch of cayenne pepper)

4 bay leaves

4 thyme sprigs

1 tablespoon chopped flat-leaf parsley

Preheat the oven to 160°C.

Heat one-third of the oil in a deep casserole dish over high heat. Add the onion and cook, stirring occasionally, until lightly coloured, then season with salt and pepper, add the garlic and cook for 2 minutes more. Remove from the heat and transfer to a bowl. Set aside.

Pat the chicken pieces dry with paper towels, season with salt and pepper and dust with the flour to coat on all sides. Heat half of the remaining oil in a large frying pan over high heat and cook the chicken for 5 minutes, or until you have a golden colour, then turn over and cook the other side for 5 minutes. Add the wine and cook for 1 minute, or until the wine is reduced by half. Transfer the chicken and the cooking juices to the casserole dish.

Clean the frying pan with paper towels. Heat the remaining oil over high heat. Add the ham or prosciutto and cook for 1 minute, or until seared, then add to the onion. Add the capsicums to the pan and cook for 10 minutes, or until they soften, then transfer to the bowl with the onion. Add the tomatoes, chilli, bay leaves and thyme and mix with the onion, ham and capsicum until well combined. Pour over the chicken.

Cover the casserole dish and cook in the oven for 45 minutes without stirring. When cooked, remove the cover and cool in the casserole dish. If you are going to serve it on the day you make it, simply reheat in the oven, uncovered, then sprinkle with the parsley.

Any leftovers can be kept in the refrigerator for 2 days, but it is so great when reheated it's sure to be eaten the next day. This dish is typically served with rice.

GRILLED CHICKEN TENDERLOIN WITH YOGHURT AND CUCUMBER

Brochette de filet de poulet au concombre

Serves 4

It is very easy these days to find chicken tenderloins but you will also find them already prepared on wooden skewers at most butchers. I prefer to buy the plain skewers and prepare my own marinade. These can be prepared with or without the curry powder. This recipe only requires a quick grilling. You could take the fillets off the skewers and serve them as an open sandwich or roll the bread around all of the ingredients.

12 chicken tenderloins on skewers from your butcher

2 tablespoons curry powder

2 cucumbers, peeled

125 g (½ cup) plain yoghurt

½ teaspoon ground cumin

4 tablespoons extra virgin olive oil

4 pita or flat breads

2 large handfuls mixed mesclun salad leaves

2 lemons, cut into wedges, to serve

Dust the chicken skewers with the curry powder to coat, then wrap in plastic wrap and refrigerate for 1 hour.

Cut one cucumber in half lengthways and use a spoon to scoop out the seeds. Cut each piece in half again, then wrap in plastic wrap and refrigerate. Use a mandoline to julienne the other cucumber, place in a strainer and sprinkle lightly with salt. Sit the strainer over the sink or a pot for about 30 minutes to let the juices drain. Squeeze dry and place in a bowl with just enough of the yoghurt to moisten, stirring well. Add the cumin and some pepper, to taste, and add salt only if needed. Put in an airtight container and refrigerate until needed.

Heat a chargrill pan or barbecue grill plate to high. Brush the pan or plate with 1 tablespoon of the oil and cook the chicken fillets for about 4 minutes, then turn and cook the other side for 4 minutes. Meanwhile, brush the pita bread with another 1 tablespoon of the oil and place on the grill to warm through, turning to lightly grill both sides.

To serve, put a pita bread on each plate with a cucumber piece, then fill the cavity of the cucumber with the cucumber salad, top with the salad leaves, drizzle with the remaining olive oil and serve with the grilled chicken and lemon wedges.

CHICKEN CONFIT WITH MUSHROOM, FENNEL AND BACON

Confit de poulet, rôtie de fenouil à la poitrine de porc fumé

Serves 4

This chicken confit is a revelatory experience, especially if you use a biodynamic or free-range chicken. The flavour of the dark meat of the chicken is enhanced, and the smoky bacon and fennel give this dish an appeal for a memorable meal.

4 chicken marylands
   (preferably organic,
   free-range or
   corn-fed)

2 French shallots, finely
   sliced

2 garlic cloves, sliced

4 bay leaves

4 thyme sprigs

100 g (⅓ cup) coarse salt
   or 50 g sea salt

750 ml (3 cups) olive oil

4 slices streaky bacon, cut
   into strips

1 fennel bulb, trimmed
   and cut into eighths

200 g Swiss brown or
   button mushrooms,
   halved

2 tablespoons butter

2 tablespoons plain flour

1 tablespoon flat-leaf
   parsley

Pat the chicken dry to remove any moisture and place in a large shallow roasting tray. Combine the shallots, garlic, bay leaves, thyme and salt and spread over the chicken. Refrigerate for 4–6 hours.

Preheat the oven to 90°C.

Rinse the chicken and pat dry with paper towels. Put the chicken in a casserole dish so the marylands fit snugly in one layer. Pour on the olive oil and cook in the oven for 40 minutes. Remove from the oven and allow to cool in the dish for 1 hour. Drain, reserving some of the oil, then refrigerate the chicken for at least 2 hours.

Preheat the oven to 160°C. Place a roasting tin in the oven to heat up, and when hot, add the bacon, fennel and a touch of oil from the confit. Cook for 20 minutes, turning the fennel from time to time to achieve a nice even colour. Remove from the oven and set aside in a warm place.

Heat a little of the reserved confit oil in a large frying pan over high heat. Add the mushrooms and butter and season with salt and pepper. Cook for 5 minutes, or until the mushrooms are cooked through, then finish with the parsley. Add to the roasting tin with the fennel.

Dust the chicken with the flour. Heat a little confit oil in a clean frying pan over medium heat and sear the chicken, skin side first. When you have a nice golden colour, turn over and cook for 2 minutes, or until the chicken is brown and crispy.

Serve the vegetables and chicken together on a large serving platter or on individual plates with the chicken in the centre and the bacon, fennel and mushrooms scattered around the chicken.

ROAST BABY CHICKEN WITH MUSHROOMS, COGNAC AND CREAM

Poussin rôti aux champignons à la crème

Serves 4

I learnt this recipe from one of the best teachers at my cooking school in Montréal. The idea was to cook the chicken in advance and then flambé the sauce to impress your guests. These days you do not see much flambéing in restaurants, but nonetheless this recipe is still special.

4 x 500 g baby chickens or spatchcocks

100 g butter, diced, softened

1 tablespoon vegetable oil

2 French shallots, finely chopped

200 g button or Swiss brown mushrooms, quartered

150 g oyster mushrooms, roughly sliced

30 ml brandy or Madeira

125 ml (½ cup) chicken stock (see page 62)

50 g dry porcini mushrooms soaked in a touch of boiling water (optional)

300 ml pouring cream

1 tablespoon tarragon or parsley

Preheat the oven to 180°C.

Trim the excess fat from the chickens, then cut the wing bones and discard. Smother the chicken with some of the soft butter. Season with salt and pepper and place the chickens in a large casserole dish. Roast in the oven, uncovered, for 15 minutes, or until the chickens are a golden colour.

Heat the oil and the remaining butter in a frying pan over high heat. Add the shallots and cook for 1 minute, then add the button and oyster mushrooms and continue to cook for 5 minutes, or until the water has evaporated and the mushrooms have browned. Season well, remove from the heat and set aside.

Remove the casserole from the oven, place over high heat and flambé with the brandy or Madeira. Add the chicken stock and porcini mushrooms with the soaking water, if using, and bring to the boil. Boil for 3–4 minutes, then add the reserved mushrooms, cream and tarragon or parsley. Reduce the heat and simmer, covered, for 5 minutes. Remove from the heat and allow to cool in the casserole dish.

Once cool, divide the chicken into halves and remove as many of the bones as possible. When ready to serve, gently reheat. This dish is best served with sautéed spinach and roast potatoes.

VARIATIONS: You could easily make this recipe with chicken breasts, except you only need to sear the breast before you add the mushrooms and stock. For something special use guinea fowl.

ROAST CHICKEN MAISON

Le poulet maison

A roast chicken should be one of the simplest meals you can make but it still takes a few crucial steps to perfect. Make sure you baste it with butter and rotate the chicken as it cooks, first on its sides and then its back. I like to roast vegetables in the same tin.

2 x 1.2—1.4 kg free-range
chickens

2 lemons, halved

2 tablespoons butter,
melted

1 tablespoon olive oil

24 small new potatoes

4 carrots, quartered
lengthways

8 small brown onions

4 tablespoons chopped
flat-leaf parsley

Preheat the oven to 220°C.

Rinse the chickens under cold running water and pat dry with paper towels. Squeeze the juice of half a lemon inside the cavity of each chicken, then drop in the lemon half with a touch of salt. Tie the legs together with kitchen string so you have a compact chicken and baste with some of the melted butter. Season the outside of both chickens with salt.

Drizzle the olive oil into a large roasting tin and add the chickens, breast side up. Scatter the potatoes, carrots and onions around the chickens, season the vegetables and then squeeze the juice from the remaining lemon halves over the top. Roast in the oven for 15 minutes and then reduce the temperature to 140°C. Baste the chickens with some more of the butter and then turn the chickens on their sides. Move the vegetables around, turning them so they do not burn, and cook for another 15 minutes. Turn the chickens to the other side, mix the vegetables again to coat them with the roasting fat — check to see if they are cooked at this stage and remove them if they are. Lastly, place the chickens breast side down and cook for another 15 minutes. To check if the chickens are cooked, pierce the legs with a knife — if the juices run clear they are done. Remove the chickens from the oven, transfer to a large dish and cover with foil. Return the vegetables to the tin to reheat while the chickens rest.

To serve, carve the chickens into smaller portions and serve them with the warmed vegetables, and some corn purée (see opposite page).

VARIATIONS: You can roast a whole guinea fowl or pheasant in this way and make a simple sour lemon jus with the pan juices. Just remove the vegetables, discard the top layer of fat, and then heat the roasting tin on the stovetop, whisking in a touch of water and some cold butter.

CORN PURÉE

Purée de maïs

Corn is a very versatile vegetable — you can turn it into a soup, a purée, eat the kernels on their own, use them in a pie or enjoy them straight from the cob. When cooked it does not lose its colour like many green vegetables, and even overcooked it is forgiving.

4 corn cobs, peeled
1 onion, peeled
50 g butter

Put the corn cobs and onion in a large saucepan. Pour in enough water to cover and season with salt. Bring to the boil, then reduce the heat and simmer for 60 minutes, or until cooked. You may need to add more water to keep the vegetables covered as they cook. Remove from the heat, drain the corn and onion, reserving the cooking liquid. Allow the corn and onion to cool, then cut the corn kernels from the cobs, discarding the cores, and quarter the onion.

Put the corn and onion in a food processor, season with salt and pepper and add a touch of the cooking liquid. Process to make a smooth purée, adding more of the cooking liquid as needed to achieve the right texture. Add the butter and process to combine.

To serve, gently reheat in a saucepan over medium heat until warmed through.

VARIATIONS: If you would prefer to make a soup you can simply add more of the cooking liquid to the purée to thin it out. If you wish to have a very smooth purée, strain through a coarse metal strainer.

ROAST QUAIL WITH POMEGRANATE AND CITRUS

Cailles rôties à la grenade et agrumes

Serves 4

Quail used to be a very popular entrée in restaurants and is still a favourite of mine.
I find this recipe quite foolproof, as you do not need to worry about cooking the quail
to pink — it is better to cook them through. To serve this dish as an entrée, cook one
quail per person instead of two.

1 tablespoon olive oil
1 tablespoon butter
8 extra-large quail, 150 g each, butterflied
4 French shallots, sliced
250 ml (1 cup) white wine
1 pinch of ground cinnamon
100 g (½ cup) sugar
150 ml apple or orange juice
250 ml (1 cup) chicken stock (see page 62)
2 pomegranates, halved, seeds scraped
1 grapefruit, peeled and segmented
1 orange, peeled and segmented
1 lemon, peeled and segmented

Preheat the oven to 180°C.

Heat the oil and butter in a large frying pan over high heat. Season the
quail with salt and pepper and sear on all sides — you may have to do this
in batches. When they have plenty of colour remove to a roasting tin and
set aside.

Reduce the heat to medium, add the shallots and wine and cook for
1 minute, or until the wine reduces slightly but does not fully evaporate.
Add the cinnamon, then pour over the quail in the tin. Cover the tin
with foil and roast in the oven for 10 minutes. Reduce the heat to 130°C
and cook for 1 hour, or until the meat literally falls off the bone.

Meanwhile, prepare the pomegranate sauce by combining the sugar and
1 tablespoon water in a small saucepan over medium heat. Keep stirring
until the sugar dissolves and makes a caramel, swirling the pan to prevent
burning. When it is a nice caramel colour, remove from the heat and
carefully pour in the fruit juice and chicken stock. Return to the heat
and reduce by half. Add the pomegranate seeds and stir through. When
cool, add the citrus fruits and any juices.

The quail can be cooked a day in advance or on the morning you wish
to serve it. Reheat the quail in a frying pan or over a hot barbecue plate
with a touch of oil or place in a 220°C oven for 5 minutes.

Serve the quail on a large platter with the pomegranate and citrus.

VARIATIONS: You can use partridge, pigeon or even pork belly in this
recipe and adjust the cooking time to suit the size of the bird or meat
you are using. Use a variety of citrus for best effect and grapes
if you can't obtain pomegranates.

PARTRIDGE WITH WALNUT STUFFING

Perdreaux à la farce aux noix

Serves 4

If you like to entertain at home and serve different foods, a main course of partridge is a good option. It is a game bird, available from specialist butchers, and will usually need to be ordered in. Poaching the bird first retains a lot of its moisture.

4 x 500 g partridges

8 garlic cloves

1 litre (4 cups) vegetable or chicken stock (see pages 61–62)

1 carrot, roughly diced

1 leek, white part only, rinsed and chopped

1 bouquet garni (see NOTE)

140 g butter

80 ml (⅓ cup) vegetable oil

1 brown onion, finely chopped

50 g (½ cup) walnuts, chopped

200 g Swiss brown mushrooms, finely chopped

1 tablespoon sage leaves, chopped

2 thick pork sausages, skin removed

100 g (1 cup) dry breadcrumbs

8 slices long streaky bacon

Clean the partridges and trim the wings and knuckles. Add the garlic and some salt to the cavities of each bird. Tie with kitchen string to hold the legs and body together.

Put the stock, carrot, leek and bouquet garni in a large saucepan or stockpot and bring to a gentle simmer. Allow the stock to simmer for 15 minutes, then add the partridges, making sure they are immersed in the stock. Bring back to a simmer, then turn off the heat and leave the partridges in the stock for 1 hour to continue poaching.

Heat 1 tablespoon of the butter and half of the oil in a frying pan over medium heat. Add the onion and cook for 5 minutes, or until it is soft. Add the walnuts and cook for 3–4 minutes, then add the mushrooms and sage. Increase the heat to high and continue cooking until any liquid has evaporated. Remove to a plate and set aside.

Heat another 1 tablespoon of the butter and the remaining oil in the same pan over high heat. Add the sausage mince and cook until brown all over. Return the onion and mushroom mixture to the pan and mix well to combine. Add enough of the breadcrumbs to make a dry mix.

Remove the partridges from the stock and reserve stock for another use, such as pork and duck cassoulet (see page 239). Cut the string from the partridges and discard. Remove the backbone of each bird by inserting a heavy knife into the cavity and cutting the backbone, leaving the breasts attached. Butterfly the bird so that it sits flat and remove the rib cage bones. Divide the stuffing among the birds and reshape. Wrap the bacon slices around each bird and secure with kitchen string. Wrap in plastic wrap and refrigerate for 2 hours.

1 bunch watercress, trimmed

12 pencil leeks, trimmed, cleaned and blanched, to serve

Blanch the watercress in a saucepan of salted boiling water for 1 minute, then refresh immediately and pat dry. Place in a food processor or blender with salt, pepper and half of the remaining butter. Process to make a smooth purée.

Preheat the oven to 160°C.

When ready to serve, remove the plastic wrap from the partridges. Heat the remaining butter with a touch of oil in a large frying pan. Sear the partridges on both sides, add the pencil leeks and reserved garlic, then transfer to a baking dish and continue cooking in the oven for 10 minutes while you warm up the watercress purée. Put a spoonful of watercress purée onto each serving plate. Remove the string from the birds, cut each partridge in two and arrange over the watercress purée with the leeks and garlic on the side.

VARIATIONS: You can use a free-range chicken or pheasant, but only use one chicken or pheasant per two people. Use Brussels sprouts or savoy cabbage instead of the pencil leeks if you prefer.

NOTE: A bouquet garni is a bundle of aromatic herbs tied together with kitchen string. I like to make them using 2 celery stalks and a few sprigs of thyme, parsley stalks and bay leaves. You can also tie them in a piece of muslin (cheesecloth) to stop them from coming apart.

A Picnic in the Vines

Tomato salad with fresh
curd cheese and cucumber

Country-style pork and walnut terrine

Rabbit pies

Chicken parfait with spiced bread

Almond jam tartlets

ROAST GUINEA FOWL WITH CABBAGE PARCEL

Rôtie de pintade au choux

Serves 4

This recipe is rather elaborate but the result makes for a stunning winter dinner.
I cook the guinea fowl legs separately from the breast, both left on the bone.
I simmer the legs gently and use them to form a cabbage parcel. The rest of the
cabbage is used to make a wonderful compote.

2 x 800 g guinea fowl

500 ml (2 cups) chicken
stock (see page 62) or
water

1 carrot, roughly diced

1 onion, roughly
chopped

3 bay leaves

3 sprigs thyme

1 whole clove

1 savoy cabbage

125 g butter

125 ml (½ cup) olive oil

300 ml pouring cream

Rinse the guinea fowl and dry well with paper towels. Remove the legs
from the breast cage with a sharp knife. Separate the legs and set the
breasts aside.

Put the legs in a saucepan, add the stock, carrot, onion, herbs and
clove and bring to the boil, then reduce the heat and gently simmer
for 1 hour, topping up with enough water to keep the legs covered at all
times. Remove from the heat and allow to cool in the stock for a further
1 hour. Remove the meat from the bones and roughly shred with your
fingers; set aside. Strain the stock and return to the pan over medium
heat. Continue to simmer until it has reduced by half. Remove from the
heat and set aside.

Trim the cabbage and discard the damaged leaves. Remove four of
the best green leaves and blanch for 2 minutes in a saucepan of salted
boiling water, then refresh immediately under cold running water. Pat
dry with paper towels and trim the rib of the cabbage to make the leaves
sit flat. Divide the leg meat between the four cabbage leaves and fold up
to form four small parcels. You could use a square pastry cutter to help
form a neat shape if you wish. Wrap firmly in plastic wrap and refrigerate
until needed.

Shred the remaining cabbage leaves with a sharp knife. Heat half of the
butter and half of the oil in a saucepan over medium heat. Cook the
cabbage for 10 minutes, or until it wilts. Add the cream, season with
salt and pepper, and cook until the cream has reduced by half and the
cabbage is cooked. Set aside and keep warm.

Preheat the oven to 180°C.

Add half of the remaining butter and oil to a large ovenproof frying pan over medium heat and seal the guinea fowl breasts on both sides to give them good colour. Season with salt and pepper and baste with the remaining butter. Transfer to the oven and roast the guinea fowl for about 20 minutes, turning them first to cook on each side and then resting on their cavities. After 10 minutes, add the cabbage parcels (remove the plastic wrap first) to the pan to heat through. Remove the pan from the oven and transfer the guinea fowl to a plate. Cover with foil and set aside to rest briefly. Heat the pan over high heat, add some of the reduced stock and stir to lift the pan juices from the base of the pan, then season and strain.

Set the cabbage parcels on four warm serving plates. Remove the guinea fowl breasts from their bones using a sharp knife and arrange on each plate. Add a good spoonful of cabbage compote, drizzle the pan juices over and around and serve with straw potato cake (see opposite page).

VARIATIONS: Use a free-range chicken or a large partridge instead of the guinea fowl to make this recipe. You can try serving it with sautéed potatoes or seared gnocchi or replace the cabbage compote with slow-cooked red cabbage and roast apples.

STRAW POTATO CAKE

Pomme galette

These potatoes are cooked over low heat in a frying pan to become deliciously crispy. They are perfect to serve with quail or game birds or with a veal or chicken fillet in cream sauce. You can make small individual cakes or a large one the size of a frying pan. If you wish, you could use an egg ring to create perfect shapes. For best results use desiree or Toolangi delight potatoes.

4 potatoes, peeled

1 tablespoon vegetable oil

100 ml clarified butter
 (see Note below)

Finely grate the potatoes using a mandoline or use the largest hole of a hand grater. Once grated, squeeze the moisture out of the potatoes but do not wash them; dry them on a clean tea towel. Select the size of the potato cake you will make and then form the potatoes into small pancake-like portions, or small patties in egg rings or a large one that can be cut into four portions once cooked.

Heat the oil in a frying pan over medium heat. Add the clarified butter and set the potato in the pan. Reduce the heat to low and cook for about 10 minutes, or until the bottom is crisp and brown. Turn and cook the other side for 10 minutes. Adjust the temperature as needed to ensure slow, even cooking. Once cooked, remove from the pan and serve immediately.

VARIATIONS: You could add a little diced speck or salted smoked pork belly to the grated potato before you cook them.

NOTE: To make clarified butter, put 500 g of salted butter in a pan or in a double boiler and gently melt over a very low heat. Once the butter is melted, skim the surface to remove the foam, then pour the liquid into a clean container, making sure to leave the residual water and sediment in the base of the pan. When making clarified butter it is best to make more than you need and use any leftover for another recipe. Clarified butter will keep in the refrigerator for a couple of weeks or can be frozen for 2 months.

DUCK CONFIT WITH QUINCE AND RED CABBAGE

Confit de canard au coing

Serves 4

Duck confit has a long history and has got to be one of the ultimate foods as it has a lot of flavour, is rewarding, versatile and easy to make. The cooked duck will keep for up to 2 weeks in the refrigerator and much longer if covered with duck fat. These days I mostly use olive oil to cook confit as it is healthier and less expensive than duck or goose fat, and always in stock at home.

4 duck legs

2 French shallots, finely sliced

2 garlic cloves, sliced

4 bay leaves

4 thyme sprigs

100 g (⅓ cup) coarse salt or 50 g cooking salt

750 ml (3 cups) olive oil

½ head red cabbage, trimmed, core removed, finely shredded

1 tablespoon butter

1 onion, finely sliced

50 ml good-quality red wine vinegar

250 ml (1 cup) red wine

1 tablespoon dark brown sugar

Stewed quince

2 quinces

200 g (1 cup) caster sugar

1 cinnamon stick

To make the stewed quince, peel the quince, remove the cores and cut the flesh into quarters. Wrap the peel and core in a small piece of muslin (cheesecloth) and tie to seal, then place in a saucepan with the quince. Add the sugar, cinnamon and 1 litre (4 cups) water and bring to the boil over high heat. Reduce the heat to low, cover the pan with a sheet of baking paper, and simmer for 1 hour, or until cooked. Remove from the heat and set aside to cool.

Pat the duck legs dry with paper towels to remove any moisture and place in a large shallow roasting tin. Mix the shallots, garlic, bay leaves, thyme and salt together and spread all over the duck legs, tipping the rest on top of the duck. Marinate in the refrigerator for a minimum of 4 hours and a maximum of 8 hours.

Preheat the oven to 90°C.

Brush the salt and herbs off the duck, then rinse the duck legs and pat dry with paper towels. Put the duck legs in a casserole dish so they fit snugly in one layer. Pour over the olive oil and cook in the oven for 1½–2 hours. Remove from the oven and allow to cool in the oil overnight. (If you are cooking the legs on the day you wish to serve them, be careful when handling as they will be quite soft.) Drain, reserving some of the oil, then refrigerate the duck for at least 2 hours.

Put the cabbage in a colander over the sink and sprinkle lightly with salt. Allow any excess moisture to drain away. Rinse well, then dry with a clean tea towel or in a salad spinner.

Heat the butter in a large saucepan over medium heat. Add the onion and I tablespoon of cooking oil from the duck. Cook for 10 minutes, or until soft but without much colour. Add the cabbage and cook for 30 minutes over low heat, or until wilted. Add the vinegar, red wine and sugar and cook over medium heat until the liquid has evaporated. Remove from the heat, transfer to a bowl and set aside.

To serve, dust the duck legs in a touch of flour then pan-fry, skin side down, for 5 minutes, or until golden. Then turn the duck legs over, add the stewed quince and cook for 5 minutes. Reheat the cabbage and serve with the duck, quince and roast potatoes.

VARIATIONS: Duck confit is quite unique but you could certainly try to make it using goose legs if you can get your hands on them. They will require an extra 30 minutes of curing in the salt and an additional I hour cooking time.

SAUTÉED DUCK LIVER WITH PICKLED ONIONS AND GRAPES

Sautéed foie de canard au onion mariné   Serves 4

Serving up liver for dinner can be challenging for some families but in the right environment, like in the country or at a farm, I think it is perfect. Chicken livers are easily obtainable, but they are better prepared in a pâté. Duck livers have a softer taste and are much more versatile. Try them with a beetroot tapenade (see page 87).

400 g duck livers, trimmed

200 g (1 cup) caster sugar

50 g (½ cup) walnuts, roughly chopped

1 red onion, roughly chopped

125 ml (½ cup) white wine vinegar

4 fresh bay leaves

2 tablespoons olive oil

30 ml Muscat liqueur

4 slices sourdough bread, toasted, to serve

200 g large red grapes, halved and seeds removed, to serve

Put the duck livers in a bowl, cover with milk and soak for 1 hour.

Preheat the oven to 160°C.

Put the sugar and 250 ml (1 cup) water in a saucepan over high heat. Bring to the boil, stirring until the sugar dissolves, then add the walnuts and cook for 5 minutes. Drain the walnuts, reserving the syrup, and place them on a baking tray. Cook in the oven for 10–15 minutes, or until lightly roasted and crisp. Set aside.

Put the onion and reserved sugar syrup in a small saucepan over medium heat. Add the vinegar and bay leaves and cook for 15 minutes, or until the onion is soft. Remove from the heat, allow to cool and set aside.

Drain the duck livers, discarding the milk, and pat dry with paper towels. Season both sides with salt and pepper. Heat the oil in a frying pan over high heat. Add the livers and cook for about 5 minutes on both sides, or until well seared. Add the Muscat and deglaze the pan. Remove from the heat and roughly chop half of the livers.

Place the toasted sourdough on serving plates and spoon some of the chopped liver on top. Put the whole livers over this, cutting them if they are too big. Top with the onion, a bay leaf, the walnuts and grapes to serve.

VARIATIONS: Chicken livers are a good variation but you can even use roasted field mushrooms, and spinach instead of the grapes, to turn this into a hearty vegetarian meal. Try substituting a variety of sautéed mushrooms and top them with some fresh goat's curd or ricotta.

ROAST DUCK WITH ROOT VEGETABLES

Canard roti à la broche

Duck is certainly my favourite meat. When I first started cooking roast duck for my family it seemed exotic to me and I instantly fell in love with its unique flavour. The fact that most people I serve it to don't often cook duck for themselves works in my favour to impress them.

2 x 1.8–2.2 kg free-range ducks

16 potatoes, skin on, washed and scrubbed

16 large French shallots, skin on

4 parsnips, halved lengthways

8 beetroot, washed and scrubbed

white pepper

Prepare the ducks by removing some of the excess fat from the cavity. Remove and discard the wings and neck. Salt the duck cavities and skin.

Preheat the oven to 220°C. Use kitchen string to tie the duck legs together and close the cavity. Sit the ducks on a rack in a roasting tin and cook in the oven for 15 minutes, or until they acquire a nice golden colour. Turn the ducks over and cook for a further 15 minutes, then reduce the oven temperature to 160°C and cook for 90 minutes, turning halfway through cooking. Remove to a plate and cover with foil. Drain some of the excess fat — you can reserve this for another use, such as for cooking the crispy potatoes cooked in duck fat (see page 231).

Meanwhile, put the potatoes, shallots, parsnips and beetroot in the same roasting tin, season with salt and white pepper and cook for 30 minutes. Increase the oven temperature to 180°C, return the duck to the tin and cook for a further 10 minutes, or until the ducks are heated through.

When the ducks and vegetables are cooked, cut the ducks into portions by first removing the legs and then carving the breast meat off the bone. Serve with the roast vegetables and any cooking juices.

CHICKEN LIVER PARFAIT

Parfait au foie de volaille

Once a year for Christmas I purchase a log of French foie gras and feast on it with my wife, Yvette, and friends, but a homemade chicken or duck liver parfait is also a nice treat. If you wish, you can enrich it with a small amount of foie gras mousse, which is available from most good delicatessens. The parfait needs to be prepared two days before you wish to serve it as the chicken livers will need a night to marinate and the parfait will take another night to set in the fridge.

500 g chicken livers, trimmed of fat

60 ml (¼ cup) brandy or Madeira

250 ml clarified butter (see Note page 203)

1 onion, diced

1 garlic clove, sliced

2 bay leaves

2 thyme sprigs

250 g butter, diced, softened

100 g foie gras mousse or chicken liver mousse (optional)

1 pinch of allspice

brioche, sliced and toasted, to serve

Put the chicken livers and brandy in a bowl and marinate overnight in the refrigerator.

Drain the chicken livers and set aside, reserving the brandy. Heat 2 tablespoons of the clarified butter in a large frying pan over medium heat. Add the onion, garlic, bay leaves and thyme and cook for 5 minutes, or until the onion is soft, but without colour. Add the reserved brandy and continue to cook until the liquid has nearly evaporated; season with salt and pepper. Remove from the heat, discard the bay leaves and thyme and set aside to cool.

Heat another 2 tablespoons of the clarified butter in a frying pan over high heat. Add half the chicken livers and cook for 5 minutes, turning regularly, until just coloured — they need to be left pink and fairly soft on the inside. Season with salt and pepper, then remove from the heat and set aside. Clean the pan with paper towels and repeat with 2 tablespoons of clarified butter and the remaining chicken livers until all are just cooked.

When the livers are cool, place them in a food processor with the onion and process, adding the diced butter a little at a time, to make a smooth purée. If you are using foie gras mousse add it once all the butter is combined. Season with salt and pepper and add the allspice, processing to combine. Push through a fine sieve set over a clean bowl.

RABBIT WITH MUSHROOM AND LEEK PIES

Lapin de compagne en aumônière

I love these little aumônière or 'coin purses'. Wrapped in crisp puff pastry and filled
with a beautiful ragoût and rabbit salad they make an appealing and memorable
dish. You see these little pies throughout France, sometimes made with truffles,
sometimes chicken or other game birds. No matter what they are made with, they
always taste delicious.

1 kg whole rabbit, cut
into 8 portions (ask
your butcher to do this
for you)

1 carrot, chopped

1 onion, diced

250 g button
mushrooms, trimmed

1 celery stalk, peeled and
halved

1 leek, trimmed, rinsed
and halved lengthways

250 ml (1 cup) white
wine

1 litre (4 cups) chicken
stock (see page 62)

2 bay leaves

2 thyme sprigs

1 tablespoon butter

2 tablespoons plain flour

4 sheets butter puff
pastry

1 free-range egg, well
beaten with a pinch of
salt, for egg wash

Put the rabbit in a large casserole dish with the carrot, onion,
mushrooms, celery, leek, wine, chicken stock, bay leaves and thyme.
Season with salt and pepper and bring to a simmer, skimming regularly
to remove any scum that rises to the surface. Cook for 1 hour, adding
more water if needed to keep the rabbit covered. Remove the carrot,
celery, leek and mushrooms after 30 minutes and reserve on a plate.
Remove from the heat and let the rabbit cool in the stock — even better
if you can refrigerate it overnight.

Remove the rabbit from the stock and remove the meat from the bones,
discarding the bones. Dice the meat roughly or use your fingers to break
into small pieces. Chop the carrot, celery, leek and the mushrooms if they
are large. Place the rabbit and vegetables in a large bowl and set aside.

Strain the stock back into a clean saucepan and place over high heat.
Bring to the boil and cook until it reduces to about 500 ml (2 cups).
Strain again.

Melt the butter in a small saucepan over medium heat. Add the flour and
stir to make a roux. Add the warm stock and stir to produce a fairly thick
sauce. Remove from the heat and cool in the refrigerator.

When the sauce is cold, stir just enough of it through the rabbit and
vegetables to coat — the mixture should not be too saucy, just moistened.
Refrigerate until needed.

Preheat the oven to 240°C. Lightly oil a baking tray with oil spray.

Place the puff pastry sheets on a clean work surface. Trim to make sixteen 12 cm squares. Place a spoonful of rabbit mixture in the centre of each pastry square. Brush the edges of each pastry square with the egg wash and gently fold the four corners towards the centre to seal — try not to seal completely so a little steam can escape. Cut little pastry decorations if you have any excess dough and use the egg wash to stick them to the top of each pie. Refrigerate for 10 minutes to firm the dough. You can freeze any excess pies for up to 4 weeks.

Put the pies on the prepared tray and cook in the oven for 15 minutes, or until golden brown. Remove from the oven and set aside to rest for 5 minutes. Serve with a salad made of watercress, sliced radishes and frisée (curly endive) dressed with a basic vinaigrette (see page 75).

RABBIT RILLETTES
Rillettes de lapin

Rillettes make a fabulous dish. I grew up on cretons (see page 230), much like pork pâté but made with pork mince as opposed to meat that has been boiled or cooked in fat and then shredded by hand. If you find it too hard to use or purchase rabbit, just double the amount of pork shoulder.

1.5 kg whole rabbit

500 g pork shoulder, cut into large dice

2 bay leaves

2 thyme sprigs

6 juniper berries

1 pinch of allspice

300 ml white wine (optional)

400 g pork or duck fat, melted, or 200 ml clarified butter (see NOTE page 203)

1 sourdough baguette, sliced and toasted, to serve

Cut the rabbit into pieces by first removing the legs and shoulders. If you wish, keep the saddle or the middle part to roast for another meal. Cut the legs and shoulders into smaller pieces and place in a large saucepan with the pork shoulder. You could ask your butcher to do this for you.

Add the bay leaves, thyme, juniper berries and allspice to the pan with the meat. If you are using the white wine add it to the saucepan, then add enough water to just cover the meat. Season with salt, bring to a very gentle simmer and cook for 4 hours, skimming regularly and topping up with more water as required — the meat should be very tender when done. Remove from the heat and allow to cool a little.

Remove the meat from the pan and use your fingers to shred all of the meat into small pieces. Add half of the pork fat to moisten the meat, stirring to coat. Season with salt and pepper and mix well. Pour into 12 small dishes or a 24 x 6 cm terrine mould. Pour the remaining pork fat over the top and refrigerate overnight to set.

Serve the rillettes with toasted baguette slices so people can help themselves.

VARIATION: Use goose fat for an extra special taste instead of the pork or duck fat or clarified butter. You will need about 400 g of goose fat, which is readily available from specialist food stores.

LOIN OF VENISON WITH MUSHROOM AND LIVER PANADE AND ONION JAM

Longe de cerf à la panade de foie de canard

Serves 4

Venison is a lean meat but its gamey flavour suits winter. It is beautiful for a dinner at home or makes a special meal for friends. I serve this with a panade, which is really a bread stuffing, made with duck liver that I sometimes enrich with foie gras. To complement this I like balancing the sourness of the liver with a sweet onion jam.

80 ml (⅓ cup) vegetable oil

1 large onion, finely diced

2 garlic cloves, finely chopped

200 g button mushrooms, finely chopped

1 teaspoon thyme leaves

200 g duck liver, cleaned

100 g foie gras (optional)

4 slices sourdough bread, diced and toasted in the oven

100 ml chicken stock (see page 62)

Onion jam

5 large onions, finely diced

150 ml balsamic vinegar

2 tablespoons caster sugar

Venison

4 x 200 g venison loin

1 tablespoon vegetable oil

100 g butter

To make the mushroom and liver panade, heat 2 tablespoons of the oil in a large heavy-based saucepan over medium heat. Add the onion and cook for 5 minutes, or until soft and golden. Add the garlic and mushrooms and cook until most of the moisture has evaporated. Season with salt and pepper, add the thyme leaves and set aside.

Heat 2 tablespoons of the oil in a saucepan over medium heat and sauté the duck livers for 5 minutes until they are firm. Remove from the heat and when they are cool enough to handle, finely chop them and add to the mushroom mixture. Add the diced foie gras, if using, and the toasted sourdough cubes and mix well to make a firm stuffing. Add just enough chicken stock to moisten so the stuffing has a smooth consistency. Season if needed and set aside.

Meanwhile, make the sweet onion jam. Put the onions, vinegar and caster sugar in a frying pan over low heat and cook until the onions are dry and caramelised — they should resemble a thick jam.

To cook the venison, season each loin with salt and pepper. Heat the oil and butter in a large frying pan over high heat and sear the loins on both sides until they have a good colour — it is best to leave them fairly rare.

To serve, arrange the venison on a warm platter and serve with the mushroom and liver panade and onion jam and some steamed broccoli.

VARIATIONS: Use beef tenderloins instead of the venison, or even try it with roasted duck. I also like to serve this with beetroot tapenade (see page 87) as it gives different textures, colours and tastes on the plate.

MEAT

Meat

Good cooking is often defined by the quality of the produce, but it is also important to select the right cooking technique to enhance the dish. So much joy can be derived by serving a great tender veal cutlet with a melting herb butter, or from savouring the stock of a slow-cooked pot-au-feu, not to mention the pleasure of a fragrant cauliflower gratin that comes to the table or an anchoïade that is tasted for the first time.

VEAL ESCALOPES WITH TARRAGON

Escalopes de veau à l'estragon

This is an easy, everyday recipe that can be used for a variety of meat and fish cuts. I use tarragon for a classic taste but any herb would do. The braised lettuce makes a welcome change and tastes great served with straw potato cake (see page 203) to mop up the sauce.

2 heads butter lettuce
100 g butter, diced
4 x 600–800 g veal escalopes
2 tablespoons plain flour
50 ml vegetable oil
4 French shallots, finely chopped
125 ml (½ cup) white wine
1 handful tarragon
juice of 1 lemon

Preheat the oven to 180°C. Lightly grease a large baking dish with oil spray.

Trim the outside leaves of each lettuce and cut each in half, making sure they remain attached at the core. Blanch the lettuce in a saucepan of salted boiling water for 3 minutes, then plunge into iced water to refresh. Drain and squeeze out any excess water, then place, cut side up, in the prepared baking dish. Scatter half of the butter on top, season well with salt and pepper and cover with baking paper. Cook in the oven for 30 minutes and set aside.

Pat the veal dry with paper towels and dust with flour to coat. Heat the oil and the remaining butter in a frying pan over medium heat. Add the shallots and cook for 3–4 minutes until they are soft, but without much colour. Add the veal and cook for 2 minutes on each side, or until most of the blood is extracted. Add the wine, tarragon and the lemon juice. Bring to the boil and cook just enough to reduce and have a nice coating. Serve with the warm lettuce.

VARIATIONS: You could use thin chicken breast, pork escalopes or even some white fish fillets instead of the veal. For a different taste you could use Champagne or vermouth instead of the white wine.

OLD-FASHIONED VEAL BLANQUETTE

Blanquette de veau à l'ancienne

I first learnt to make a *blanquette* at school and ever since I've loved the flavour and the classic method of making this ragoût. The major principle is to poach the meat in the liquid before the resulting stock is thickened. There is a subtle flavour of clove that comes through, and is perfect served with rice.

50 ml vegetable oil

1 kg diced veal shoulder

6 carrots, chopped

2 celery stalks, chopped

2 garlic cloves, peeled

1 leek, white part only, rinsed and cut into 4 lengths

24 button mushrooms, stems trimmed and reserved

1 onion, peeled

2 whole cloves

12 small pickling onions, peeled

50 g butter

50 g (⅓ cup) plain flour

Heat half of the oil in a large casserole dish over high heat. Add the veal and cook for 10 minutes, turning to seal the meat without colouring it. Remove from the dish and drain the meat in a colander.

Rinse the dish clean and return to the heat with the veal. Add half of the carrots with the celery, garlic, leek and the mushroom stems. Spike the onion with the cloves and add to the dish. Pour in enough water to cover, season with salt and pepper, and bring to a simmer. Cook for about 1½ hours, skimming regularly, until the meat is cooked through and tender. Strain and reserve the meat and stock separately, discarding the vegetables.

Meanwhile, put the pickling onions in a saucepan over medium heat with just enough water to cover. Season with salt and cook for 10 minutes, or until they are nearly cooked through, then add the mushrooms and remaining carrots and continue cooking for 5 minutes longer, or until the carrots are cooked but not soft. Remove from the heat, drain and set aside.

Melt the butter in the cleaned casserole dish over low heat. Add the flour and stir to make a roux. Add the warmed reserved stock and cook for about 10 minutes, or until you have a thick sauce. Add the veal to the dish to heat through for 10 minutes, and lastly add the carrots and onions. Serve immediately with steamed rice or flat noodles on the side.

VARIATIONS: You could enrich the sauce by mixing together 2 egg yolks and 250 ml (1 cup) pouring cream and adding to the sauce at the last minute. You could also substitute the veal with 2 chickens cut into portions to make a chicken blanquette.

VEAL AND CHICKEN POT-AU-FEU

Pot-au-feu de poule et jarret de veau

4 small veal shins
(300 g each) or 1 large
veal shank (about 1 kg)

2 onions, peeled

2 whole cloves

2 leeks, white part only,
rinsed

2 carrots, quartered

4 celery stalks, trimmed,
peeled and cut into
5 cm lengths

6 small kipfler potatoes

8 baby turnips or 1 large
turnip, peeled and cut
into eighths

16 radishes, halved

1.4 kg free-range chicken

Wash the veal under cold water and place in a large saucepan or stockpot. Add 4 litres (16 cups) water and bring to the boil over medium heat. Remove from the heat and discard the water. Keep the veal in the pan, cover with another 4 litres water. Spike the onions with the cloves and add to the pan with the leeks. Season with salt and pepper and bring to a simmer for 2–3 hours (depending on the size of the veal), skimming regularly. Remove the leeks after 5 minutes, or when tender, and add the carrots, cooking for a further 3 minutes, or until cooked. Add the celery and in turn the potatoes, turnips and finally the radishes. As the vegetables cook and become tender, remove them from the pan and reserve. When the veal falls off the bone it is done.

Once the veal has cooked, remove all the meat and vegetables from the pan and set aside. Add the chicken to the stock with extra water if needed to cover, and bring to a simmer over low heat, skimming regularly. As soons as it simmers, cover with a lid and turn off the heat. Leave the chicken to poach in the liquid for 1 hour. Remove the chicken and set aside. Reserve the stock.

Preheat the oven to 140°C. Once the chicken is cool enough to handle, divide it into eight portions and place in a large ovenproof serving dish that will fit in the oven. Portion the veal shank and arrange with the chicken, then distribute the vegetables in and around the meat. Cover the dish with foil and place in the oven to reheat.

While the meat and vegetables are reheating, strain the stock back into a clean saucepan and continue cooking over medium heat until the liquid has reduced to 2 litres (8 cups). Remove from the heat and transfer to a soup tureen. Serve alongside the meat and vegetables so that guests can ladle the warm soup into their dish.

This dish is best prepared a few hours before you wish to eat it and reheated just before serving — the veal and chicken will still be moist and juicy.

GRILLED VEAL RACK WITH MONTPELLIER BUTTER AND PARMESAN ASPARAGUS

Côte de veau grillée, beurre Montpellier, asperges au parmesan　　　　Serves 6

Whenever I see beautiful racks of veal at the butcher I always think of this recipe — it is the perfect way to cook them. The great advantage of this dish is it can be pre-roasted to medium rare and left for up to a day, before being cut into cutlets and grilled, making for a very tender piece of meat.

2 kg veal rack of six bones, cutlet bone cleaned and shin bone removed

2 tablespoons vegetable oil

3 bunches large asparagus spears, trimmed and lightly peeled

50 g (½ cup) finely grated parmesan cheese

100 g butter, melted

Montpellier butter

1 bunch watercress

½ bunch flat-leaf parsley

½ bunch tarragon, leaves picked

4 French shallots, finely chopped

1 garlic clove, finely chopped

3 anchovy fillets (optional)

250 g butter, softened

To make the Montpellier butter, blanch the watercress in a saucepan of boiling water for 1 minute, then plunge into iced water to refresh. Drain well and set aside. Repeat with the parsley and set aside. Cut and discard the stems of the watercress and parsley and place the leaves in a food processor with the tarragon, shallots, garlic and anchovies. Process until finely chopped. Add the butter, salt and pepper and blend well to combine. Refrigerate until ready to serve.

Preheat the oven to 220°C.

Pat the veal rack dry with paper towels, then season well with salt and pepper. Heat the vegetable oil in a large frying pan and sear the veal well on all sides. Place the veal on a roasting tray, reduce the oven temperature to 140°C and cook for 45–60 minutes depending on the size of the veal — pierce the centre of the veal with a skewer, it should be lukewarm, not cold or searing hot.

Remove the veal from the oven and set aside to rest for 10 minutes before serving. Alternatively, see the variation for grilling on page 230.

Increase the oven temperature to 220°C. Blanch the asparagus in a saucepan of salted boiling water for 2 minutes, then plunge immediately into iced water to refresh. Place in a gratin dish, sprinkle over the parmesan and melted butter and cook for about 10 minutes, or until the cheese is golden.

Cut the veal rack into individual cutlets and serve with a generous dollop of Montpellier butter on top and the asparagus and crispy potato cooked in duck fat (see page 231) on the side.

VARIATION: Cook the veal in advance to medium rare, then leave the veal to cool before cutting the flesh off each end to remove the seared meat. Cut six cutlets out of the rack so each person will get a bone. Wrap the bone loosely in foil to stop the bone from burning. Heat a barbecue grill to high and brush with a wire brush to make sure it is perfectly clean. Wipe with an oiled paper towel and set the veal cutlets on the grill. Set at a slight angle and after 3 minutes change to the opposite angle. Repeat to cook the other side. Serve with a good dollop of Montpellier butter.

PORK PÂTÉ

Cretons au porc

Serves 12

I was raised on cretons, the French Canadian pork pâté that was eaten mostly at breakfast time. Canadian winters are cold and you do require a diet rich in meat and fat to survive those long frosty days. This dish is similar to a French rillette but is made with fewer ingredients — typically it is easier to prepare, making it a great option for entertaining. This pâté is great with spiced bread (see page 213).

500 g minced pork

500 ml (2 cups) chicken stock or water

1 onion, finely chopped

¼ teaspoon ground cinnamon

¼ teaspoon ground cloves

¼ teaspoon ground nutmeg

¼ teaspoon ground sage

Put all of the ingredients into a heavy-based saucepan over low heat and simmer for 1 hour, or until all the stock has evaporated from the pan. Adjust the seasoning to taste and place in a small serving dish. Refrigerate for at least 8 hours to set before serving.

Serve the pork pâté with small slices of warm toast.

CRISPY POTATO COOKED IN DUCK FAT

Pomme salardaise

Serves 4–6

These potatoes require a bit of work but the result is a crispy textural joy. You will need to make them the day before you wish to serve them.

6–8 large potatoes, peeled

500 ml (2 cups) warmed duck fat

60 ml (¼ cup) vegetable oil or clarified butter (see Note page 203)

Preheat the oven to 180°C. Line a 25 cm square baking dish with baking paper, just enough to fit the base and overlap the sides.

Finely slice the potatoes using a mandoline or a sharp knife.

Put a small ladle, about 60 ml (¼ cup), of the warmed duck fat in the baking dish. Lay two layers of the potato on top, season with salt, then pour in another ladle of the duck fat. Repeat layering until all the potato and duck fat are used, finishing with a layer of potato. Cover with a sheet of baking paper and then with foil and cook for 25 minutes. Lower the oven temperature to 150°C and cook for a further 30 minutes. Remove from the oven and allow to cool for 1 hour. Press a similar-sized dish over the top of the first and weigh down with food tins to flatten the potatoes. Refrigerate overnight.

Turn the dish upside down to remove the potato slice, discarding the baking paper and foil. Cut the potato into portions, ideally 8 x 3 cm rectangles. Heat the oil or clarified butter in a frying pan over high heat. Add the potato portions and cook for 2 minutes, turning to make sure that both sides are evenly cooked and crispy. Serve warm.

PORK MEDALLIONS WITH APPLE AND CIDER SAUCE

Médaillons de porc aux pommes et au cidre

I grew up eating plenty of pork. My grandmother lived in the Quèbec countryside in an area famous for its apple orchards and cider, so to me the combination of pork and apple seems a very natural pairing. This dish can be made without cream if you prefer — simply substitute with 250 ml (1 cup) of reduced stock. If you have Calvados, don't be afraid to add a small glass to flambé the fillets while they are cooking.

2 x 400 g skinless pork
    fillets, trimmed

2 tablespoons olive oil

4 apples, peeled, cored
    and quartered

100 g butter

1 tablespoon sugar

300 ml apple cider

2 tablespoons plain flour

300 ml pouring cream

2 tablespoons chopped
    sage

Cut the pork fillets into about eight small medallions, about 100 g each. Working with one medallion at a time, place between two sheets of plastic wrap that have been lightly drizzled with 1 tablespoon of the oil. Use a meat cleaver or a small, heavy saucepan to pound the medallions so they are flattened and thinned. Set aside.

Trim the apple pieces so they are all an even shape. Heat 1 tablespoon of the oil and half the butter in a frying pan over medium heat. Add the apples and cook for 15 minutes, reducing the heat once they start acquiring some colour. Add the sugar and caramelise for another 5–10 minutes until golden and glazed, then remove the apples to a plate.

Put the apple cider in the pan over high heat and cook until reduced by half. Strain.

Season the medallions with salt and pepper and dust with the flour. Heat the remaining butter in a large frying pan over medium heat. Cook the pork for about 4 minutes, then turn and cook the other side for 4 minutes, or until cooked but still slightly pink. Remove the pork to a plate; wipe the pan clean with paper towels.

Add the reduced cider, cream and sage to the clean pan and bring to a simmer. Season with salt and pepper, stir to combine, then return the pork to the pan and cook in the sauce for 5 minutes, turning the pork once, until the cream has thickened. Add the apples and bring back to a simmer just before serving. This dish is great served with potato and leek boulangère (see page 234).

VARIATIONS: You can use pork cutlets instead of a fillet but add a finely chopped onion when cooking the apple to create a more rustic dish. You can then reduce the cream by half and add I tablespoon of wholegrain mustard. Serve with diced leeks and potatoes cooked in chicken stock until nearly dry or a warm potato salad dressed with cider vinegar, or vegetable and walnut oil and some blanched finely chopped Swiss chard.

POTATO AND LEEK BOULANGÈRE

Pomme boulangère aux poireaux   **Serves 4**

I tablespoon butter

I large leek, white part only, rinsed and sliced

4–6 medium waxy potatoes, such as bintje, halved

I litre (4 cups) chicken or vegetable stock (see pages 61-62)

Melt the butter in a deep casserole dish over medium heat. Add the leek and sweat to soften for about 10 minutes. Remove the leek and set aside.

Put the potato in the casserole, add the stock and cook over medium heat for 10 minutes, or until the potatoes are nearly cooked. Add the leeks, season well with salt and pepper and cook for another 10 minutes, or until the potatoes are fully cooked and the liquid is partly absorbed. Rest for at least 10 minutes before serving.

PORK AND VEAL PIE

Tourtière du Québec

Serves 6

This meat pie is a speciality from the French part of Canada. Every mother and grandmother has a recipe and every region has their own variation. This is the recipe I grew up with and it is easy to make and delicious to eat.

750 g minced pork

500 g minced veal

1 large potato, peeled and diced

1 onion, finely chopped

1 teaspoon ground cinnamon

1 teaspoon ground cloves

1 teaspoon ground nutmeg

500 g shortcrust pastry (see page 95)

plain flour, for dusting

1 free-range egg, well beaten with a touch of milk, for egg wash

Combine the pork, veal, potato, onion and spices in a large saucepan and season with salt and pepper. Add enough water to just cover the meat. Bring to a simmer and cook for 90 minutes, stirring occasionally. If the meat seems too dry, add a touch more water (the idea is that at the end of the cooking time all the water should be absorbed and evaporated and the potato broken down, which will help bind the meat). Remove from the heat, adjust the seasoning to taste, and allow to cool for about 30 minutes.

Preheat the oven to 200°C. Lightly grease a 20 cm round baking dish with oil spray.

Roll out the pastry on a lightly floured work surface to 3 mm thick. Cut a 24 cm round from the pastry. Gently press the pastry into the prepared dish, making sure you leave no air pockets around the base. Trim the edges and refrigerate for 10 minutes. Re-roll the dough and cut another 20 cm round to use for the lid. Refrigerate for 10 minutes.

Spoon the filling into the dish and lay the pastry lid on top, trimming as needed and pinching to seal and enclose the filling. Refrigerate for 10 minutes to firm up the top. Brush the top with the egg wash and make a small slit in the lid to allow the steam to escape. Place in the oven and cook for 10 minutes, or until the crust is golden. Allow to cool slightly, cut into slices and serve.

VARIATIONS: You could substitute the potato for 50 g (½ cup) dry breadcrumbs as is done in some regions of Canada. If the spices are not to your liking they can be replaced by a teaspoon of mustard powder and some dried sage.

A Dinner Party

Saffron and mussel soup

Pan-roasted lamb rump with
heirloom carrots and potato gratin

Floating islands

Coffee with almond tuiles

PORK AND DUCK CASSOULET

Cassoulet de porc et au confit de canard

Serves 6—8

In winter I love to prepare one-pot dishes and this cassoulet is a hearty meal that will satisfy hungry guests. I often prepare the cassoulet the day before and warm it up in front of the fireplace so it can acquire a nice smoky flavour. Just return it to a hot oven to form a crust on the top before serving.

1 kg (5 cups) dried white beans, soaked in cold water for 4 hours

1 onion, peeled

2 whole cloves

4 bay leaves

2 carrots, peeled and quartered

4 garlic cloves, peeled

2 tablespoons olive oil

1 kg pork flank, sliced into 8 cm lengths and 2 cm thick

500 ml (2 cups) chicken stock (see page 62)

500 ml (2 cups) strong beef stock (see page 62) or game stock (see page 196)

6—8 confit duck legs (see page 205)

2 tablespoons plain flour

200 g (2 cups) dry breadcrumbs

125 g butter, melted

Rinse the beans, drain well, then place them in a large saucepan with enough water to cover. Bring to the boil over high heat and, once boiling, remove from the heat. Rinse again and drain, discarding the cooking water. Return the beans to the saucepan and cover with fresh water. Spike the onion with the cloves and add to the pan with the bay leaves, carrots, garlic and a couple of tablespoons of salt. Bring to the boil, then reduce the heat and simmer for about 2 hours, or until the beans start to split — you may need to top up with fresh water every now and then to keep the beans covered. Drain, reserving 500 ml (2 cups) of the cooking liquid. Set the beans aside; discard the vegetables.

Preheat the oven to 180°C.

While the beans are cooking, heat the oil in a frying pan over high heat. Add the pork flank and cook for 10 minutes, or until well seared. Transfer to a roasting tin, pour in the chicken stock, cover with foil and cook in the oven for about 2 hours, or until tender. Remove from the heat, strain the stock and reserve.

Combine the reserved stock and the beef stock and bring to the boil, skimming regularly, until you have a dark, rich sauce. Strain, adjust the seasoning to taste and set aside.

Dust the duck legs with the flour. Place in a frying pan over high heat and cook for 10 minutes, or until well seared on all sides. Remove from the heat.

Put a layer of beans in a large, deep casserole dish and place the duck legs on top. Add another layer of beans and then the pork flank, filling the pot with the remaining beans. Add the sauce, scatter the breadcrumbs on top and drizzle with the melted butter.

Reduce the oven temperature to 130°C. Cover and cook for 2 hours. Check after 30 minutes to make sure the oven is not too hot, otherwise the cassoulet will dry out too quickly. Top up with the leftover bean stock if needed. About 30 minutes before the end of the cooking time, remove the lid and let the breadcrumbs toast to form a crust.

Remove from the oven and allow to cool for 30 minutes, then serve in the middle of the table with a green salad.

VARIATIONS: You could use goose confit if you are able to source any and include plenty of duck fat, although I have omitted it for a lighter result. If you do not have dark beef stock or game stock add 2 tablespoons of tomato paste to 1 litre (4 cups) of the bean cooking stock and add a 400 g tin of diced tomatoes. Cook over high heat until reduced by half. You could also add some sliced chorizo or chopped smoked bacon.

SLOW-COOKED PORK BELLY WITH CABBAGE AND PEAR

Longe de porc braisé, compote de choux Serves 10

This slow-cooked pork belly takes some time to cook so is best done in the morning or early afternoon and reheated for dinner. Once cooked it does not require many steps to put it together, leaving plenty of time for relaxing with guests. It is best served with cabbage compote and pear purée.

2 kg skinless pork belly, bone removed

1 tablespoon vegetable oil

2 onions, chopped

2 carrots, chopped

2 celery stalks, chopped

1 litre (4 cups) vegetable stock (see page 61)

Pear purée

200 g (1 cup) caster sugar

10 pears, peeled, cored and chopped

Cabbage compote

300 ml pouring cream

50 g butter

6 French shallots, finely chopped

2 garlic cloves, finely chopped

1 savoy cabbage, finely shredded

Preheat the oven to 180°C.

Season the inside of the pork belly with salt and pepper, then roll up into a log and tie with kitchen string to secure (you can ask your butcher to do this). If you feel the belly is too long for your frying pan, then cut it in half.

Heat the oil in a large frying pan over high heat. Cook the pork for 10 minutes, searing on all sides. Transfer to a large saucepan or stockpot and add the onions, carrots and celery. Add the stock and cover with a tight-fitting lid, reduce the heat to low and simmer for 2½ hours, or until tender. Remove from the heat and allow the pork to cool in the stock to room temperature. Remove the pork and wrap it tightly in several layers of plastic wrap, forcing any excess liquid and fat out and compacting the meat. Refrigerate for a few hours or even overnight.

To make the pear purée, put the sugar and 1 tablespoon water in a saucepan over medium heat. Stir until the sugar dissolves, and continue to swirl the pan gently to make sure the caramel cooks evenly — the mixture should be almost boiling. As soon as the mixture turns golden, add the pears and continue cooking over medium heat for 10 minutes, or until soft. Remove from the heat and allow to cool slightly, before transferring to a food processor or blender and pulsing to make a smooth purée. Refrigerate until needed.

To make the cabbage compote, heat the cream in a small saucepan over medium heat and cook for 10 minutes, or until the cream has reduced by half. Melt the butter in a separate saucepan over medium heat. Add the shallots and cook for 2 minutes, or until soft but without much colour. Add the garlic and cabbage and cook for 20 minutes over low heat, or until the cabbage is cooked. Add the cream, stir to combine and cook for 10 minutes, or until the cream coats the cabbage and is not runny. Season to taste and set aside.

Preheat the oven to 180°C.

Cut and discard the string from the pork. Wrap the pork in foil, place in a roasting tin and cook for 30 minutes to heat through before serving. Reheat the pear purée and cabbage compote. Slice the pork and serve on the cabbage compote with the pear purée on the side.

VARIATIONS: You could use a pork shoulder instead of the belly to achieve something similar but still with plenty of flavour. You could also make a sauce from the braising stock by simmering until reduced and thickened, skimming regularly. Strain and serve with the pork.

LAMB LOIN WITH OLIVE CRUST AND CAPSICUM FONDUE

Canon d'agneau à la croûte d'olives

Serves 4

I am not that enamoured of raw capsicum, but when cooked they are delicious and pair beautifully with black olives. Both are perfectly matched with this tender lamb.

4 x 180 g lamb loins from the neck or backstrap

150 ml extra virgin olive oil

2 French shallots, finely chopped

1 garlic clove, finely chopped

60 ml (¼ cup) verjuice or water

100 g (⅔ cup) black olive tapenade

1 handful flat-leaf parsley or oregano, finely chopped, plus extra to serve

100 g (1¼ cups) fresh breadcrumbs

150 g butter, diced

2 red capsicums, roasted and peeled (see page 71)

2 yellow capsicums, roasted and peeled (see page 71)

8–12 baby zucchini, trimmed

Pat the lamb dry with a paper towels and season with salt and pepper. Heat 1 tablespoon of the oil in a frying pan over high heat. Add the lamb and cook for 5 minutes, turning to seal on all sides. Remove from the heat.

Put the shallots, garlic and verjuice in a small saucepan over low heat. Season and bring to a simmer, cooking until nearly dry. Remove from the heat and allow to cool.

Put the olive tapenade in a food processor with the shallot mixture and parsley or oregano and process to a rough paste. Add the breadcrumbs and the butter and pulse until all the ingredients are well blended. Spread the mixture on a sheet of baking paper, put another piece of paper on top and roll out to 4 mm thick. Place on a tray and refrigerate for 20 minutes. When the olive butter is firm, remove the top layer of paper, lay the lamb directly on top and cut to fit the lamb loin. Put the lamb in a deep roasting tin and cook in a pre-heated oven at 120°C for 18 minutes for the neck or 10 minutes if using the lamb backstrap. You could do this a couple of hours before you wish to serve. To finish cooking, increase the oven temperature to 160°C and cook for 5 minutes. Remove from the oven and set aside to rest for a few minutes before serving.

While the lamb is resting, increase the oven temperature to 250°C. Cut the roasted capsicum into small strips. Put the zucchini on a roasting tray and drizzle with 4 tablespoons of the oil. Cook for 10 minutes, then add the capsicum and cook for a further 5 minutes, or until the zucchini are soft and the capsicum heated through. Trim the lamb at each end and cut into slices. Serve with the capsicum, zucchini and any remaining olive oil and a few leaves of parsley or oregano.

VARIATIONS: You can use veal loins or even tuna steaks. I have also used swordfish, which I served with oven-roasted tomatoes with wonderful results.

LAMB CUTLETS WITH ROSEMARY AND CHICKPEA CRÊPES

Côtelette d'agneau au romarin, socca niçoise　　　　　　Serves 4

**In the Côte d'Azur near Nice you can often find little chickpea pancakes like these,
which make a pleasant change from serving the lamb with the usual potato side dish.**

250 g chickpea (besan)
　flour

80 ml (⅓ cup) extra
　virgin olive oil, plus
　extra for drizzling

2 pinches of salt

4 rosemary sprigs, leaves
　of half chopped

2 medium zucchini,
　skin on, grated and
　drained

8 double or 16 single
　lamb cutlets

12 small zucchini, halved
　lengthways

2 red capsicums, roasted,
　peeled and diced (see
　page 71)

12 kalamata olives

4 garlic cloves, sliced

Put the chickpea flour in a bowl and add 250 ml (1 cup) water in a steady
stream, stirring while adding. Add 2 tablespoons of the oil, the salt, the
chopped rosemary and grated zucchini and stir to combine. Refrigerate
for at least 2 hours.

Pat the lamb cutlets dry with paper towels, season with salt and pepper,
drizzle with 1 tablespoon of the oil and top with the remaining rosemary
sprigs. Cover with baking paper and set aside at room temperature.

Heat 1 tablespoon of the oil in a frying pan over medium heat. Add
2 tablespoons of the chickpea mixture at a time to make pancakes. Cook
for 1 minute, before turning and cooking the other side, or until cooked
through. Repeat with the remaining chickpea mixture to make at least
12 small pancakes. Transfer to a low oven to keep warm.

Clean the frying pan with paper towels and heat half of the remaining oil
over high heat. Add the zucchini halves and sear until brown. Season to
taste, then transfer to a dish in the oven to keep warm. In the same pan,
heat the rest of the oil, then add the capsicum, olives and garlic and cook
for 3 minutes to warm through. Season to taste, then transfer to a dish
in the oven to keep warm while you cook the lamb.

Heat the barbecue plate to high. Pat the lamb with paper towels to
remove any excess oil and cook the cutlets for about 2 minutes on each
side, or until cooked to your liking.

Assemble the dish by putting the pancakes and zucchini on a plate. Add
the cutlets and scatter the capsicum, olives and rosemary on top. Drizzle
with extra virgin olive oil and serve.

VARIATIONS: You could roast some kipfler potatoes instead of making
chickpea pancakes, and baby eggplant would make a great addition.

BRAISED LAMB SHANKS WITH ONION AND POTATOES

Souris d'agneau, pomme boulangère

Serves 4 to 8

Lamb shanks are very popular these days. I have doubled the quantities in this recipe so you will have leftovers to reheat. The braised onion and potatoes can be prepared earlier in the day and reheated before serving. For a dinner party meal that leaves you plenty of time for your guests, this is a good choice.

8 lamb shanks, French-trimmed

60 ml (¼ cup) olive oil

2 carrots, chopped

2 onions, chopped

2 celery stalks, chopped

1 garlic bulb, halved

4 tablespoons plain flour

2 tablespoons tomato paste

2 litres (8 cups) beef stock (see page 62)

250 ml (1 cup) white wine

2 bay leaves

4 thyme sprigs

2 rosemary sprigs

Braised onion and potatoes

2 tablespoons butter

1 tablespoon vegetable oil

4 onions, sliced

8 potatoes, peeled and thinly sliced

4 thyme sprigs

4 bay leaves

1 litre (4 cups) vegetable or chicken stock (see pages 61–62)

Preheat the oven to 150°C.

Pat the lamb dry with paper towels and season with salt and pepper. Heat 1 tablespoon of the oil in a large frying pan over high heat. Add four lamb shanks at a time and cook for 10 minutes, turning to seal well on all sides. Remove to a plate and repeat with another 1 tablespoon of oil and the remaining shanks until all are sealed.

Heat the remaining oil in a large casserole dish over high heat. Add the carrots, onions, celery and garlic and cook for 5 minutes, or until the vegetables acquire some colour. Add the flour, mix well to coat, then add the tomato paste and cook for 3–4 minutes, stirring to combine. Add the shanks, then pour in the stock and wine, add the herbs and season with salt and pepper. Bring to the boil, then reduce the heat and simmer for 10 minutes. Transfer to the oven and cook for 1–1½ hours, depending on the size of the shanks, skimming at regular intervals. Test with a fork and if the meat comes off the bone easily it is cooked. Remove from the oven, lift out the shanks and set aside in a warm place. Strain the cooking stock into a saucepan over medium heat and reduce to a thick sauce, skimming regularly.

To make the braised onion and potatoes, heat the butter and oil in a large saucepan over medium heat. Add the onions and cook for 15 minutes, or until soft but without much colour; season with salt and pepper. Layer the potatoes and onions in the base of a 2 litre (8-cup) capacity baking dish, with the thyme and bay leaves. Pour in just enough stock so that it is level with the potatoes, cover with a layer of baking paper then foil, but do not completely seal the dish so that steam can escape. Cook in the oven for 1 hour. Halfway through, remove the foil to form a crust.

Pour the hot sauce over the shanks and reheat them without boiling the sauce. Serve with cauliflower gratin, steamed green beans and braised onion and potatoes on the side.

VARIATIONS: You could use lamb neck or lamb chops instead of the shanks. Serve with roasted root vegetables or soft polenta in place of the braised onion and potatoes.

CAULIFLOWER GRATIN
Gratin de choux fleur   Serves 8

It is important to have the right cheese to form the gratin — Gruyère is best, although I also use cheddar when it's all I have in the fridge.

1 kg cauliflower, cut into florets

40 g butter

40 g plain flour

500 ml (2 cups) full-cream milk

250 g (2 cups) grated Gruyère or cheddar cheese

Preheat the oven to 220°C.

Put the cauliflower in a large saucepan and cover with salted water. Place over high heat and bring to a simmer. As soon as the cauliflower comes to a simmer it is nearly cooked — check by piercing the stems with a sharp knife; it is best if you have a touch of resistance. Drain and place in a 2 litre (8-cup) capacity baking dish.

Melt the butter in a small saucepan over medium heat. Add the flour and stir for 1 minute, then add the milk a little at a time, whisking vigorously until smooth. Once all the milk had been added, bring to a simmer and cook for 3 minutes, or until the sauce is thick and smooth. Remove from the heat and season with salt and pepper. Stir in one-third of the cheese to combine, then pour the sauce over the cauliflower. Sprinkle the remaining cheese over the top and bake in the oven for 15 minutes, or until golden — you may have to place the baking dish under a hot grill for a few minutes to achieve good colour on top. Serve immediately.

BRAISED LAMB NECK WITH CHICKPEAS

Agneau braisé aux pois chiche

Serves 4

There are certain cuts of lamb that rarely get used, like the neck, that are full of flavour and really worth trying. Serve it with the bone in. This dish is best cooked in advance and reheated before serving to allow the flavours to develop.

2 kg lamb neck, cut into 12 thick rounds

80 ml (⅓ cup) olive oil

4 small onions, halved

2 tablespoons plain flour

2 x 400 g tins diced tomatoes

1 carrot, cut into large dice

1 celery stalk, cut into large pieces

2 bay leaves

2 rosemary sprigs

4 garlic cloves

1 litre (4 cups) vegetable or chicken stock (see page 61–62)

400 g tinned chickpeas, rinsed and drained

4 small zucchini, peeled and chopped

Preheat the oven to 140°C.

Pat the lamb dry with paper towels and trim any excess fat. Season with salt and pepper. Heat 1 tablespoon of the oil in a large frying pan over high heat. Add the lamb in batches and cook for 10 minutes, turning to seal on all sides. Transfer to a large casserole dish and allow to cool.

Wipe the pan clean with paper towels. Heat 1 tablespoon of the oil over medium heat. Add the onion, cut side down, and cook for 10 minutes, or until they are well coloured. Remove from the pan and set aside.

Heat 2 tablespoons of the oil in an ovenproof casserole over medium heat. Add the lamb and sprinkle with the flour, stirring to coat all sides. Cook for 5 minutes, stirring from time to time. Add the tomatoes, carrot, celery, onions, bay leaves, rosemary and garlic and finally the stock; bring to the boil on medium heat for 5 minutes. Cover the casserole and cook in the oven for 2½ hours, skimming from time to time to remove any surface fat. Top with a touch of water if needed to keep the lamb covered with liquid during the cooking.

Check the lamb to ensure it is cooked — the meat should be falling off the bone; if not cook for a further 30 minutes. When cooked, remove the lamb neck only to a dish and reserve. Add the chickpeas to the cooking stock and cook for 30 minutes or until the chickpeas are tender. Remove from the oven and return the meat to the stock to warm up.

Heat the remaining oil in a frying pan over high heat. Add the zucchini and cook for 5 minutes, or until golden. Season with salt and pepper. Serve the lamb neck and vegetables in a large serving dish at the table with the zucchini.

SLOW-COOKED LAMB SHOULDER WITH ROAST POTATOES AND ONIONS

Épaule d'agneau aux onions

Serves 4

This is one of the simplest meat dishes to prepare. The secret is the long, slow cooking and the very low heat. I normally put this in the oven before I go to bed and check it in the morning. You can feed 10 to 12 people with two shoulders.

4 tablespoons olive oil

1–1.2 kg lamb shoulder on the bone, trimmed (ask your butcher to do this)

4 onions, unpeeled and halved

12 small potatoes, such as kipfler or new potatoes scrubbed and halved lengthways

500 ml (2 cups) vegetable or chicken stock (see pages 61–62)

1 tablespoon butter

1 tablespoon plain flour

3–4 drops Parisian browning essence (see Note page 252)

4 rosemary sprigs

4 thyme sprigs

Preheat the oven to 250°C.

Drizzle 1 tablespoon of the oil into the base of a large roasting tin (just big enough to fit the lamb) and set the lamb shoulder inside. Drizzle the remaining oil on top and season with salt and pepper.

Put the lamb in the oven and cook for 15 minutes to seal the meat, then cover with foil. Reduce the oven temperature to 120°C and continue cooking the lamb for 9 hours, or until the meat is so tender it falls off the bone when you test it with a fork. Remove from the oven, transfer to a tray, cover with a clean tea towel and set aside at room temperature to rest.

Once the lamb is out of the roasting tin, add the onions and potatoes to the tin. Increase the oven temperature to 160°C and cook for 1 hour, turning the potatoes halfway through. Cook the onions until very soft, then remove from the oven and when cool enough to handle, carefully peel off the skins.

Drain the excess oil and fat from the roasting tin, place over medium heat and add the stock. Bring to the boil and scrape the bottom of the tin to lift off any meat and juices. Melt the butter in a saucepan over medium heat and add the flour, stirring to make a roux. Cook for 2–3 minutes, then strain the lamb stock into the pan, stirring continuously with a whisk. Continue cooking over medium heat for 5 minutes, or until the sauce has thickened and reduced, skimming regularly. Adjust the seasoning to taste and add a few drops of Parisian browning essence to darken the colour. Strain and add half the rosemary and thyme. Cover with plastic wrap and set aside to let the flavours infuse.

About 30 minutes before you wish to serve, preheat the oven to 140°C. Place the lamb, uncovered, in a roasting tin with the potatoes, onions and balance of the herbs and cook for 5 minutes, until heated through. Gently reheat the sauce.

Tear the lamb away from the bone and serve with the vegetables and sauce and some glazed carrots — you could also add a salad or some sautéed beans or spinach. If you do not wish to make the sauce you could serve the lamb with lemon wedges instead.

NOTE: Browning essence, also called Parisian browning essence, can be found in your supermarket. It is used to add colour to sauces, gravies, soups and broths as well as cakes and puddings. You only need to use a few drops.

GLAZED CARROTS
Carottes glacées au beurre   **Serves 4**

4 medium carrots
1 tablespoon butter
1 teaspoon caster sugar
1 pinch of salt

Peel the carrots and trim both ends. Cut each carrot into 5 cm lengths and use an apple corer to remove the hard core of the carrots. Discard the cores. Choose a saucepan to cook the carrots in and trace the base of the pan onto a sheet of baking paper — this will be cut out and used as a lid for the pan while the carrots are cooking.

Put the carrots in the saucepan with the butter, sugar, salt and 60 ml (¼ cup) water over low heat. Place the circle of baking paper on top to act as a lid and cook for 5 minutes, stirring from time to time, until the carrots are tender but still firm. Remove from the heat and serve.

VARIATION: You can use honey to glaze the carrots instead of sugar but be careful not to use too much as it will become overly sweet.

ROAST SADDLE OF LAMB ON THE BONE WITH ONION AND RICE PURÉE

Longe d'agneau rôtie, soubise

Serves 4

Most people are not familiar with lamb saddle. It is cut into noisettes or stuffed, but I think as a roast without the bone it is pretty good.

4 onions, peeled

12 baby new potatoes

2 tablespoons butter

1 tablespoon mixed dried herbs (rosemary, thyme and marjoram)

2 short lamb saddles (about 800 g each), bone in

2 tablespoons olive oil

370 g (2 cups) cooked long-grain white rice

Preheat the oven to 180°C.

Wrap the onions together in foil and place in a roasting tin. Wrap the potatoes in foil with 2 teaspoons of the butter and a pinch of the dried herbs. Add to the roasting tin and bake for 30 minutes, or until soft to touch. Remove the potatoes and cook the onions for a further 15 minutes, or until nice and soft. Remove to a plate and set aside.

Increase the oven temperature to 220°C. Put the lamb saddles, fat side up, in a roasting tin (if the butcher left the flap or sides untrimmed, fold them under the saddle to protect the fillets). Brush with the oil and sprinkle with the remaining herbs. Cook for 10 minutes, then reduce the oven temperature to 160°C and cook for a further 20 minutes, or until the centre of the meat is lukewarm when pierced with a fork. Remove from the oven, cover with foil and set aside to rest for 10 minutes before serving. Return the potatoes to the oven to reheat.

Put the onions in a food processor with the cooked rice and process to make a smooth purée; season with salt and pepper. Transfer to a saucepan over medium heat. Add the remaining butter and a touch of water if the purée seems too thick, stirring to combine until the rice mixture is warmed through.

Carve the lamb off the saddle following the backbone. Slice the fillet on the underside and the flap. Put a generous spoonful of the onion and rice purée on the plate with the lamb and serve with the warm potatoes.

VARIATIONS: Instead of using mixed dried herbs you could smear the lamb with Dijon or wholegrain mustard. You can make a fennel purée instead of the onion or you could simply serve a green salad with the lamb and potatoes.

PAN-ROASTED LAMB RUMP WITH HEIRLOOM CARROTS

Agneau poêlé aux carottes   Serves 4

I will always remember a meal that I had at my friend Jean Luc's Parisian restaurant, Pétrelle, where I ate some perfect veal sweetbreads simply served with carrots. Simplicity sometimes requires courage, but it's worth taking a chance.

4 x 250 g lamb rump

4 garlic cloves, sliced

1 rosemary sprig, leaves picked

2 tablespoons chopped flat-leaf parsley

100 ml olive oil

750 g heirloom or baby carrots

100 g butter

1 tablespoon aged red wine vinegar

1 tablespoon sugar

4 bunches spinach, trimmed, rinsed and drained

2 lemons, cut into wedges

Trim any excess fat from the lamb, but not all of it. Place in a large container with the garlic, rosemary, parsley and 75 ml of the oil and mix well to coat the lamb. Cover with plastic wrap and marinate in the refrigerator overnight.

Trim the carrot tops, leaving a small green stem. Scrub the carrots but do not peel them. Heat half of the butter in a large saucepan over low heat. Add the carrots and cook for 5 minutes, or until they acquire a touch of colour. If some of the carrots are smaller, remove them when they are nearly cooked. When all the carrots are nearly cooked, return them all to the pan and add the vinegar and sugar, mixing gently as the sugar caramelises and glazes the carrots — you may need to add a touch more butter. Season with salt and pepper, then remove the carrots and set aside in a baking tray.

Remove the lamb from the refrigerator 1 hour before you wish to cook it. Clean off most of the oil, garlic and herbs to prevent burning.

Preheat the oven to 160°C. Heat an ovenproof frying pan over high heat and sear the lamb on all sides, then reduce the heat to medium-low, turn the lamb on the fatty side, and let the fat render or slow-cook for 10 minutes. Turn over, then transfer to the oven for about 10 minutes until the lamb is cooked to a nice pink colour. Remove the lamb from the oven, cover with foil and set aside to rest for 5 minutes before serving.

While the lamb is resting, heat the remaining butter in a frying pan over high heat. Add the spinach and cook for 3–4 minutes, or until just wilted. Season with salt and pepper. Place in a strainer to drain off any excess liquid — you can either serve the spinach as is, or transfer to a food processor with a little extra butter and process to make a smooth purée. Reheat the carrots in the oven.

Divide the spinach between serving plates, slice the lamb and lay over the spinach. Set the carrots on top and serve with the potato gratin and lemon wedges on the side for squeezing.

VARIATIONS: If you cannot find a baby carrots, use parsnips, salsify, baby turnips or radishes. Make an onion purée or some potato purée (see page 286) instead of the spinach if you prefer.

POTATO GRATIN
Gratin dauphinois   Serves 8

This definitive potato gratin differs in taste and texture to most due to the cooking technique. I learnt this method from a great friend in France, and the important thing is to first cook the potato in milk before adding the cream.

2 kg desiree potatoes, peeled

1 litre (4 cups) full-cream milk

600 ml pouring cream

1 garlic clove, peeled

400 g (3 cups) grated Gruyère cheese

Preheat the oven to 160°C. Lightly grease a 2 litre (8-cup) capacity baking dish with butter. Cut the potatoes in half lengthways and slice them into fairly thick ovals. Place in a large saucepan with the milk and season with salt and pepper. Cook over medium heat for 10 minutes, or until tender but retaining some firmness. Drain and discard the milk. Arrange the potatoes in the prepared dish, making sure you do not press down on them so the cream can drizzle through.

Put the cream in a small saucepan over medium heat and bring to a simmer. Add the garlic and simmer for 5 minutes, then discard the garlic and season well. Pour the cream over the potato in the dish, top with the cheese and bake in the oven for 30 minutes. Lower the oven temperature to 140°C and cook for a further 30 minutes. If you feel the potatoes are not brown enough, put them under a hot griller for a few minutes. This dish will reheat easily if prepared ahead of time and will actually have an improved taste.

LAMB RAGOÛT WITH SPRING VEGETABLES

Navarin d'agneau printanier

Serves 6–8

This classic lamb stew does not require special ingredients. You could easily use water instead of stock and larger onions if you cannot find the smaller pickling onions. You can use dried lamb from the shoulder if you ensure it is trimmed well or use meat from the leg.

60 ml (¼ cup) olive oil

2 carrots, diced

2 onions, diced

4 garlic cloves, peeled

1.2 kg diced lamb, trimmed of fat

1½ tablespoons caster sugar

3 tablespoons plain flour

1 tablespoon tomato paste

1 bouquet garni (see Note page 197)

1 litre (4 cups) vegetable stock (see page 61) or water

1 tablespoon butter

24 small pickling onions, peeled

12 baby carrots, halved lengthways

200 g (1⅓ cups) fresh peas

1 French baguette, sliced, to serve

Preheat the oven to 160°C.

Heat half of the oil in a large casserole dish over medium heat. Add the carrots and onions and cook for 3 minutes, or until soft but without much colour. Add the garlic cook for 3–4 minutes. Strain and reserve the oil and reserve the vegetables.

Return the reserved oil to the dish with the remaining oil over high heat. Add the lamb a few pieces at a time, cook for 5 minutes, turning to seal on all sides. Remove to a plate and repeat with the remaining lamb.

Return all of the lamb and cooked vegetables to the dish, add 1 tablespoon of the sugar and stir for 3–4 minutes, or until it starts to caramelise, then sprinkle the flour into the dish, stirring to coat. Add the tomato paste, bouquet garni and the stock. Bring to a simmer, mixing gently to remove any solids from the base of the dish. Season with salt and pepper, cover with a lid, then transfer to the oven and cook for 1–1½ hours, or until tender. Remove the lamb to a large saucepan and reserve.

To make the sauce, strain the cooking stock into a separate saucepan, discarding all of the vegetables, but making sure you squeeze all the flavour into the stock first. Cook the stock over medium heat, or until thickened and reduced; adjust the seasoning to taste.

Heat the butter in a small frying pan over low heat. Add the pickling onions and cook for 10 minutes, or until nearly cooked. Add the baby carrots, remaining sugar and a pinch of salt and cook for 2 minutes until the carrots are nearly cooked, then add the peas — adding 2 tablespoons of water if necessary — and cook for 5 minutes further. Remove from the heat and set aside.

Pour the sauce over the lamb, add the pickling onions, baby carrots and peas and reheat over low heat, barely mixing the vegetables. Serve with toasted crusty bread on the side.

VARIATIONS: You can use broad beans instead of peas or boil some white beans and serve with the ragoût. If you prefer another meat just use chicken legs and reduce the cooking time to 45 minutes with a good 30 minutes to rest in the sauce.

PEPPER STEAK

Steak au poivre noir

When I started cooking in Canada, pepper steak was a big favourite. Many restaurants used to do the flambé and I developed a special appreciation for this dish. These days I tend to make this steak for friends at home, much to their delight!

2 tablespoons whole
  black peppercorns

4 x 250 g sirloin steaks,
  trimmed

250 ml (1 cup) red wine
  sauce (see page 272)

50 g butter, diced

1 tablespoon vegetable oil

30 ml brandy

potato gratin (see
  page 256), to serve

1 French baguette, sliced,
  to serve

Crush the black peppercorns in a mortar and pestle; this will require a bit of force but to make a memorable fragrant pepper it is best done fresh.

Season both sides of each steak with salt and the crushed pepper and press with the palm of your hand so the pepper is stuck to the flesh.

Put the red wine sauce in a saucepan over medium heat. Once it is heated through, taste to make sure it is well balanced, season if necessary. Whisk in half the butter and keep warm while you cook the beef.

Heat the oil in a large frying pan over high heat. Add the steaks and cook for about 3 minutes, then turn over and cook for a few more minutes until both sides are well seared — the length of time will depend on how thick the steaks are. Add the brandy and let it flambé — it should light immediately if you are cooking with gas but you might need a match if you are using an electric stovetop. Once the flames have ceased, add the red wine sauce and reduce until the sauce just coats the steak. Remove the steaks to warm serving plates.

Whisk the remaining butter into the sauce over medium heat until completely combined. Pour over the steaks and serve with potato gratin and some crusty bread on the side.

VARIATIONS: Use sirloin steak for an authentic dish and if you wish to make a richer sauce add 250 ml (1 cup) pouring cream instead of the butter and let it boil and reduce for a couple of minutes with the beef sauce. You could also try using green peppercorns for a different flavour.

DINNER
259

SKIRT STEAK WITH ANCHOÏADE SAUCE

Bavette de boeuf grillé, sauce anchoïade

Serves 4–6

Many people have never tried skirt steak. This is one cut that is worth sourcing the best quality you can — try wagyu or heavily grain-fed beef. It goes perfectly with this anchoïade — anchovy sauce.

1 garlic bulb, halved

16 tinned Spanish anchovies in oil

1 tablespoon red wine vinegar

2 tablespoons Dijon mustard

125 ml (½ cup) extra virgin olive oil

1–1.5 kg whole skirt steak, trimmed

4 tablespoons vegetable oil

Preheat the oven to 160°C.

To make the anchoïade sauce, wrap both garlic halves in foil with a drizzle of oil from the anchovy tin (or olive oil if you prefer) and roast for 20 minutes in the oven. Allow to cool, then press the garlic cloves out of the husk. Use a mortar and pestle, or a fork in a bowl, to mash together the anchovies, garlic and red wine vinegar and make a rough paste. Add the mustard and pound to combine. Using a whisk, start adding the extra virgin olive oil in a thin stream, whisking continuously until all the oil is incorporated. Set aside.

Heat the barbecue grill plate to high. Pat the steak dry with paper towels. Season sparingly with salt but use plenty of pepper. Dip a paper towel in the vegetable oil and wipe it over the barbecue grill. Set the skirt steak on the grill at an angle and reduce the heat to medium. Cook for 5 minutes, then move to the opposite angle to create a diamond pattern. Cook for a further 5 minutes, then turn over and repeat on the other side — depending on your barbecue you might need to set the temperature to low or even to high; what you need is a steady heat that will not burn the steak. Once cooked to your liking, remove from the grill, cover with foil and set aside to rest for 5–10 minutes.

To serve, cut large strips across the grain or across the narrow part of the steak. Place on a platter and serve at the table with the anchoïade sauce, French-style peas (see page 262) and sautéed potatoes (see page 262).

VARIATIONS: A fresh vine-ripened tomato per person, cut first and seasoned, is also delicious as the tomatoes go very well with anchovies. Rib steak could be used instead of the skirt steak. If anchovies are not to everyone's taste you could make a béarnaise sauce (see page 267) instead.

SAUTÉED POTATOES

Pomme de terre à la Lyonnaise

Serves 4

8 medium potatoes,
    desiree, spunta or
    sebago, skin on

125 ml (½ cup) clarified
    butter (see Note
    page 203)

4 brown onions, sliced

100 g butter

1 tablespoon chopped
    flat-leaf parsley

Cook the potatoes in a saucepan of boiling salted water until just tender. Drain and cool. (This could be done a day ahead to have firm, cooked potatoes.) Peel the potatoes, cut in two and then into 5 mm thick slices.

Heat half of the clarified butter in a large frying pan over medium heat. Cook the onion for 20 minutes, or until soft and golden. Set aside. Heat half of the remaining clarified butter in a large heavy-based frying pan over high heat. Add half of the potatoes and sauté until lightly coloured, turning gently with a flat spatula. Add half of the butter and continue to sauté the potatoes until crisp and golden. Add half of the onion and mix well by moving the pan, being careful not to break the potatoes. Season generously with salt and pepper and finish with half the parsley. Transfer to a baking dish and keep warm in a low oven. Wipe the pan clean with paper towels, and repeat with the remaining clarified butter, potato, butter, onion and parsley. Serve immediately.

FRENCH-STYLE PEAS

Petits pois à la Française

Serves 4

100 g pickling onions,
    peeled

300 g (2 cups) fresh peas

40 g butter, softened

40 g plain flour

1 tablespoons vegetable oil

200 g sliced speck or
    bacon, cut into strips

1 tablespoon chopped
    tarragon or parsley

1 head cos lettuce, finely
    chopped

1 teaspoon sugar

Put the onions in a saucepan and cover with water. Season with salt and pepper and cook over medium heat for 20 minutes, adding more water if needed. Add the peas and cook for 10 minutes, or until the peas are nearly cooked. Strain the peas, place on a plate and cool in the refrigerator. Reserve the onions and cooking liquid separately; allow to cool. Mix the butter and flour in a bowl to form a paste. Return the cooking liquid to the pan over medium heat and bring to a simmer. Slowly stir in the butter mixture, adding just enough to thicken.

Heat the oil in a frying pan over high heat. Add the speck and cook for 2 minutes, or until seared on all sides. Add the peas, onions, herbs, lettuce and sugar and season with salt and pepper. Add some of the thickened stock. Cook until warmed through and the lettuce has wilted. Transfer to a large serving dish and serve immediately.

STEAK DIANE WITH CREAM AND BRANDY

Steak Diane

Serves 4

Steak Diane is another old-fashioned classic that was once a constant on most restaurant menus, but is seen less and less these days. The mushroom, brandy and cream makes for a pretty enticing flavour and as an occasional treat it is quite simple to put together.

4 x 200 g beef tenderloins, butterflied (ask your butcher to do this)

2 tablespoons vegetable oil

50 g butter

4 French shallots, finely chopped

200 g mushrooms, trimmed and quartered

30 ml brandy or cognac

200 ml pouring cream

2 teaspoons Worcestershire sauce

250 ml (1 cup) strong beef stock (see page 62)

1 tablespoon Dijon mustard

1 tablespoon chopped flat-leaf parsley

Season the beef with salt and pepper on both sides. Heat half of the oil in a frying pan over high heat. Add the beef and cook for 3 minutes on each side to sear well, making sure it is still rare in the centre. Remove to a plate.

Heat the remaining oil in the same pan with the butter and shallots. Cook for 1 minute, or until the shallots are softened, then add the mushrooms and cook for 3 minutes, or until they have a good colour. Return the beef to the pan and flambé with the brandy or cognac. Once the flame has subsided, add the cream, Worcestershire sauce, stock and mustard and bring to the boil. If you like the beef rare, then remove it at this point and continue to reduce the cream over medium heat until you have a coating consistency. Add the parsley just before serving and season with salt and pepper, to taste.

Serve the beef with a little sauce poured over the top and crispy potatoes.

VARIATIONS: You could use chicken breast or veal mignonettes made out of veal fillet instead of the beef. This dish can be made without the beef stock. Just use 300 ml pouring cream with the mushrooms. If your kitchen does not have a naked flame, just use a match to light the brandy.

GRILLED BEEF TENDERLOIN

Boeuf tournedos

This is the most tender part of the beef and also the most expensive so it is well worth following a few tips before you start cooking your tournedos. It is best to bring the steak to room temperature to ensure the cooking is even and you don't end up with a rare core. The next step is to dry your meat with paper towels to remove any moisture on the meat surface. This will help build a crust when grilling. I like my steak medium rare and depending on the thickness of the steak it will take 6–8 minutes to cook. I try to only move the beef four times, twice on each side. If your guests prefer theirs cooked a little more, start cooking their steak first so they will all be ready at the same time.

4 desiree potatoes, peeled, thinly sliced

3 tablespoons vegetable oil

4 x 200 g beef tenderloins

24 asparagus spears, trimmed and lightly peeled

béarnaise sauce (see opposite page), to serve

Preheat the oven to 220°C.

Wash the potatoes and pat dry with paper towels. Drizzle 2 tablespoons of the oil into a roasting tin. Arrange the potatoes in an even layer in the tin. Roast for about 15 minutes, then turn and cook for a further 10 minutes, or until they are golden on both sides and cooked through. Remove from the heat and set aside.

Heat a barbecue grill plate to high. Dip a paper towel in half the remaining oil and wipe over the grill. Set the steak on the grill at an angle and cook for 2 minutes, then move to the opposite angle to create a diamond pattern. Cook for a further 2 minutes, then turn over and repeat on the other side. Season the steak on both sides before removing from the heat, then set aside for 5 minutes to rest before serving.

Meanwhile, toss the asparagus in the remaining oil and grill on the barbecue for 4 minutes, or until cooked but still crunchy.

Put the steak, potatoes and asparagus on a warm plate and serve with the béarnaise sauce on the side.

BÉARNAISE SAUCE

Sauce béarnaise

Makes 2 cups

It takes a small amount of skill to make a béarnaise sauce but if you like a rich sauce, it is well worth mastering the technique. When I go camping with my son Sasha, I often help with the cooking with the other fathers or friends, and no matter where we camp I can always manage to make a hollandaise (see page 32) or a béarnaise sauce, depending on the ingredients I have. In any case, either sauce is always well appreciated. Béarnaise sauce works perfectly served with grilled meats.

4 French shallots, finely chopped

1 bunch tarragon, leaves chopped

80 ml (⅓ cup) red or white wine vinegar

1 tablespoon black peppercorns, crushed

250 g butter

3 free-range egg yolks

1 tablespoon lemon juice or to taste

Put the shallots, tarragon and vinegar in a saucepan over medium heat. Add the crushed peppercorns and cook for 5 minutes, or until the liquid is nearly dry. Remove from the heat and allow to cool.

Melt the butter in a saucepan over low heat and skim to remove any foam or impurities that rise to the surface. Once the butter is fully melted and the surface is clear, transfer to a clean container, making sure you discard the sediment and water left at the bottom of the pan, so you are left with a pure clarified butter.

Put 250 ml (1 cup) boiling water in a small saucepan over low heat. Place a heatproof bowl with the egg yolks on top and whisk the eggs over the heat until they are pale and creamy. Take the bowl off the heat from time to time, making sure you do not cook the egg yolks. Add the clarified butter in a thin stream, a little at a time, whisking continuously until all the butter is incorporated — if it is too thick add a little boiling water — and finish with the lemon juice. Add the shallot mixture, stirring to combine, and adjust the seasoning, to taste. Keep warm, but not near a heat source or the béarnaise may separate. Serve as directed.

NOTE: A béarnaise or hollandaise sauce will not keep for more than a couple of hours. If it gets too cold the butter will solidify, and if it is kept hot the sauce will start to break down, so it is best to prepare the sauce just before you're ready to serve.

STEAK TARTARE

Steak tartare

Serves 4

Like eating your first oyster, the first time you taste a steak tartare will seem like a defining moment in your culinary life. Once you get used to making this dish, adjust the ingredients to your personal taste. The quality and freshness of the beef is very important so ask your butcher to select a piece of meat that has preferably not been stored in plastic and make sure all the silver skin and fat have been trimmed.

800 g beef tenderloin

4 free-range egg yolks

2 tablespoons Dijon
    mustard

I teaspoon
    Worcestershire sauce

3–4 drops Tabasco sauce

4 French shallots or
    I onion, finely diced

2 tablespoons salted
    capers, rinsed,
    drained and chopped

2 tablespoons chopped
    flat-leaf parsley

4 tablespoons extra
    virgin olive oil

I head butter lettuce

vinaigrette or dressing
    of your choice (see
    pages 75–76)

12 slices sourdough bread
    or brioche, toasted, to
    serve

Pat the beef dry with paper towels, then cut into large pieces that will fit into a meat grinder. Pass through the grinder twice to ensure a fine mince. Alternatively, you could cut it by hand. Set aside.

Put the egg yolks, mustard, Worcestershire sauce and Tabasco in a large cold bowl and mix well. Add the beef, shallots or onion, capers and parsley and season with sea salt and pepper. Mix well, then slowly stir in the oil until well combined. Adjust the seasoning, to taste. Cover with plastic wrap and refrigerate until needed.

Clean the lettuce under cold water, drain and spin dry, discarding the outer leaves. Toss in the vinaigrette and set in a bowl. Put the toast in a basket and the steak tartare in a serving bowl and let your guests take as much or as little as they like.

VARIATIONS: You can use well-trimmed sirloin steak or scotch fillet. Add chopped anchovies or gherkins if you like. Sometimes I also like to empty the centre of a baguette and fill it with the steak tartare and slice it into thick rounds to serve.

A good kitchen doesn't require many tools, just good ones. A sturdy, sharp knife, a large cutting board and a few heavy pots are a great base. I particularly love my copper pots.

BAKED BEEF FILLET WITH MUSHROOMS IN PASTRY CRUST

Boeuf en croûte

Serves 4

If ever there was a dish worthy of a truffle sauce then this is it — simply make the red wine sauce and add some chopped truffle and whisk in 2 tablespoons of cold butter.

800 g beef tenderloin, centre cut

4 tablespoons vegetable oil

100 g butter

500 g large field mushrooms, peeled, stems removed and roughly chopped

4 French shallots, finely chopped

1 teaspoon thyme leaves

12 slices prosciutto

1 x 25 cm sheet butter puff pastry

2 free-range egg yolks, well beaten, for egg wash

red wine sauce (see page 272), to serve

Pat the beef dry with paper towels and season well with salt and pepper. Heat half of the oil and 1 tablespoon of the butter in a large frying pan over high heat. Add the beef and cook for 5 minutes on all sides, or until well seared. Remove to a plate and allow to cool.

Place the mushrooms in a food processor and process until very finely chopped. Heat the remaining oil and remaining butter in a frying pan over high heat. Add the shallots and sweat for 1 minute, then add the mushrooms and cook for 15 minutes, or until all the liquid has evaporated and the mushroom mixture is very dry. Remove from the heat, season to taste, then add the thyme leaves. Set aside to cool for 15 minutes.

Arrange half the prosciutto slices on a sheet of plastic wrap so they are as wide as the tenderloin — the slices should slightly overlap. Spread the mushrooms over the prosciutto. Lay the beef on mushrooms and roll the plastic wrap over to cover the beef. Refrigerate for 1 hour.

Preheat the oven to 220°C.

Remove the plastic wrap and lay the prosciutto-wrapped beef in the centre of the pastry sheet. Brush the egg wash along the sides of the pastry, fold the pastry over to cover the beef, trim the excess pastry, then fold and seal each end to make a neat parcel. Brush the top with the egg wash. Add some cut pastry leaves for decoration and brush with the egg wash. Use the tines of a fork to press and seal the edges of the pastry and refrigerate for 10 minutes.

Place the beef in the oven and cook for 5–10 minutes until golden, then reduce the oven to 140°C, opening the oven door for a minute to help lower the temperature. Cook for a further 20 minutes until you have a nice, juicy pink result. Rest for 5 minutes.

Place the beef on a cutting board, cut both ends, then cut in two in the middle and each half in two again to achieve four portions. Place each portion on a warm plate and serve with red wine sauce and sautéed green beans (see opposite page).

VARIATIONS: I use prosciutto to prevent the moisture of the mushrooms soaking the dough but you could use sliced ham or some thin crêpes.

RED WINE SAUCE

Sauce au vin rouge   **Makes about 2 cups**

A red wine sauce is an essential element of French cooking. This sauce is perfect for roast beef and many other meat dishes.

2 tablespoons olive oil

4 French shallots, finely chopped

I onion, finely chopped

I teaspoon white and black peppercorns, crushed

I field mushroom, sliced

2 garlic cloves, finely chopped

500 ml (2 cups) red wine

500 ml (2 cups) strong beef stock (see page 62)

2 thyme sprigs

2 rosemary sprigs

Heat the oil in a large saucepan over high heat. Add the shallots and onion and cook for 5 minutes or until the onion caramelises. Add the peppercorns, mushroom and garlic and cook for 2 minutes. Add half of the wine, and simmer until nearly dry. Pour in the remaining wine and cook for 10 minutes, or until reduced by three-quarters. Add the stock, bring to the boil, then reduce the heat and simmer for 20 minutes, or until reduced by half, skimming the surface regularly. Strain through a fine sieve into a small saucepan and bring back to a simmer, skimming again to make sure the sauce is free from impurities. Simmer for 10 minutes, or until it is glossy and has the consistency of pouring cream. Remove from the heat, add the herbs, cover with plastic wrap and set aside for 10 minutes to allow the flavours to infuse. Pass through a fine sieve to remove the herbs and keep the sauce warm until needed. Any excess sauce can be stored in an airtight container in the refrigerator for up to 5 days.

SAUTÉED GREEN BEANS

Haricots vert sauté

To really enjoy green beans it is important to get the cooking just right. Undercooked beans are not that enjoyable to eat and even less so if they are overcooked. The main thing when cooking beans is to cook them in plenty of boiling water and have a bowl of iced water ready to quickly stop the cooking. In my opinion, smaller, young green beans are best left with a good crunch while larger beans should not be served crunchy — the following method reveals their flavour best.

---

400 g green beans, trimmed

60 g butter, diced

Bring a large saucepan of salted water to the boil — as a guide use double the quantity of water to the volume of beans. Once the water is boiling, plunge in the beans and cook for 5 minutes, or until they are just past the crunchy point — being careful not to overcook them as they will lose their colour and flavour. Drain and immediately plunge them into a bowl of iced water to refresh and retain their vibrant green colour. Drain again and dry on a clean tea towel.

Heat the butter in a large frying pan over high heat. Add the beans and cook for 3 minutes, or until they are slightly caramelised. Season with salt and pepper.

VARIATIONS: You could add some chopped or sliced garlic when you sauté the beans or sprinkle them with roasted sliced almonds for a more complex taste.

For me a kitchen is like a studio. I have my favourite tools, I have my rituals and I find inspiration amongst my collection of pots, plates and platters.

SLOW-COOKED BEEF CHEEKS WITH POTATOES COOKED IN ASH AND PENCIL LEEKS

Joue de boeuf braisé, pomme à la cendre   Serves 4

I love cooking over an open flame. There is something primitive about making a fire and cooking a meal directly over it. This dish is all about controlling the temperature — if you cook the cheeks in a casserole dish in the ash, check it often as you may need to move the dish closer or further away from the flame. The idea is to time the cooking of the potatoes and beef. The beef will take 2 hours and the potatoes, if you are using large ones, about 45 minutes in the ash. If you are cooking this at home in the oven, a potato gratin (see page 256) makes a great accompaniment.

4 x 300 g beef cheeks, trimmed

4 tablespoons vegetable oil

1 carrot, roughly chopped

1 onion, roughly chopped

1 small leek, white part only, rinsed and chopped

2 celery stalks, lightly peeled and chopped

2 tablespoons plain flour

500 ml (2 cups) red wine

2 tablespoons tomato paste

1 litre (4 cups) beef stock (see page 62)

2 garlic cloves, peeled

2 bay leaves

2 thyme sprigs

12 pencil leeks, trimmed and washed

1 tablespoon butter

Remove the beef cheeks from the refrigerator about 1 hour before you are going to start cooking to bring them to room temperature. Dry with paper towels to remove any moisture. Season with salt and pepper.

Heat half of the oil in a large braising casserole dish over high heat. Working with two beef cheeks at a time, add the beef and cook for 5 minutes on each side to seal well and give plenty of colour. Remove and set aside while you cook the remaining beef. Remove the beef to a plate.

In the same oil, or a little more if necessary, add the carrot, onion, leek and celery to the dish and cook for 10 minutes to colour. Add the flour, mix well, then pour in the wine to deglaze. Bring to the boil and cook until the liquid has reduced by half. Add the tomato paste, stock, garlic and herbs and mix well. Return the beef cheeks to the dish, pour in enough water to cover and bring to a simmer.

While you bring the beef to a simmer, preheat the oven to 140°C.

Season with salt and pepper, put a close-fitting lid on the casserole and cook in the oven for 1½ hours, skimming regularly and topping up with water as needed. When cooked, the meat will break away easily when tested with a fork — if not cook them a bit longer without the lid to let the sauce reduce and to allow it to acquire a dark colour.

4 large roasting potatoes
or 12 new potatoes

1 teaspoon Parisian
browning essence

100 g butter

Meanwhile, lay the leeks on a large piece of double thickness aluminium foil and spread the butter over them. Add a tablespoon of water and season with salt and pepper. Wrap carefully, but not too tightly, so that steam can build up inside. Put near the fire, on the ash, or in a hot oven and cook for 20 minutes. Open the foil parcel to check that the leeks are cooked, then rewrap and keep warm.

To cook the ash potatoes, gather some hot ash in the corner of the fireplace with no burning embers in it. Put the potatoes directly in the ash and cover well. Add some hot embers on top and cook for 20 minutes. Make another pile of ash in the other corner and repeat with some more potatoes and warm ash. Check with a skewer to see when they are ready. When the potatoes are cooked brush the ash off and keep warm by wrapping in a clean tea towel.

Remove the beef cheeks from the dish with a slotted spoon and reserve on a plate. Strain the stock into a saucepan, discarding the vegetables, and bring to a simmer over medium heat. Reduce heat, again skimming regularly. When you have the right consistency, check the seasoning and add a touch of Parisian browning essence to darken the colour. Return the beef cheeks to the sauce and heat through.

When ready to serve, split the ash potatoes in half and fluff with a fork. Place a good knob of butter on top of each and serve hot with the warm beef cheeks and pencil leeks.

VARIATIONS: You can use beef brisket, beef ribs or chuck steak cut into large dice instead of the beef cheeks if you prefer. This dish is also delicious with roast garden vegetables (see opposite page) in place of the leeks.

ROAST GARDEN VEGETABLES

Légumes du potager rôties

This is a wonderfully rustic way to serve vegetables to highlight their natural beauty and focus on pure flavour. It is a lovely dish served with the beef cheeks on the previous page. It is best to leave the vegetables unpeeled and cook and eat them the way nature intended.

125 ml (½ cup) extra virgin olive oil

4 carrots, trimmed

4 parsnips, trimmed

4 red onions, lightly peeled, tops and tails left on

1 butternut pumpkin, seeded, halved and cut into 16 wedges

1 fennel bulb, trimmed

1 celeriac, trimmed and cut into 8 wedges

1 garlic bulb

125 g butter

Preheat the oven to 180°C.

Heat one-third of the oil in a large frying pan over medium heat. Put one-third of the vegetables in the pan, then add one-third of the butter and cook until they start to caramelise. The idea is to slow-cook the vegetables but still have enough heat to colour them. The red onion can be pan-fried quickly but will not require much colour. When you have coloured them on all sides put them in a roasting tray. Repeat with the remaining oil, vegetables and butter until all the vegetables are cooked; season with salt and pepper.

Bake in the oven for about 20 minutes, checking every 10 minutes or so and removing any vegetables that are fully cooked. The carrot, parsnip, celeriac and pumpkin will cook first, followed by the fennel and garlic, then the onion. Keep warm until ready to serve, then simply pile on a large serving platter and enjoy.

COUNTRY-STYLE BEEF AND POTATO PIE

Tourte de boeuf parmentier

Serves 4–6

This pie is easy to make as it doesn't use pastry. If you have leftover veal and chicken pot-au-feu (see page 226) or even cooked lamb shank it will work perfectly baked under a layer of potato and breadcrumbs. In fact, I have also varied this pie over time, using braised lamb neck or leftover beef stew (see page 282). You can make smaller individual pies or one large pie, depending on the occasion.

125 ml (½ cup) vegetable oil

60 g (½ cup) plain flour

1 kg beef brisket cut into 4 cm cubes

2 onions, peeled

1 carrot, chopped

2 bay leaves

4 thyme sprigs

1 litre (4 cups) strong beef stock, (see page 62)

white pepper, to taste

1 leek, white part only, rinsed and diced

6 large potatoes, unpeeled

150 g butter, melted

50 g (½ cup) dry breadcrumbs

2 tablespoons chopped flat-leaf parsley

1 garlic clove, finely chopped

Heat half of the oil in a large frying pan over high heat. Lightly flour the beef and fry to give it some colour — do this in two or three batches, putting each batch into a braising pot when done. Dust the beef with a touch more flour, mix well and add the onions, carrot, bay leaves and thyme. Pour in enough hot stock to cover and season with salt and white pepper. Bring to the boil, reduce the heat and simmer for 1–1½ hours, skimming regularly and topping up with water if needed. Remove the carrot and onions to a plate once tender — about 30 minutes. Add the leek and continue cooking for another 30 minutes, or until cooked. Discard the herbs, set the leek aside and drain the meat. While still warm, use a fork to break the beef down.

Put the potatoes in a saucepan of salted water over high heat and cook for 15 minutes, or until tender but firm — the point of a sharp knife should easily pierce the centre. Drain and cool, then peel and slice.

Preheat the oven to 180°C.

Roughly cut the carrot and onion, mix with the beef and leek and put into a large 2 litre (8 cup) capacity baking dish. Arrange the potato slices on top so they are just overlapping. Brush the potatoes with some of the melted butter. Combine the breadcrumbs, parsley and garlic with the remaining melted butter and scatter on top of the potatoes. Cook in the oven for about 30 minutes, or until golden.

VARIATIONS: You could add a corn purée (see page 193) to the top of the beef or purée the potatoes instead of slicing them. I used to make this pie with boiled beef tongue, about a quarter of tongue for the beef brisket, with excellent results.

BEEF STEW WITH ONIONS

Ragoût de boeuf aux onions

Serves 6–8

This is a very satisfying ragoût and relatively easy to make as there are not too many ingredients. The onions give the stew its sweetness and softness, making them just as important in this dish as the meat. This stew is best when made in advance and reheated and served with either boiled potatoes or thick sourdough toast.

1.5 kg diced chuck steak

4 large brown onions

170 ml (⅔ cup) vegetable oil

4 tablespoons plain flour

1.2 kg tinned diced tomatoes

2 fresh bay leaves

4 thyme sprigs

1 garlic clove

1 teaspoon Parisian browning essence (see Note page 250)

Remove the beef from the refrigerator 1 hour before you wish to start cooking to bring to room temperature. Peel the onions and cut each onion into quarters so the quarters are still attached at the cores if possible.

Preheat the oven to 130°C.

Heat 2 tablespoons of the oil in a large casserole dish over high heat. Add half of the beef and cook for 10 minutes, turning to sear on all sides. Transfer to a strainer to allow the oil and juices to drain. Wipe the dish with paper towels and repeat with another 2 tablespoons of the oil and the remaining beef until well seared, then strain. Remove all of the beef to a plate.

Heat 2 tablespoons of the remaining oil in the casserole dish over medium heat. Add the onions and cook for 10 minutes, or until they have attained some colour. Remove the onions to a plate.

Return the beef to the dish with 2 tablespoons of the oil, then add the flour, stirring to coat. Cook for 2–3 minutes, then add the tomatoes and 1 litre (4 cups) water. Add the herbs and garlic and season well with salt and pepper. Mix well, add the onions and bring to the boil. Cover with a tight-fitting lid and cook in the oven for about 3 hours, stirring every hour or so and testing after 2 hours to see if the meat is cooked. After 2 hours, if the sauce is too pale, add a few drops of Parisian browning essence, mix and cook in the oven, uncovered, for another 30–60 minutes, or until the beef is tender and cooked.

Remove from the oven and allow to cool. At this stage you can divide the ragoût into two portions and either freeze the second half or keep it stored in an airtight container in the refrigerator for up to 4 days.

Reheat in a saucepan over medium heat to serve.

VARIATIONS: Use beef that is suitable for stewing, such as chuck, shin or even flank. I prefer cuts that have a bit of visible fat, which provides extra flavour and juiciness. This stew could also be made with diced lamb shoulder or venison. Sometimes I add 2 chopped carrots for the last 20 minutes of cooking. You can slice the onion instead of cutting into quarters; if you do, then it is best to add 4 tablespoons of mild paprika and a touch of chopped caraway seeds and call it a goulash.

RUMP STEAK WITH SHALLOTS AND RED WINE AND MATCHSTICK POTATOES

Boeuf à l'échalote et pomme allumettes

Serves 4

If you are serious about steak and want a great sauce to go with it, then this shallot sauce is perfect. The steak also goes very well with a béarnaise sauce (see page 267) or a pepper sauce.

2–3 large potatoes

vegetable oil or peanut oil, for deep-frying

120 g butter, diced

1 kg spinach leaves, trimmed

4 x 300 g thick rump steaks

1 tablespoon vegetable oil

8 French shallots, finely chopped

375 ml (1½ cups) red wine, such as Shiraz or Merlot

100 ml strong beef stock (see page 62)

Preheat the oven to 180°C.

Peel the potatoes, cut into 5 mm thick slices, then cut again into matchsticks. Wash in plenty of cold water, then dry well with a clean tea towel.

Fill a deep-fryer or large heavy-based saucepan one-third full with the vegetable or peanut oil and heat to 180°C, or until a cube of bread dropped into the oil browns in 15 seconds. Add the potato matchsticks and fry for 3 minutes, or until golden. Drain well, season with salt and keep warm.

Heat 1 tablespoon of the butter in a large frying pan over high heat. Add the spinach, season with salt and pepper and cook for 2 minutes, or until the spinach has wilted. Drain and squeeze out any excess liquid. Set aside and keep warm.

Pat the steak dry with paper towels and season on both sides with salt and pepper. Heat the vegetable oil in a large frying pan over high heat. Add the steaks and cook for 2 minutes on each side to sear well. Remove from the pan. Place on a baking tray and finish cooking in the oven for 3 minutes, or until the sauce is ready.

Add half of the remaining butter to the same pan over medium heat. Add the shallots, season, and cook for 5 minutes, stirring regularly, until soft but not caramelised. Add the red wine and bring to the boil, then reduce the heat and simmer until reduced by two-thirds. Add the stock and continue cooking until reduced by half, then add the remaining butter and stir through until melted and combined.

Put the steaks on serving plates with the spinach and matchstick potatoes. Spoon some sauce over the beef and serve with a good glass of red wine.

BRAISED BEEF RIBS WITH VEGETABLES
Plat de côte de boeuf braisé

Serves 4

I have made this dish countless times and often serve it for lunch. I sometimes vary the vegetables, adding mushrooms, swede or peas, but the basics never change. It also goes well with homemade potato purée (see page 286). This dish improves after a day, so reheating leftovers will make a meal that is just as impressive the second time around.

6 x 300 g beef ribs, cut in half

125 ml (½ cup) vegetable oil

2 tablespoons plain flour

2 tablespoons tomato paste

1 litre (4 cups) beef stock (see page 62)

2 bay leaves

2 thyme sprigs

250 ml (1 cup) red wine (optional)

8 pickling onions, peeled

4 carrots, cut into thirds

1 turnip, quartered

Preheat the oven to 150°C.

Tie each beef rib half in a bundle with kitchen string to hold together during the cooking process. Dry with paper towels.

Heat half of the oil in a large frying pan over high heat. Add the beef and cook for 10 minutes, turning to sear well on all sides. Transfer to a deep casserole dish and add the flour, tossing to coat the beef on all sides. Add the tomato paste, stock, herbs and wine, then season with salt and pepper and slowly bring to the boil. Reduce the heat and simmer while you cook the pickling onions.

Heat the remaining oil in the clean frying pan over high heat. Cook the pickling onions for 5 minutes to give them a touch of colour, then add to the casserole with the carrots and turnip. Cover the casserole, place in the oven and cook for 1 hour. Remove the carrots, turnip and onions to a plate. Cover the casserole and continue to cook the ribs for a further 1 hour, skimming from time to time, until the beef is tender and comes apart when tested with a fork.

Remove the ribs to a tray. Strain the stock into a large saucepan and bring to a simmer, stirring until the sauce thickens. Check the seasoning and adjust if necessary. Skim to remove any fat and strain the sauce.

Cut the string off the beef. Return the beef and vegetables to the pan with the sauce and gently reheat before serving.

HOMEMADE POTATO PURÉE
Pomme purée maison

Serves 4

This is the potato purée I prepare regularly at home — as it is both quick and easy.
I use a flat potato masher and find that the best potatoes to use are either desiree or
Toolangi delight.

4 large potatoes, peeled
and cut into large dice

250 ml (1 cup)
full-cream milk

1 pinch of ground
nutmeg

50–100 g butter, diced

Put the diced potatoes in a large saucepan and pour in just enough water
to cover. Season with salt and bring to a simmer over medium heat.
Cook for 15 minutes, or until tender. Drain in a colander and return
the potato to the pan. Add most of the milk, reserving about 60 ml
(¼ cup), then place over high heat and bring to the boil. As soon as the
milk starts to boil, remove from the heat, add the nutmeg and season
with salt and pepper. Add the diced butter and start mashing until you
have a soft purée. Add a touch more milk if you prefer a creamier purée.

VARIATION: You can use a rice masher instead of a regular potato
masher, which will produce an excellent purée. I do put a lot of butter in
my purée, so try it first with a smaller quantity of butter and increase it if
you like a velvety rich taste.

BURGUNDY-STYLE BEEF

Boeuf à la Bourguignonne

Serves 4 –6

There is no French recipe more typical than beef bourguignon, and despite the slight variation from chef to chef it almost always includes speck lardons, onion, mushroom and red wine. If you can't find pickling onions use the smallest onions you can find or use French shallots. Like all stews, this dish is best prepared in advance and reheated to give the flavours a chance to develop.

1 kg diced chuck steak

100 g smoked speck, skin removed and reserved

200 ml (¾ cup) vegetable oil

24 small pickling onions, peeled

200 g mushrooms, stems trimmed and reserved

1 carrot, cut into large dice

1 onion, cut into large dice

2 garlic cloves, peeled

375 ml (1½ cups) red wine such as a heavy shiraz or merlot

2 tablespoons plain flour

2 tablespoons tomato paste

2 fresh bay leaves

4 thyme sprigs

1 tablespoon chopped parsley

1 litre (4 cups) strong beef stock

Preheat the oven to 140°C.

Bring the beef to room temperature and dry with paper towels to remove any moisture.

Cut the speck into small strips or lardons. Heat 2 tablespoons of the oil in a large casserole dish over high heat. Add the lardons and pickling onions and cook for 5 minutes, stirring to sear the speck on all sides and colour the onions. Remove to a bowl and set aside.

Heat another 4 tablespoons of the oil and add the mushroom caps to the dish. Cook for 5 minutes, stirring regularly. Remove the mushrooms to a bowl with the pickling onions and speck. Add the carrot, diced onion, garlic and mushroom stems to the dish and cook for 5 minutes. Remove to a bowl and set aside.

Wipe the dish clean with paper towels. Heat 2 tablespoons of the oil over high heat. Add half of the beef and cook for 10 minutes, turning to seal on all sides, then remove to a colander to drain. Repeat with another 2 tablespoons of the oil and the remaining beef. Return all the beef to the dish, then add the flour and toss to coat. Add the tomato paste, red wine, the reserved vegetables, the herbs, the reserved speck skin and the stock and bring to the boil. Cover and cook in the oven for 1½ hours. Check the beef to ensure it is cooked; if not remove the cover and cook for a further 30 minutes.

When the meat is cooked, remove the dish from the oven, drain the stock into a large saucepan, reserving the beef, onions, speck and mushrooms and discarding all the other vegetables. Continue to cook the stock until it has reduced and thickened into a sauce. Return the beef, onions, speck and mushrooms to the pan and simmer for a few minutes to heat through. Adjust the seasoning, to taste, then remove from the heat and allow to cool for a few hours for the flavours to develop. Store in the refrigerator until you are ready to reheat and serve.

VARIATIONS: Towards the end of the cooking time you could add some large carrots in chunks. Turnips and potatoes also work well. You could make this dish using a free-range chicken cut into eight portions and chicken stock (see page 62) instead of the beef stock — you would only need to cook the chicken for 1 hour.

DESSERTS AND BAKING

French dessert names are often evocative – clafoutis, gâteaux, brûlée and millefeuille, to name a few. I suspect they are designed to create temptations and to help break resolutions, so maybe it is best to live by the French saying 'everything in moderation'. Hone your skills with these delicious recipes and your family and friends will love you forever.

PASSIONFRUIT FLOATING ISLAND

Ile flottante aux fruits de la passion

Serves 4

Floating Island or 'Ile flottante' is a classic light French dessert that is made mostly of egg white. It can change with the fruit of each season — try it with rhubarb, mangoes, strawberries or serve it simply with custard. I use sorbet in my recipe to give it an extra dimension.

Floating islands

4 free-range egg whites

200 g (1 cup) caster
    sugar

Passionfruit custard

300 ml pouring cream

50 ml passionfruit juice

6 free-range egg yolks

100 g (½ cup) caster
    sugar

250 g tropical fruit or
    raspberry sorbet

2 passionfruit, pulp only

Caramel

200 g (1 cup) caster
    sugar

60 ml (¼ cup) water

Preheat the oven to 150°C. Select four 8 cm round ramekins or soufflé dishes, about 5 cm deep — or I often use coffee cups of about 200 ml capacity — and lightly grease with oil spray.

To make the floating islands, put the egg whites and sugar in a heatproof bowl and place over a saucepan of simmering water. Whisk continuously until the sugar has dissolved and the egg whites are warm. Transfer to the bowl of an electric mixer and beat until stiff peaks form. Spoon or pipe the mixture into the ramekins and smooth the top with a wet spatula.

Place the ramekins in a deep roasting tin and pour in enough water to come two-thirds of the way up the ramekins. Cook in the oven for 15 minutes, then turn the tray around and continue to cook for another 15 minutes, or until the egg white is firm. Remove from the oven and allow to cool. When cool, use an ice-cream scoop or similar to make a hollow in each island where you can place the sorbet just before serving.

To make the passionfruit custard, put the cream in a saucepan over medium heat and bring to the boil. Put the passionfruit juice in a separate saucepan over medium heat and bring to the boil. Use a whisk to beat the egg yolks and sugar together until light and fluffy. Gradually pour in the hot cream, then the juice, whisking continuously. Return to a saucepan and cook over medium heat for 3 minutes until the custard thickens and coats the back of a spoon. Remove from the heat and immediately dip the base of the pan into a sink filled with iced water. Strain into a clean bowl and refrigerate until cool.

To make the caramel, put the sugar and water in a small saucepan over high heat. Stir to dissolve the sugar and until it starts to boil — move the saucepan in a circular motion to ensure it cooks evenly. As soon as the syrup turns golden, remove from the heat and add a touch of water and stir to make a smooth caramel. You should make the caramel just before you are ready to serve the floating islands. If the caramel hardens or thickens too much, just heat it up again.

When ready to serve, put the ramekins in a large dish and pour cold water over them to get the islands to float out of their ramekins — do not be afraid; the water will not damage them.

To serve, pour some passionfruit custard into each serving bowl. Scoop a ball of sorbet into the hollow of each island and invert onto the passionfruit sauce. Spoon some passionfruit pulp over the floating islands. Using a tablespoon, drizzle with the hot caramel.

VARIATIONS: You can serve the floating islands with a citrus salad and lemon gelato in the winter months or use fresh currants with a cassis and blueberry sorbet during the summer.

APPLE GÂTEAU WITH CALVADOS SYRUP

Gâteau aux pomme, sirop de calvados

This cake requires minimum skills to put together and is very forgiving, so there is no excuse for not trying it. It is quite a rustic country-style cake that also travels well and requires little refrigeration. Make it to take on a picnic, boat ride or enjoy it at the vineyard!

---

5 green apples, peeled, cored and quartered

300 g (1½ cups) caster sugar

200 g butter, softened

25 ml calvados or brandy

50 g raisins

3 free-range eggs

90 ml pouring cream

160 g plain flour, sifted

2 pinches of ground cinnamon

Preheat the oven to 180°C. Lightly grease a 20 cm round springform cake tin with butter.

Place the apples in a baking dish and sprinkle with 50 g (¼ cup) of the sugar and 50 g of the butter. Bake in the oven for 20 minutes, turning the apples from time to time, or until softened and cooked. Remove from the oven and transfer to the prepared tin.

Combine 50 g (¼ cup) of the sugar and 50 ml water in a saucepan and bring to the boil. Add the calvados or brandy and raisins, reduce the heat to low and simmer for 10 minutes. Strain and reserve the raisins and syrup separately.

Put the eggs and the remaining sugar in the bowl of an electric mixer with a paddle attachment and beat until light and creamy. Melt the remaining butter and add to the bowl with the cream, mixing well to combine. Gradually add the flour, cinnamon and raisins and mix well. Pour over the apples and bake in the oven for 25 minutes, or until firm and dry in the middle when tested with a skewer. Remove from the oven, allow to cool and then remove the tin. Turn the cake over and brush the reserved syrup over the apples. Serve with vanilla bean ice cream (see page 327).

VARIATIONS: You could make this cake with pears, cooked quince, cherries or poached rhubarb.

FRENCH APPLE TART
Tarte fine aux pommes

Serves 4

This is one of the simplest desserts to make and one of my personal favourites, although I rarely come across it in restaurants in Australia. I like to add a thin base of almond frangipane under the apples to make this tart truly stunning. You will need to prepare the almond frangipane ahead of time so that it can rest overnight, otherwise it will just run off the pastry when you bake it.

100 g butter, plus
    2 tablespoons extra,
    melted

100 g icing sugar

2 free-range eggs

100 g (1 cup) ground
    almonds

40 g plain flour

4 sheets butter puff
    pastry

5 Granny Smith apples

2 tablespoons butter,
    melted

4 tablespoons caster
    sugar

To make the frangipane, put the butter and icing sugar in the bowl of an electric mixer fitted with a paddle attachment. Mix on medium speed until light and fluffy. Add the eggs, one at a time, until well combined, and then add the ground almonds and flour, mixing well. Wrap in plastic wrap and refrigerate for at least 8 hours or preferably overnight.

Cut the pastry sheets to make four 20 cm rounds and sit on baking trays lined with baking paper. Dock the pastry with the tines of a fork. Spread a couple of tablespoons of the frangipane over each pastry round, spreading almost to the edges, and refrigerate for 20 minutes.

Preheat the oven to 180°C.

Peel the apples, cut into quarters and remove the cores. Slice thinly and arrange them neatly over the pastry so they slightly overlap and cover the frangipane; leave a 1 cm border around the edges. Brush the melted butter over the top and sprinkle on the sugar. Bake for 20 minutes, or until the apples and pastry are cooked.

Remove from the oven and serve on warm plates, topped with a scoop of your favourite ice cream (calvados or Armagnac ice cream would be great).

VARIATIONS: The apples in this tart are pretty essential but the classic apple tart does not use frangipane, so make a few without and see what you prefer.

RASPBERRY AND YOGHURT CHEESECAKE

Gâteau au fromage blanc et à la framboise

Serves 8

This is my version of a set cheesecake, as opposed to a baked one. It is lighter but make no mistake, it is still quite rich. I got the idea from Café Marly in the Musée du Louvre in Paris.

300 g digestive biscuits

100 g butter, melted

200 g fromage blanc or cream cheese, diced and softened

300 ml sweetened condensed milk

125 g (½ cup) plain yoghurt

125 g (½ cup) sour cream

1 tablespoon lemon juice

2 x 5 g gelatine sheets, soaked in cold water

125 g raspberries, washed

berry coulis (see page 315), to serve

Crush the digestive biscuits in a food processor or put them in a bag and crush them with a rolling pin. Stir in the melted butter until well combined. Use the crumbs to line the base and side of a 20 cm round springform cake tin. Refrigerate for at least 1 hour to firm up.

Put the fromage blanc or cream cheese in the bowl of an electric mixer fitted with a paddle attachment. Beat on low speed for 5 minutes, then increase the speed to medium for a further 5 minutes until smooth. Gradually add the condensed milk on low speed, again increasing the speed to high for 5 minutes, making sure there are no lumps in the mixture. Add the yoghurt and sour cream and continue mixing on medium speed for 5 minutes, scraping the side and bottom of the bowl from time to time, until well combined.

Heat the lemon juice in a small saucepan. Squeeze the water from the gelatine leaves and then stir them into the lemon juice until they melt. Strain over the cheesecake mixture and continue mixing for 5 minutes at high speed until all the ingredients are well combined. Pour the cheese filling over the cake base until it is filled to halfway. Sprinkle the raspberries all over the cheesecake and then top with the remaining filling mixture. Refrigerate for 4 hours. Once set, remove from the tin, cut the cake into wedges and serve with the berry coulis.

VARIATIONS: You can use blueberries or any other berries instead of the raspberries. If you prefer you could make a chocolate crumb base instead, simply follow the instructions for the base of the dark chocolate and raspberry tart recipe (see page 338) — you do not need to cook it, just spread the crumbs into the base of the tin, refrigerate briefly, then pour the cheesecake filling on top.

BAKED CHEESECAKE

Gâteau au fromage

This baked cheesecake is more of a tradition in Montréal than France. I used to love going to the Jewish delicatessens established in Montréal. There is no question that I always finished my meal with a cheesecake like this one.

200 g sugar pastry (see page 26)

600 g cream cheese, diced

200 g (1 cup) caster sugar

1 tablespoon plain flour

3 free-range eggs

70 ml pouring cream

finely grated zest and juice of 1 lemon

1 teaspoon vanilla bean paste

Preheat the oven to 180°C. Lightly grease a 20 cm round springform cake tin with butter and line the base and side with baking paper.

Take the pastry out of the refrigerator about 10 minutes before you wish to start rolling. Roll out the pastry on a lightly floured work surface to about 2–3 mm thick. Use the base of the cake tin to cut out a 20 cm round circle. Place on a baking tray and refrigerate for 15 minutes.

Cook the pastry base in the oven for about 20 minutes, or until golden. Remove from the oven and allow to cool.

Put the cream cheese in the bowl of an electric mixer fitted with a paddle attachment and beat for 4 minutes until soft and smooth. Add the sugar, flour and eggs, and continue mixing on low speed for 2 minutes until well combined. Add the cream, lemon zest and juice and vanilla and continue to mix until smooth.

Place the cooled pastry base in the cake tin and spoon the cheesecake mixture on top. Reduce the oven temperature to 160°C and bake for 40 minutes — when cooked the cake should have a touch of colour. Remove from the oven and cool completely in the tin before removing from the tin and serving.

VARIATIONS: You could add blueberries, pitted cherries, or even prunes to the cheesecake filling, or simply top with fresh fruit or a fruit compote after baking.

BANANA TART TATINS

Tarte tatins à la banana

Serves 4

A classic tarte tatin is made with apples, which acquire a super-sweet flavour and an incredibly good taste. I tried making it some time ago with bananas and it was an instant hit. If you have a choice of which ice cream to serve it with, go for a lighter flavour, such as vanilla, coconut or ginger. You could prepare these 1 or 2 hours ahead of time, then reheat them in their dishes just before serving so the caramel gets softer, making them easier to remove from the dish.

125 g (⅔ cup) caster sugar

125 g butter, softened

4 bananas, cut into 2—3 cm pieces

4 sheets butter puff pastry

vanilla bean ice cream (see page 327), to serve

Lightly grease four 10 cm round baking dishes or pie tins, about 3 cm deep, with oil spray. Sit them in a deep roasting tin.

Put the sugar and 1 tablespoon water in a saucepan over medium heat. Cook for 5—10 minutes, swirling the pan to ensure even cooking, until the sugar dissolves and caramelises to a nice golden colour. To avoid the caramel burning, brush the sides of the pan with a wet pastry brush regularly. Remove from the heat, then stir in the butter until well combined. Pour 2 tablespoons of the caramel into each dish.

Divide the bananas among the dishes, laying them over the caramel so they are tightly packed. Cut the pastry into four 12 cm circles. Dock with the tines of a fork and set over the dishes, tucking the pastry around the bananas, down the side of the dishes. Refrigerate until you are ready to cook them.

Preheat the oven to 180°C.

Bake in the oven for 20 minutes, or until crisp and golden brown. Remove from the oven and allow to rest for 10 minutes before inverting onto serving plates — the caramel can be extremely hot so take care. Pour any leftover caramel around the tarts and serve with a scoop of ice cream.

VARIATION: To make an apple tarte tatin, the apple would need to be partly cooked by sautéing in butter until golden before arranging over the caramel.

CHERRY CLAFOUTIS

Clafoutis aux cerises   Serves 4 (makes 2 large or 4 small)

When I was at cooking school we only ever used tinned cherries to make clafoutis.
Once you try it with fresh cherries it is hard to go back. The taste is almost
incomparable, with the fresh cherries being less sweet but more flavoursome. The
beauty of clafoutis is the range of fruit you could use — so go with whatever is in season
and buy locally whenever you can. Mangoes, peaches, plums and figs all work well.

500 g cherries

150 g (¾ cup) caster
    sugar

3 free-range eggs

5 free-range egg yolks

375 ml (1½ cups)
    pouring cream

30 g (¼ cup) plain flour,
    sifted

75 g (⅔ cup) ground
    almonds

1 pinch of salt

icing sugar, for dusting

Preheat the oven to 170°C. Lightly grease two 20 cm round baking
dishes or four 8 cm x 10 cm round ramekins with oil spray.

Use a cherry-pitter to remove the cherry stones. Pat the cherries dry with
paper towels to remove any excess juice and cut in half. Put the cherries
into the prepared baking dishes and place in a deep roasting tin.

Put the sugar, eggs and egg yolks into the bowl of an electric mixer fitted
with a paddle attachment. Beat together for 2–3 minutes on medium
speed to dissolve the sugar, then add the cream and beat for 1 minute, or
until smooth.

In a separate bowl, combine the flour, ground almonds and salt and
mix to combine. Make a well in the centre and slowly add the egg and
cream mixture, stirring constantly until well combined and smooth.
Pour into the baking dish to just cover the cherries. Pour enough boiling
water into the tin to come two-thirds of the way up the side of the dish.
Bake for 20–25 minutes, or until firm to the touch. Remove from the
oven and allow to cool for at least 15 minutes, then dust with icing sugar
and serve.

VARIATIONS: You could vary the flavour of the clafoutis by adding a little
ground ginger or cinnamon. If nuts are an issue, replace the ground
almonds with the same quantity of flour.

QUINCE CAKE

Gâteau aux coings

Serves 8

Every winter I make a version of this cake as small individual cakes for the restaurant or as a large cake for home. I always believe in using the fruit of the season so there is no reason to pass up the offerings of late autumn — this cake is the perfect way to unlock the glorious flavours of slow-cooked quince. You will need to cook the quince a day before you wish to make the cake.

3 quinces

500 g (2½ cups) caster sugar

375 ml (1½ cups) white wine

1 cinnamon stick

1 star anise

6 whole cloves

juice of 1 lemon

100 g butter

125 g (⅔ cup) caster sugar

1 free-range egg

125 ml (½ cup) pouring cream

1 teaspoon vanilla bean paste

125 g (1 cup) plain flour

1 teaspoon bicarbonate of soda

½ teaspoon baking powder

1 teaspoon ground cinnamon

2 pinches of ground ginger

1 pinch of ground cloves

Scrub the quinces under running water to remove any mould or dust. Peel the quinces and set aside the peelings, then cut into quarters and remove all the cores. Put the peelings in a piece of muslin (cheesecloth) and tie with kitchen string to make a little bundle.

To poach the quince, put the sugar, wine, cinnamon stick, star anise, cloves, lemon juice and 2 litres (8 cups) water in a saucepan. Add the peelings in the muslin bag to improve the flavour and colour of the poaching water. Bring to a gentle boil over medium heat and boil for 10 minutes to extract all the flavours. Reduce the heat to low and plunge the quince into the syrup. Cover with baking paper, making sure the quinces are completely submerged in the liquid, and simmer for up to 1 hour, or until tender. Remove from the heat, allow to cool and refrigerate overnight to firm up the quince.

When you are ready to make the cake, preheat the oven to 180°C. Lightly grease a 20 cm round springform cake tin with oil spray.

Put the butter and sugar in the bowl of an electric mixer fitted with a paddle attachment and beat together on medium speed for 5 minutes until light and fluffy. On low speed, add the egg, cream and vanilla bean paste and mix well, stopping to scrape the side of the bowl and incorporate all of the mixture.

Sift the flour, bicarbonate of soda, baking powder and all the spices together and gradually add to the bowl, mixing on low speed for 1 minute, and then on medium speed for 2 minutes until well combined.

Dry the quince pieces on a clean tea towel and set them in the base of the cake tin, cut side up. Pour the cake batter over the top and bake in the oven for about 40 minutes, or until the top is golden brown and the middle of the cake springs back when touched. Remove from the oven and allow to cool in the tin for 20 minutes, before removing the tin and cooling completely on a wire rack. Turn the cake over so the quince is on top and serve cold or warm with a caramel sauce or lightly sugared whipped cream or vanilla bean ice cream (see page 327).

VARIATIONS: You can use persimmons, pears or apples instead of the quince in this cake.

LEMON TART

Tarte citron à la crème

This is a cooked lemon tart and is different to a lemon curd tart, which is made with only egg and butter and doesn't require cooking in the pastry shell. This tart contains cream to produce a silky, refined tart. It will need to be refrigerated to firm it up before you cut and serve it.

250 g sugar pastry
(see page 26)

6 free-range eggs

250 g (1¼ cups) caster
sugar

juice of 6 lemons

300 ml pouring cream

finely grated zest of
2 lemons

Preheat the oven to 180°C. Lightly grease a 24 cm round fluted tart tin with oil spray.

Roll out the pastry on a lightly floured surface to about 3 mm thick. Lay over the tart tin and gently press the pastry into the base, making sure you leave no air pockets around the base. Trim the edges and refrigerate for 30 minutes.

Line the tart shell with baking paper and pour in enough baking beads or uncooked rice to fill. Bake in the oven for 15–20 minutes, or until the dough is firm and lightly crisp. Remove the beads and baking paper and continue cooking for another 5 minutes until the pastry is a nice golden colour. Remove from the oven and allow to cool.

Put the eggs and sugar in the bowl of an electric mixer fitted with a whisk attachment. Whisk together on medium speed until creamy and fluffy. Add the lemon juice and mix on medium speed until combined, then gradually add the cream until well combined. Strain the mixture into a clean bowl. Add the lemon zest and fold in by hand.

Place the tart shell on a baking tray and pour the lemon custard directly into the shell so that it is nearly level with the rim. Cook in the oven for 40–45 minutes, or until set — to test, give the pie a little knock and if the centre wobbles like jelly it will need to be cooked a touch longer. Remove from the oven and allow to cool, then refrigerate for 2 hours to firm up. Once the tart is chilled, remove from the tin and cut into wedges. Serve plain or with a touch of whipped cream.

Afternoon Tea

Cinnamon biscuits

Strawberry eclairs

Apricot millefeuille

Dark chocolate and raspberry tart

RHUBARB CHARLOTTE

Charlotte à la rhubarbe

This is a classic dessert that you do not see very often. It will require some patience to assemble but it is an impressive way to serve what is essentially a bread pudding.

2 bunches rhubarb, trimmed and cut into 2 cm pieces

200 g light brown sugar

375 ml (1½ cups) sparkling wine or water

1 vanilla bean, split lengthways

1 loaf day-old sliced white bread

250 g butter, melted

2 free-range eggs

100 g (½ cup) caster sugar

250 ml (1 cup) full-cream milk

crème anglaise (see page 314), to serve

Preheat the oven to 120°C. Lightly grease a 20 cm round charlotte tin or 10 x 20 cm rectangular cake tin with butter.

Place the rhubarb into a baking dish. Put the brown sugar and wine in a small saucepan. Scrape the vanilla bean seeds into the pan, then add the vanilla bean. Bring to the boil and boil over medium heat for 10 minutes, or until slightly reduced. Pour over the rhubarb, cover with foil and cook in the oven for 30 minutes, or until the rhubarb is tender. Remove from the oven, discard the foil and allow the rhubarb to cool in the syrup. Remove the vanilla bean. Increase the oven temperature to 190°C.

Cut the crusts from the bread with a serrated knife and put the crusts in a bowl. Cut the bread slices into thirds. Brush both sides of half of the bread slices with the melted butter, and as you work and start overlapping them in the base of the prepared tin. Reserve half of the remaining bread slices to seal the charlotte and dice the rest, including the crusts.

Put the eggs, sugar and milk in a bowl and whisk until the sugar has dissolved. Add the diced bread and crusts and set aside to soak briefly. Add the cooked rhubarb and mix well by hand to combine. Spoon into the tin to fill — you should have one part bread to two parts fruit.

Brush the remaining melted butter over both sides of the reserved bread slices and overlap them to cover the filling; press lightly to smooth the top. Bake for 30—40 minutes, or until the bread is crisp and browned. If the top browns too quickly, cover loosely with a piece of foil to prevent it from burning. Remove from the oven and allow to cool for 10—15 minutes. Carefully remove from the tin and serve with crème anglaise.

VARIATIONS: Use apples, pears, dates or custard apples instead of the rhubarb. You can also brush warm orange jam glaze over the top of the charlotte to give it a pleasant shine.

CRÈME ANGLAISE

Crème Anglaise

Crème anglaise is a classic French cream sauce and pastry kitchen essential. It was probably inspired by the English custard of the time, although these days it is hard to imagine cooking French-style pastry without this signature egg and vanilla sauce.

500 ml (2 cups) full-cream milk
500 ml (2 cups) cream
1 vanilla bean, split lengthways
12 free-range egg yolks
200 g (1 cup) caster sugar

Put the milk and cream in a saucepan over medium heat. Scrape the vanilla bean seeds into the mixture, then add the vanilla bean and bring to the boil. Remove from the heat and set aside. Remove the vanilla bean, rinse and reserve for another use.

Meanwhile, whisk the eggs yolks and sugar in a large bowl until creamy. Whisk in a touch of the hot mixture until smooth. Mix in the remaining mixture, then return to a clean saucepan over low heat, stirring constantly, for 10 minutes, or until the mixture thickens and coats the back of a wooden spoon. Make sure the custard does not boil. Remove from the heat, strain into a bowl and dip the base of the bowl in iced water to stop the anglaise from cooking any further. Refrigerate until ready to use.

The anglaise can be stored in an airtight container in the refrigerator for up to 4 days.

VARIATIONS: You could add a limitless number of flavours, either on their own or combined. Think coffee and caramel, cardamom, cinnamon, cognac, orange marmalade and many others.

POACHED PEACHES WITH BERRY COULIS

Pêches aux fruits rouges

Berries and peaches are both at their best during summer, which is the perfect time to make this dessert. If the peaches are ripe, just blanch them in boiling water to remove the skin, otherwise slow-cook them in the poaching syrup first.

500 g (2½ cups) caster sugar

1 lemon, halved

1 cinnamon stick

8 large ripe peaches

500 g mixed berries, such as raspberries, blackberries or currants, to serve

Berry coulis

100 g frozen blueberries

100 g frozen raspberries

100 g frozen blackberries

100 g frozen strawberries

200 g icing sugar

To poach the peaches, put the sugar, lemon halves, cinnamon and 1 litre (4 cups) water in a large saucepan and bring to the boil over high heat for 5 minutes. Reduce the heat to low, add the peaches and simmer for about 5–10 minutes, or until the skins have softened — the time will depend on how ripe the peaches are. Remove from the heat and put the peaches directly in iced water to stop the cooking process, then peel and discard the skins. Strain the syrup, discarding the lemon and cinnamon. Place the peaches in the remaining syrup and refrigerate until needed.

To make the berry coulis, put all the fruit in a bowl and dust with the icing sugar. Allow to defrost for at least 2 hours. Blend with a stick blender or in a food processor until you have a smooth purée. Strain through a fine sieve and refrigerate until ready to use.

When ready to serve, drain the peaches and place them in small bowls. Garnish with the mixed berries and spoon over the berry coulis.

VARIATIONS: You could use nectarines or large apricots instead of the peaches, or roast the peaches (see page 10).

NOTE: Coulis can be prepared with a sugar syrup that the fruit was cooked in, but I find the method above much more simple and the fruits are always available. The result is a deep coloured coulis perfect to use with any dessert.

ORANGE CAKES

Gâteaux à l'orange

Makes 8

This is a very interesting dessert that uses a whole orange that is first boiled and then puréed. The texture of the cake is moist and sticky, but perfectly balanced and flavoursome.

1 orange

5 free-range eggs

200 g (1 cup) caster sugar

100 g (1 cup) ground almonds

100 g plain flour, sifted

1 teaspoon baking powder

2 oranges, peeled

2 tablespoons icing sugar, plus 1 tablespoon extra for dusting

Wash the orange and dry it with a clean tea towel. Finely grate the zest and set aside. Put the uncut orange in a small saucepan and pour in just enough water to cover. Bring to the boil over medium heat, then reduce the heat and simmer for 2 hours, topping up with water as needed, until soft and cooked. Remove from the heat and allow to cool, then transfer the orange to a food processor and process to a fine purée.

Preheat the oven to 180°C. Lightly grease eight 10 cm round cake tins with butter.

Put the eggs and sugar in the bowl of an electric mixer fitted with a paddle attachment and beat until you have thick, creamy ribbons. Fold in the orange purée by hand, either using a whisk or a spatula. Add the ground almonds, reserved orange zest, the flour and baking powder and continue mixing by hand until combined. Pour into the prepared tins and bake for 25–30 minutes, or until a skewer inserted in the centre comes out clean. Remove from the oven and allow to cool completely in the tins.

Meanwhile, cut the peeled oranges into segments and put in a bowl. Squeeze the remainder of the orange centre to gather all the juice. Strain the juice into a separate bowl and add the icing sugar to make a sweet syrup.

Remove the cakes from their moulds and when ready to serve dust with the extra icing sugar. Top with the orange segments and drizzle with the orange syrup.

VARIATIONS: You can use a tangelo or mandarin instead of an orange although you will have to remove the pips after boiling. Sprinkle with slivered almonds before baking the cake or even shredded coconut for a different flavour.

LEMON CREAM
Crème au citron

In France most creams are set with egg, but this one, originating in England, uses the acidity from the fruit to set, creating a surprisingly light and unctuous dessert that is both refreshing and memorable.

600 ml pouring cream

250 g (1¼ cup) caster sugar

80 ml (⅓ cup) lemon juice, strained

Put the cream and sugar in a small saucepan and bring to the boil. Boil for 4 minutes, then add the lemon juice and cook for another 4 minutes. Remove from the heat and allow to cool slightly. Pour the cream into small glasses and refrigerate for 4 hours to firm up before serving.

VARIATIONS: You can dice your favourite fruit and place a teaspoon in the bottom of each glass before topping with the cream — try in-season passionfruit or pineapple.

FIGS WITH CHAMPAGNE SABAYON

Sabayon au Champagne et aux figues

Serves 4

Figs are an intriguing fruit. They can be pale, green, reddish or even a shiraz colour. They can have light flesh, be brilliant red or even have a brownish tinge. A friend in Montréal who taught me much about food told me to pick figs when they are quite ripe. For him a little black fig surrounded by tiny fermentation flies was a sign of great pleasure ahead, so do not be afraid to pick soft or even bruised figs. Serve with a sabayon or a sweet version of a hollandaise sauce.

6 free-range egg yolks

100 g (½ cup) caster sugar

250 ml (1 cup) Champagne or sweet dessert wine

4 large or 12 small ripe figs

Put the eggs, sugar and wine in a large stainless steel or ceramic bowl over a saucepan of simmering water and whisk for 2–4 minutes — the sabayon will slowly form, increasing in volume and thickness. Once it is creamy and light in colour, remove from the heat and allow to cool so the sabayon stabilises.

Cut the figs or tear them apart with your fingers and place in serving glasses or bowls. When ready to serve, return the sabayon to medium heat and whisk for 1–2 minutes to warm up and to give it more volume. Pour the sabayon over the figs and serve immediately.

VARIATIONS: The sabayon could be prepared ahead of time and served cold, in which case just whisk the cooked sabayon over a bowl of ice to firm it up. You could also spoon the warm sabayon over your fruit in small bowls and place under a hot grill to brown a little, but traditionally it is served warm and prepared at the last minute.

GRAPEFRUIT SOUFFLÉ

Soufflé au pamplemousse

This is a simple fruit juice soufflé that is light and quite easy to make. A traditional soufflé is made with a custard base and is heavier and more like a very light cake. This grapefruit soufflé is ideal for a small dinner party and is good served with candied orange and Grand Marnier ice cream on the side.

50 g (¼ cup) caster sugar, for dusting

8 free-range eggs, separated

200 g (1 cup) caster sugar

125 ml (½ cup) grapefruit juice

1 tablespoon icing sugar, for dusting

Preheat the oven to 200°C.

Lightly grease four 10 cm round soufflé dishes, about 6 cm deep, with butter and then sprinkle the sides with the caster sugar. The best way is to put all the sugar in one of the greased moulds and turn the dish in your hand to coat the inside. Pour the remaining sugar from the first dish into the next dish and repeat until all the dishes have been greased and sugared. Set the dishes on a baking tray.

Put the egg whites in the bowl of an electric mixer fitted with a whisk attachment. Mix on high speed until firm peaks form. Add half of the sugar and continue mixing until very stiff peaks form. Gently place into another bowl.

Wash the bowl of the electric mixer and dry thoroughly. Put the egg yolks and remaining sugar in the bowl and whisk until pale and creamy. Add the grapefruit juice and mix gently to combine. Gently fold through the egg whites, a little at a time until all combined. Scoop this mixture into the soufflé dishes and fill almost to the top. Bake for 10–15 minutes, or until well risen — the soufflés should have a good crust on top. Remove from the oven, dust with the icing sugar and serve immediately.

VARIATIONS: You could use any type of citrus in place of the grapefruit, or try passionfruit or guava juice.

DEEP-FRIED APPLE FRITTERS

Beignets aux pommes

Serves 8

This is an unusual recipe. The light and tasty coating for the apple bares no similarity to the batter that is often used when frying. Served with the prune and Armagnac ice cream, this dessert is truly sensational.

250 g rice flour

100 g plain flour

2 tablespoons baking powder

250 ml (1 cup) apple cider vinegar

100 g (½ cup) caster sugar

1 teaspoon ground cinnamon

juice of 1 lemon

6 large Granny Smith apples

vegetable oil, for deep-frying

prune and Armagnac ice cream (see page 326), to serve

To make the apple fritters, put the rice flour, plain flour, baking powder, vinegar and 170 ml (2/3 cup) water in a bowl and stir to make a smooth paste. Set aside for 30 minutes.

Put the sugar and cinnamon in a large bowl and stir to combine — the bowl needs to be large enough for dipping the fried apple into after it is cooked.

Put the lemon juice in a bowl with some water to make acidulated water — this will prevent the apples from browning. Peel and core the apples, then place in the acidulated water as you go. Drain, then square the top and bottom of each apple, discarding the trimmings. Cut the apples into thick rings, about six per apple. Soak them again in the acidulated water.

Fill a deep-fryer or large heavy-based saucepan one-third full of the oil and heat to 180°C, or until a cube of bread dropped into the oil browns in 15 seconds. Working with two or four apple rings at a time, dry the apple on a clean tea towel, dip into the batter to coat and then gently lower into the oil. Cook for 5 minutes, or until golden. Toss in the cinnamon sugar to coat and place on a tray lined with paper towels. Repeat with the remaining apple rings, batter and cinnamon sugar until all are cooked. Stack the apple rings into eight portions and serve with a scoop of homemade prune and Armagnac ice cream.

VARIATIONS: You could use pears instead of apples, or try using peaches, pineapple, or mangoes, depending on the season.

PRUNE AND ARMAGNAC ICE CREAM

Glace au pruneau et à l'Armagnac

Makes 1 litre (4 cups)

This type of ice cream is hard to find in a shop. If you have an ice-cream maker then treat yourself with this unctuous ice cream. Armagnac is the oldest distilled alcohol in France and is quite similar to cognac. It is produced in the Gascony region in the southwest of France. You will need to soak the prunes the night before you wish to make the ice cream and allow time for it to freeze before serving. This ice cream tastes terrific with deep-fried apple fritters (see page 325).

12 prunes, pitted and chopped

100 ml Armagnac or cognac

400 ml full-cream milk

300 ml pouring cream

1 vanilla bean, split lengthways, seeds scraped

8 free-range egg yolks

200 g (1 cup) caster sugar

Put the prunes and Armagnac in a bowl and leave to soak overnight.

Place the prunes and any leftover juices in a food processor or use a stick blender to make a coarse purée.

Put the milk, cream and vanilla seeds in a saucepan over medium heat and bring to a simmer. Once simmering, remove from the heat and set aside.

Put the eggs yolks and sugar in a bowl and whisk until creamy and fluffy. Add a touch of the warm milk mixture to the egg mixture to dilute it, mixing well, then add the remaining warm milk. Place the egg mixture in a clean saucepan over medium heat, stirring constantly with a wooden spoon to make sure the custard does not stick to the base of the pan — the custard will thicken but be careful to make sure it does not boil. Remove from the heat and strain into a clean bowl, then dip the base of the bowl into iced water to stop the cooking and to cool. Cover with plastic wrap and refrigerate for at least 4 hours.

Add the prune purée to the chilled custard. Transfer to an ice-cream machine and freeze according to the manufacturer's instructions.

VANILLA BEAN ICE CREAM

Glace à la vanille

There is nothing like homemade ice cream. This ice cream is the base for many other flavours so if you have an ice-cream machine at home you can vary the ingredients to produce an amazing array of colour and flavour combinations.

400 ml full-cream milk

300 ml pouring cream

1 vanilla bean, split
   lengthways

8 free-range egg yolks

200 g (1 cup) caster
   sugar

Put the milk, cream, vanilla bean and seeds in a saucepan over medium heat. Bring to a simmer, stirring for a few minutes. Set aside for about 10 minutes for the flavours to infuse. Remove the vanilla bean and gently reheat over medium heat.

Whisk the eggs yolks and sugar in a large bowl for 2 minutes until pale and creamy. Whisk in a touch of the warm milk mixture until smooth. Mix in the remaining milk mixture, then return to a clean saucepan over low heat, stirring constantly, for 5 minutes, or until the mixture thickens and coats the back of a wooden spoon. Make sure the custard does not boil. Remove from the heat, strain into a bowl and dip the base of the bowl in iced water to cool slightly. Refrigerate until cold.

Transfer to an ice-cream machine and freeze according to the manufacturer's instructions.

LIME CRÈME BRÛLÉE

Crème brûlée au citron vert

6 free-range egg yolks

100 g (½ cup) caster sugar

4 drops of lime oil or finely grated zest of 1 lime

500 ml (2 cups) pouring cream

100 g (½ cup) caster sugar, extra, for caramelising

Preheat the oven to 130°C. Select four 200 ml capacity ramekins or moulds.

Put the egg yolks, sugar and lime oil or zest in the bowl of an electric mixer and whisk until pale and creamy. Put the cream in a saucepan and bring to the boil. Remove from the heat and pour the hot cream into the egg mixture, continuing to mix at medium speed until combined.

Pour the egg mixture into the ramekins until three-quarters full. Sit the ramekins in a deep roasting tray, or a dish a little deeper than the height of your ramekins. For added safety you could line the tray with a few pages of newspapers or tea towel to avoid the dishes slipping around when the water is added. Set the tray on an oven shelf which has been partly pulled out, pour in enough hot water to come two-thirds of the way up the ramekins, and carefully push the shelf and tray back into the oven.

Cook for 30–40 minutes, or until set. Remove from the oven and place the ramekins on a wire rack to cool before chilling in the refrigerator for at least 2 hours. A skin will form on the custard, which is fine.

Remove the ramekins from the refrigerator. Sprinkle the extra sugar over the top of each custard to coat and use a kitchen blowtorch to caramelise the top. The trick here is to try to burn the sugar evenly, but if the sugar starts burning in just a few places, just top quickly with another pinch of sugar and continue to burn the entire surface. Clean the sides of the dishes by scraping away any burnt sugar and serve — the tops will remain crisp for a couple of hours so they could be burnt ahead of time.

VARIATION: You could add a split vanilla bean to the cream as it boils to add complexity, or try adding orange zest or candied ginger to the cream for an infusion of flavour.

APRICOT MILLEFEUILLE

Napoléon aux abricot

Serves 4

Known in France as a *Napoléon aux fruits*, this dessert was created in Denmark to honour one of the French Emperor's visits. It is made with layers of sweet puff pastry, a custard cream and poached fruit to make a wonderfully delicate pastry dessert.

I sheet butter puff pastry

8 apricots

200 g (I cup) vanilla custard (see page 352)

2 tablespoons peach liqueur or Grand Marnier

200 ml pouring cream, whipped

I tablespoon icing sugar, for dusting

Preheat the oven to 200°C. Line two baking trays with baking paper.

Cut the pastry sheets into eight 6 x 12 cm rectangles. Sit the pastry rectangles on the prepared trays, lay a sheet of baking paper over the top and set another tray on top to prevent the pastry from rising. Bake in the oven for 20 minutes. Remove from the oven and allow to cool on a wire rack.

Blanch the apricots in a saucepan of boiling water for I minute, or until the skin comes loose. Immediately plunge into iced water to refresh and allow to cool. Peel and discard the apricot skins, cut in half and remove the stones.

Put the custard in a bowl and whisk to remove any lumps. Add the peach liqueur or Grand Marnier and mix well, then add the whipped cream, a little at a time, until combined.

Set four pastry rectangles on four plates and arrange two apricot halves on each pastry. Spoon on some custard cream, top with another pastry rectangle and add another layer of fruit. Dust with the icing sugar and serve.

VARIATIONS: You could use peaches, plums or nectarines, or as the seasons change you can use a mixture of berries or pitted cherries, mangoes and passionfruit instead of the stone fruit with excellent results.

RASPBERRY MERINGUES
Vacherin glacé à la framboise

The French word *vacherin* describes a meringue dessert and also a cheese from the Jura region of France. *Vacherin*, the dessert or more precisely *vacherin glace*, only have their shape in common — both resemble a small camembert.

8 free-range egg whites

400 g (2 cups) caster sugar

500 g raspberry sorbet (see page 334)

375 g raspberries, rinsed

2 tablespoons icing sugar

Preheat the oven to 100°C. Use a pencil to draw about twenty circles, each with an 8 cm diameter, onto sheets of baking paper. Sit the baking paper, pencil side down, on baking trays.

Put the egg whites and sugar into the bowl of an electric mixer. Set the bowl over another larger bowl filled with hot water. Whisk until the sugar dissolves. Once the sugar has dissolved, transfer the bowl to an electric mixer fitted with a whisk attachment and beat for 4 minutes on high speed, or until stiff peaks form.

Put the meringue mixture into a piping bag fitted with a plain nozzle and fill each circle on the baking paper, in a steady stream, starting from the middle and spiralling out. Place the meringues in the oven and cook for about 2 hours, or until crisp. Remove from the oven and allow to cool.

Set half of the meringues on a tray and scoop a spoonful of sorbet on top. Layer the remaining meringue on top and press to make a 'sandwich'. Return to the freezer to firm up before serving. Alternatively, you could scoop the sorbet into egg rings and freeze them into shape before setting them between two meringues. Garnish with the raspberries and dust with icing sugar to serve.

VARIATIONS: You can use just about any fruit sorbet with these meringues. Berry coulis (see page 315) or crème anglaise (see page 314) also work well as accompaniments.

CHOCOLATE CROISSANT PUDDING

Gâteau de pain au chocolat

At Bathers' we make our own croissants and bread and there is often a surplus of the bakery items that I occasionally take home. If we have too many chocolate croissants, this pudding is a great way to use them up, but store-bought chocolate croissants work just as well.

5 free-range eggs

100 g (½ cup) caster sugar

300 ml pouring cream

300 ml full-cream milk

1 teaspoon vanilla bean paste

6–8 chocolate croissants

Put the eggs and sugar in a bowl and whisk until combined. Add the cream, stirring well to combine, then add the milk and the vanilla until incorporated. Strain into a clean jug and set aside.

Preheat the oven to 140°C. Lightly grease eight 250 ml (1 cup) capacity ramekins or a 2 litre (8 cup) capacity baking dish with butter.

Cut the chocolate croissants into pieces and place in a bowl. Pour on half of the egg mixture and let the liquid be absorbed, gently pressing with your fingers to help soak up the liquid. Divide the soaked croissants between the ramekins and pour on the remaining egg mixture, evenly distributing between each.

Put the ramekins in the base of a deep roasting tin and pour enough boiling water into the tin to come two-thirds of the way up the side of the ramekins. Bake the puddings in the oven for about 30 minutes, or until the tops are golden and crisp. If you are cooking one large pudding it may require a further 15 minutes for the liquid to set. Remove from the oven and allow to cool slightly before serving.

These puddings are best eaten still warm but not piping hot. They can be served in the ramekins or spooned out and served with crème anglaise (see page 314), pouring cream or vanilla bean ice cream (see page 327).

VARIATIONS: You can make a lovely pudding using plain croissants and adding stewed apples, pears or even rhubarb.

DARK CHOCOLATE AND RASPBERRY TART
Ganache à la framboise

The rich, dark chocolate ganache used in this tart is the ultimate filling. It can also be used as a cake filling or a dipping sauce for fruit, or when diluted with hot milk makes a decadent hot chocolate. Whichever way you use it, it's delicious!

Chocolate base
120 g unsalted butter, softened

125 g (⅔ cup) caster sugar

150 g (1 cup) plain flour

50 g cocoa powder

1 pinch of salt

Chocolate ganache
300 ml pouring cream

400 g (2⅔ cups) chopped good-quality dark bittersweet chocolate

250 g raspberries

Lightly grease the base and side of an 11 x 34 cm rectangular fluted mould or a 24 cm round fluted tart tin with a removable base.

To make the chocolate base, put the butter and sugar in the bowl of an electric mixer fitted with a paddle attachment and beat on medium speed for 2 minutes. Sift together the flour, cocoa powder and salt and gradually add to the butter mixture until combined, scraping down the side of the bowl to incorporate. Push the dough into a ball, wrap in plastic wrap and refrigerate for 1 hour to firm up.

Roll out the pastry on a lightly floured work surface to 3 mm thick. Line the base and sides of the tart tin with the pastry, but do not worry about trimming it to fit just yet — if you have bare patches break a bit of the excess dough from the side and press to cover any exposed areas. Return to the fridge for 1 hour to rest and then trim the excess dough with a sharp knife.

Preheat the oven to 180°C. Pierce the base a few times with the tines of a fork and bake in the oven for 15 minutes, or until crisp. Allow to cool. The tart base will keep for a few days in a dry environment.

To make the chocolate ganache, put the cream in a saucepan over medium heat and bring to the boil, then remove from the heat. Put the chocolate in a bowl and pour on the hot cream, stirring until the chocolate has melted and looks glossy and rich.

Place half of the raspberries in an even layer in the base of the tart and pour the chocolate ganache over the top. Refrigerate for 4 hours so the chocolate can set.

Allow the tart to come to room temperature otherwise the chocolate will be too firm. Cut into slices using a sharp knife dipped in hot water. Serve with the remaining raspberries.

CHOCOLATE FONDUE WITH FRESH FRUIT

Fondue au chocolat

This is a colourful and totally enticing dessert that everyone will love, especially children. It is a good alternative to a chocolate cake and is probably a bit healthier too!

125 g (⅓ cup) golden syrup

170 ml (⅔ cup) pouring cream

250 g good-quality dark chocolate, broken into pieces

250 g strawberries, stems removed

2 bananas, peeled and chopped

½ pineapple, peeled, core removed and chopped

24 marshmallows

24 sablé biscuits (see page 136)

To make the chocolate fondue, put the golden syrup in a saucepan over medium heat and warm up slowly. Add the cream, stirring continuously, and bring to the boil. Pour onto the chocolate pieces in a bowl and mix with a wooden spoon until the chocolate has melted. Set aside and keep warm until ready to serve.

Just before serving, arrange the strawberries, bananas and pineapple pieces on 16 wooden skewers, alternating the fruit with the marshmallows until all the fruit and marshmallows are used. You could also arrange the fruits and marshmallow on a plate. If you have little fondue dishes then serve the chocolate sauce in those, otherwise use small dipping dishes or jugs for each person. Serve with sablé biscuits.

CHOCOLATE MERINGUE AND HAZELNUT CAKE

Gâteau meringué au chocolat et à la noisette

Serves 8

This cake is sweet but light due to the crisp meringue, which will soften after a few hours for a great textural contrast to the mousse. It is best served in small portions as it is quite rich. Finish it with a good dusting of cocoa powder and it will be immensely enjoyable.

Hazelnut meringue

5 free-range egg whites

100 g (½ cup) caster sugar

150 g (1¼ cups) icing sugar

150 g (1⅓ cups) ground hazelnuts

50 g cocoa powder

½ cup chocolate shavings, for dusting

1 tablespoon cocoa powder, for dusting

Chocolate mousse

200 g good-quality dark chocolate

40 g butter

3 free-range egg yolks

5 free-range egg whites

50 g (¼ cup) caster sugar

125 ml (½ cup) pouring cream, lightly whipped

Preheat the oven to 150°C. Lightly grease a 30 x 12 x 8 cm loaf or terrine tin and line with plastic wrap — you may need to use a few sheets to make sure that you have an overhang on each long slide.

To make the hazelnut meringue, put the egg whites in the bowl of an electric mixer fitted with a whisk attachment and whisk until soft peaks form. Gradually add the sugar and whisk until stiff peaks form. Use a spoon to fold in the icing sugar, ground hazelnuts and cocoa powder. Put the mixture into a piping bag fitted with a plain nozzle and pipe the mixture in long lines, about 10 cm, on an oven tray lined with baking paper — making sure you leave a small gap between each line. Bake in the oven for 35–40 minutes, or until the meringues are crisp.

To make the chocolate mousse, melt the chocolate and butter in the microwave in short bursts, being careful as the chocolate can burn easily. This is a more efficient and safer method than using a double-boiler, however, if you do not have a microwave, put the chocolate and butter in a heatproof bowl over a saucepan of simmering water, making sure the base of the bowl does not touch the water, and stir until the chocolate melts. Allow to cool, then whisk the egg yolks into the chocolate mixture.

Put the egg whites in the bowl of an electric mixer fitted with a whisk attachment and whisk until soft peaks form. Gradually add the sugar and whisk until firm peaks form. Fold into the chocolate, a little at a time, until combined, then fold in the lightly whipped cream.

Arrange an even layer of meringue in the base of the prepared tin. Put the chocolate mousse in a piping bag fitted with a plain nozzle and pipe

over the meringue in an even layer. Arrange another layer of meringue on top followed by another layer of chocolate mousse and repeat until the tin is full. Cover with the overhanging plastic wrap and refrigerate for at least 4 hours.

When you are ready to serve, unwrap the cake and invert onto a serving plate. Top with any leftover meringue broken into small pieces, the chocolate shavings and dust with the cocoa. Cut into slices with a knife dipped in hot water.

VARIATIONS: If you like, you can add a shot (30 ml) of strong coffee to the mousse or a shot of coffee liqueur.

CRÈME CARAMEL

Crème au caramel

350 g (1¾ cups) caster sugar

1 litre (4 cups) full-cream milk

1 vanilla bean, split lengthways

4 free-range eggs

4 free-range egg yolks

Preheat the oven to 160°C.

Put 200 g (1 cup) of the sugar and 60 ml (¼ cup) water in a small saucepan over high heat and stir to dissolve the sugar. When the syrup starts to boil — move the saucepan in a circular motion to ensure it cooks evenly. As soon as the syrup turns golden, remove from the heat, add a touch of water and stir to make a smooth caramel. Pour the caramel into eight 250 ml (1-cup) capacity ramekins or similar moulds to about 5 mm deep and set aside.

Pour the milk into a saucepan over low heat, add the vanilla seeds, reserving the bean for another use, and cook for 5 minutes to allow the flavour to infuse. Remove from the heat and set aside but keep warm.

Meanwhile, in a separate bowl, whisk the eggs and egg yolks with the remaining sugar until combined. Add the warm milk and whisk vigorously to combine. Strain through a fine sieve into a pouring jug and pour the custard mixture over the caramel until three-quarters full.

Line a deep roasting tin with paper towels. Place the ramekins in the tin. Open the oven, pull a shelf out halfway and place the tin on the shelf. Pour enough boiling into the tin water to come two-thirds of the way up the ramekins and carefully push the shelf back in the oven. Cook for 35–40 minutes, until the cream is firm (shake the dish and if the cream wobbles cook it for a few more minutes and test again). Once the custard has set, remove from the oven and allow to cool on a wire rack.

When ready to serve, run the tip of a knife around the edge of each ramekin and gently invert a crème caramel onto a serving plate. Drizzle any leftover caramel from the base of each ramekin over the top.

VARIATIONS: You could make an orange crème caramel by infusing the milk with the zest of 1 orange and adding the juice of 1 orange to the eggs before adding the milk.

COFFEE CUSTARDS

Petit pots de crème au café

I love these little coffee custards as they can be baked in tiny cups or small pretty dishes. The principle behind this recipe is to flavour the sweetened milk and then set it with the egg so there is a limitless range of combinations you are able to achieve — think chocolate and orange, coconut and mango, lime, basil and strawberry. The coffee flavour of these custards is quite strong, so if you prefer a weaker strength, simply add less coffee syrup to the milk.

4 tablespoons instant coffee

100 ml boiling water

800 ml full-cream milk

8 free-range eggs

200 g (1 cup) sugar

Preheat the oven to 180°C.

Put the coffee and boiling water in a heatproof bowl and stir to dissolve the coffee to make a syrup. (Alternatively, you could make 100 ml strong espresso coffee if you have an espresso machine.) Add the milk and stir to combine.

In a separate bowl, whisk the eggs and sugar until the sugar has dissolved. Stir into the milk mixture, then strain through a fine sieve into a clean bowl and skim any bubbles off the surface, as they will look unsightly when you cook the custard.

Select some little coffee cups or demitasse and gently pour in the custard, again trying not to create bubbles. Put the cups in a deep roasting tin. Set the tin on an oven shelf which has been partly pulled out, pour in enough hot water to come two-thirds of the way up the cups, and carefully push the shelf back into the oven. Cook in the oven for 40–45 minutes, or until the custards have a firm jelly-like wobble. Remove from the oven, place the cups on a wire rack to cool, then transfer to the refrigerator for at least 4 hours before serving.

VARIATION: You can serve these custards with a touch of whipped cream and shaved chocolate.

POOR MAN'S PUDDING

Pudding chomeur

In Québec there are many brown sugar desserts and the poor man's pudding or literally 'man on the dole pudding' was one served during times of economic hardship, as it did not cost much to produce. Basically it was made using sugar, flour and margarine, or if you were lucky, butter. These days I add maple syrup and cream to enrich the flavour of the brown sugar sauce, but whatever your budget, it will still taste delicious.

200g (1 cup) caster sugar

60 g butter, softened

2 free-range eggs

1 teaspoon natural vanilla extract

250 g (2 cups) plain flour

2 teaspoons baking powder

300 ml full-cream milk

370 g (2 cups) light brown sugar

125 ml (½ cup) maple syrup

250 ml (1 cup) pouring cream

½ teaspoon vanilla bean paste

100 g butter, diced

Preheat the oven to 160°C. Lightly grease two 20 x 30 cm baking dishes or pudding moulds with butter.

Put the sugar and butter in the bowl of an electric mixer with a paddle attachment and beat on medium speed until pale and creamy. Add the eggs, one at a time, and beat until well combined, then add the vanilla extract and mix well.

Sift together the flour and baking powder and beat into the butter mixture on low speed, alternating with the milk until you have a smooth batter. Pour the mixture into the prepared dishes.

Put the brown sugar, maple syrup, 250 ml (1 cup) water, cream and vanilla bean paste in a saucepan and bring to the boil over medium heat. Cook for a few minutes until the sugar is dissolved. Add the butter, stirring continuously until smooth. Pour the sauce gently over the pudding and bake for 35 minutes, or until a toothpick comes out clean when inserted in the centre of the pudding. Remove from the oven and allow to cool in the dish for 10 minutes before serving.

SUGAR AND WALNUT PIE

Tarte au sucre et noix du Québec

There is probably no other more typical French Canadian dessert than a sugar pie or *tarte au sucre*. There are a multitude of regional recipes; some add a touch of maple syrup, others use milk instead of cream, while some omit the egg or add chopped walnuts. No matter which recipe you try the main ingredient is always brown sugar.

200 g sugar pastry (see page 26)

360 g (2 cups) dark brown sugar

250 ml (1 cup) pouring cream

2 tablespoons plain flour

50 g butter

2 free-range eggs

1 free-range egg yolk

100 g walnuts, chopped

Lightly grease a 20 cm round tart tin or pie dish with butter and dust with a little flour.

Take the pastry out of the refrigerator about 10 minutes before you wish to start rolling. Roll out the pastry on a lightly floured work surface to about 2–3 mm thick. Gently press the pastry into the base of the tart tin, making sure you leave no air pockets around the base. Trim any excess pastry from the edges. Refrigerate for 2 hours.

Preheat the oven to 200°C.

Put the brown sugar, cream, flour and butter in a small saucepan and bring to the boil over medium heat, stirring occasionally. Once boiling, remove from the heat, allow to cool for a few minutes, then whisk in the eggs and egg yolk to combine.

Pour the mixture into the pastry case and sprinkle with the walnuts. Bake in the oven for 10 minutes, then reduce the temperature to 175°C and continue cooking for a further 30 minutes, or until set. Remove from the oven and allow to cool completely in the tin. Cut into slices and serve with whipped or chantilly cream.

BASQUE CUSTARD CAKE
Gâteau Basque

215 g light brown sugar

250 g butter, diced

2 free-range eggs

310 g plain flour, sifted

1 pinch of salt

1 teaspoon vanilla bean paste

125 g ground almonds

1 teaspoon baking powder

2 tablespoons cherry jam

1 free-range egg, well beaten, for egg wash

Vanilla custard

1 litre (4 cups) full-cream milk

400 g (2 cups) caster sugar

12 free-range egg yolks

1 teaspoon vanilla bean paste

80 g (⅔ cups) cornflour

Put the sugar and butter in the bowl of an electric mixer fitted with a paddle attachment. Mix on medium speed until pale and fluffy. Reduce the speed to low and add the eggs, scraping down the sides to make sure all the ingredients are incorporated. Add the flour, salt, vanilla, ground almonds and baking powder and mix until you have a soft homogenous dough. Divide the dough into half, press into two flat squares and wrap each in plastic wrap. Refrigerate for 1 hour.

While the dough is resting, prepare the vanilla custard. Put the milk in a saucepan and heat to boiling point. Put the sugar, egg yolks and vanilla in a bowl and whisk by hand until creamy. Add the cornflour and dilute with a touch of the hot milk, then pour the egg mixture into the pan of hot milk and cook for 4 minutes, stirring often, until the custard thickens and coats the back of a spoon. Remove from the heat and plunge the pan into a sink of iced water to cool. Cover the top of the custard with plastic wrap to prevent a skin forming.

Grease a 20 cm round springform cake tin with butter. Roll out each portion of dough on a lightly floured work surface to 4–5 mm thick. Cut out a 26 cm round from each portion. Press one pastry round into the prepared tin to line the base and side. Place the other round on a plate and refrigerate both for 30 minutes.

Spread the cherry jam over the tart base and pour the custard evenly on top. Place the other pastry round over the custard. Trim the edges and tuck the dough neatly in at the sides. Return to the refrigerator for 30 minutes. Preheat the oven to 180°C.

Brush the top of the tart with the egg wash. Return to the refrigerator for 10 minutes to dry, then use a fork to make a crisscross pattern on top. Bake for 30–40 minutes, or until cooked and golden. Remove from the oven, allow to cool and slice into wedges to serve.

RASPBERRY JAM TART

Tarte à la confiture de framboise

Serves 8

This is one of my favourite tarts, which I always thought of as a Linzer tart until my Austrian pastry chef pointed out that it bears little resemblance to the real thing. A classic Linzer tart uses red currant jam and has dough made of cake crumbs, while this uses strawberry jam and plain flour. Secretly, I love this tart more, but don't tell my pastry chef!

300 g plain flour, sifted

125 g (⅔ cup) caster sugar

200 g ground hazelnuts

1 pinch of ground cinnamon

1 pinch of ground cloves

190 g butter, diced

1 free-range egg

1 free-range egg yolk

juice of 1 lemon

1–2 tablespoons full-cream milk

200 g (⅔ cup) raspberry jam

1 free-range egg, well beaten, for egg wash

Put the flour, sugar, ground hazelnuts, cinnamon and cloves in the bowl of an electric mixer fitted with a paddle attachment. Add the butter and mix on low speed until the texture resembles breadcrumbs. You will need to stop and scrape the sides of the bowl from time to time. Add the egg, egg yolk, lemon juice and just enough milk to make a firm dough. Gather the dough together, wrap in plastic wrap and refrigerate for 1 hour.

Preheat the oven to 160°C. Lightly grease the base and side of a 20 cm round springform cake tin.

Roll out two-thirds of the dough on a lightly floured work surface to about 3 mm thick. Cut out a 24 cm round and line the base and side of the tin with the dough. Trim any excess dough from the edges. Re-roll the leftover dough into a rectangle and cut into thin strips, about 20 x 1 cm, which will be used to decorate the tart.

Spoon the jam onto the base of the tart. Lay the dough strips in a lattice pattern over the top, trimming to fit neatly within the borders. Refrigerate for 15–20 minutes. Brush the egg wash over the dough strips, making sure you do not touch the jam. Bake the tart for 40–50 minutes, or until the pastry is firm to touch and golden. Remove from the oven and allow to cool completely in the tin on a wire rack before serving.

VARIATIONS: Blackberry jam makes an excellent substitute for the raspberry. If you do not like seeds, use a seedless raspberry jam.

CROQUEMBOUCHE GATEAU

Croque-en-bouche

1.5 kg choux pastry (see page 360)

Vanilla custard

500 ml (2 cups) full-cream milk

200 g (1 cup) caster sugar

6 free-range egg yolks

1 teaspoon vanilla bean paste

4 tablespoons cornflour

Caramel

500 g (2½ cups) caster sugar

100 ml water

Preheat the oven to 160°C. Prepare two baking trays by putting a touch of the choux pastry in each corner and placing a sheet of greaseproof paper on top so it sticks and does not move. First, on one baking tray, make the base by using a piping bag and a plain round piping nozzle about the same diameter as a 5 cent piece. Pipe the choux pastry to form a 20 cm square making sure it is fully filled in. This will be used as the base for your gâteau.

On the other baking tray pipe small balls, each about the size of a 20 cent piece, until all the dough is used. This will make approximately 15 to 20 balls. Cook for 20 minutes, then open the oven door to remove some moisture and allow the pastry to crisp out for 10 minutes.

Prepare the custard as per method on page 352.

When the choux balls have cooled, take a small sharp knife and poke a hole into the bottom of the ball just big enough to insert the tip of a nozzle. Set a plain nozzle in a clean piping bag. Beat the custard in an electric mixer until smooth as the custard will be quite firm when taken out of the fridge. Fill the piping bag with the custard and fill all the balls with the pastry cream. Set aside on a sheet of greaseproof paper.

Prepare the caramel as per method on page 294.

Take a choux ball and holding it from the bottom, dip the top of the ball into the caramel, only just covering the top. Place the caramel top onto the greaseproof paper. Allow to set, approximately 5 to 10 minutes. Continue dipping the remaining choux balls. If the caramel gets too thick just warm it up on the stove while mixing with a whisk.

While the choux balls in caramel are setting, take the 20 cm square base and place it onto a serving plate. Spread the remaining pastry cream over the base avoiding the sides. Arrange the set choux balls on top of the square, stacking some. Using some of the leftover caramel, dip a fork into the cramel and drizzle lightly over the cake. Serve once the caramel is set, about 10 minutes, or in the next hour as the humidity will soften and eventually melt the caramel.

ÉCLAIRS WITH STRAWBERRY CREAM

Éclairs à la fraise

750 g choux pastry (see page 360)

Strawberry purée

250 g strawberries, washed, tops trimmed and halved

100 g (½ cup) caster sugar

Cream filling

250 ml (1 cup) full-cream milk

1 vanilla bean, split lengthways

6 free-range egg yolks

100 g (½ cup) caster sugar

40 g (⅓ cup) cornflour

2 tablespoons butter, softened

100 ml pouring cream

100 ml fondant, for glazing (see Note page 360)

Preheat the oven to 180°C. Lightly grease two baking trays with oil spray and line with baking paper.

Fill a piping bag fitted with a plain nozzle with the choux pastry. Pipe thirty 8 cm x 1.5 cm logs onto the prepared trays, allowing space for spreading — the éclairs will double in size. Bake the pastries in the oven for 15 minutes, making sure you do not open the oven door during this time. Reduce the oven temperature to 160°C and cook for a further 20 minutes, opening the door from time to time to allow the steam to escape, thus producing crispy choux pastry éclairs. Remove from the oven and allow to cool.

Meanwhile, make the strawberry purée. Combine the strawberries, sugar and 1 tablespoon water in a small saucepan and cook over low heat for 10 minutes until the strawberries are soft and pulpy. Allow to cool slightly and use a stick blender or food processor to purée until smooth.

To make the cream filling, put the milk and 125 ml (½ cup) strawberry purée in a saucepan over medium heat. Scrape the vanilla seeds into the pan and slowly bring to the boil. Once boiling, remove from the heat and set aside. Whisk the egg yolks and sugar in a bowl until the sugar dissolves. Add the cornflour, mixing to combine, then add 125 ml (½ cup) of the hot strawberry milk and mix well. Add the egg mixture to the remaining hot strawberry milk in the pan and return to the heat. Bring to the boil and cook for 2–3 minutes, stirring constantly, until the mixture thickens. Remove from the heat and whisk in the butter. Strain through a fine sieve into a bowl, cover with plastic wrap to avoid a skin forming and refrigerate until cool.

Whisk the strawberry cream to remove any lumps. Whip the cream in a separate bowl until firm, then add to the strawberry cream, a little at a time, to lighten the mixture, until all the whipped cream is incorporated.

To assemble the éclairs, make a small hole in the bottom of each éclair. Put the strawberry cream in a piping bag fitted with a plain nozzle and fill each éclair with the cream — each éclair should feel heavy, but try to avoid the strawberry cream spilling out.

Put the fondant in a saucepan over low heat and gently warm it up, stirring regularly with a wooden spoon until soft and smooth. Remove from the heat and, working quickly, dip the top of each éclair in the fondant to produce a glossy white frosting. When all the éclairs are dipped, arrange on a platter and serve.

VARIATIONS: You can make éclairs with a chocolate or coffee filling and dip them in melted chocolate.

NOTE: You can buy fondant from some delicatessens or specialist food shops, or you could ask your local pastry shop to sell you a small quantity.

CHOUX PASTRY
Pâte a choux

Makes 750 g or 30 small eclairs

125 g butter, diced

250 ml (1 cup) milk

150 g plain flour, sifted

4 free-range eggs

Put the butter and milk in a saucepan and bring to the boil over medium heat. Add the flour all at once and stir on the stove with a wooden spoon until the dough comes together in a large ball that does not stick to the side of the pan. The dough should have a nice gloss. Transfer the dough to an electric mixer fitted with a paddle attachment and beat for a couple of minutes on medium speed to remove the excess heat from the dough. Add the eggs, one at a time, beating on medium speed, until well combined. The dough should be glossy but stiff enough to hold firm peaks. Use as directed.

Once cooked, these choux pastries can be stored in an airtight container and frozen for up to 2 weeks.

CHOCOLATE BROWNIES

Pavé au chocolat à la ganache

Makes 25

150 g good-quality dark chocolate

100 g butter

500 g (2½ cups) caster sugar

5 free-range eggs

3 drops natural vanilla extract

200 g (1⅔ cups) plain flour, sifted

1 teaspoon baking powder

125 g (1 cup) chopped walnuts or raisins (optional)

Chocolate ganache

300 ml pouring cream

200 g (1⅓ cups) chopped good-quality dark chocolate

Preheat the oven to 170°C. Line a 25 cm square cake tin with baking paper.

To make the brownies, put the chocolate and butter in a bowl and melt in the microwave in short bursts, being careful as it can burn easily. This is a more efficient and safer method than using a double-boiler, however, if you do not have a microwave, put the chocolate and butter in a heatproof bowl and sit it over a saucepan of simmering water, making sure the base of the bowl does not touch the water, and stir until the chocolate melts.

Put the sugar and eggs in the bowl of an electric mixer fitted with a paddle attachment and mix on medium speed for 5 minutes until combined. Add the vanilla and melted chocolate, then fold in the flour and baking powder. Lastly, add the walnuts or raisins, if using, and mix to combine. Spoon the mixture into the prepared tin and bake for 50 minutes. If you like a dry brownie, cook for a further 10 minutes. Remove from the oven and allow to cool in the tin.

To make the ganache, put the cream in a saucepan and bring to the boil over medium heat. Remove from the heat and add the chocolate, stirring well until the chocolate melts and thickens the cream. Transfer to a small container, cover with plastic wrap and refrigerate for 2–3 hours.

Before serving, cut the crust-like edges from the brownie to expose the moist cake, then spread the ganache evenly over the top. To serve, cut into small squares with a knife dipped in hot water.

VARIATIONS: You can vary this recipe slightly by adding chopped hazelnuts, pecans, sun-dried fruit or you could also soak the chocolate cake with a homemade sugar syrup (adding a splash of rum for the grown-ups).

ALMOND JAM TARTLETS

Frangipane à la confiture

These beautiful little tartlets are well worth putting a bit of effort into making. They are the perfect addition to an afternoon tea or for any occasion that requires a delicious and sophisticated sweet offering.

150 g butter, diced

150 g (¾ cup) caster sugar

2 free-range eggs

150 g (1½ cups) ground almonds

40 g (⅓ cup) flour

250 g sugar pastry (see page 26)

100 g (⅓ cup) strawberry jam

90 g (1 cup) flaked almonds

2 tablespoons icing sugar, for dusting

Put the butter and sugar in the bowl of an electric mixer fitted with a whisk attachment and whisk on medium speed until pale and fluffy. Add the eggs, one at a time, beating until combined. Reduce the speed to low and gradually beat in the ground almonds and flour, until well combined and still light in colour. Cover and refrigerate for 4 hours or best overnight.

Lightly grease twelve 5 cm round fluted tart tins with oil spray.

Take the pastry out of the refrigerator about 10 minutes before you wish to start rolling. Roll out the pastry on a lightly floured work surface to about 2–3 mm thick. Use a pastry cutter to cut twelve 7 cm circles. Gently press the pastry into the base of each tart tin, making sure you leave no air pockets around the base. Trim any excess dough from the edges. Refrigerate for a further 30 minutes.

Preheat the oven to 160°C.

Divide the jam between each tartlet. Spoon or pipe the almond filling over the jam, then smooth the tops with a spatula. Sprinkle on the flaked almonds and bake for 20 minutes, or until golden, making sure the almonds do not burn. Remove from the oven and allow to cool. Serve the almond jam tartlets dusted with icing sugar.

VARIATIONS: You can use orange marmalade or apricot jam instead of the strawberry. You can make one large tart using a 20 cm tart tin, which may require further cooking of the pastry to allow for the larger size. You could also embed some fresh berries, such as raspberries or blackberries, in the almond filling before baking.

SUGAR SHORTBREAD

Biscuits au sucre

This is a simple little biscuit dusted with sugar. They can be made into any shape
— triangles, rounds or squares — and are great for serving with afternoon tea,
or as small fingers to go with a creamy dessert, such as ice cream, clafoutis or
lemon cream. I also use this recipe to make the base for some cakes, such as baked
cheesecake (see page 302).

250 g butter, diced

150 g (¾ cup) caster
sugar, plus extra for
dusting

360 g plain flour, plus
extra for dusting

Rub the butter and sugar together in a bowl. Add the flour and work
with your fingertips to make a firm dough. Gather into a ball, wrap in
plastic wrap and rest in the refrigerator for 1 hour.

Preheat the oven to 180°C. Line a baking tray with baking paper.

Roll out the dough on a lightly floured work surface to form a rectangle
about 1.5 cm thick. Cut the dough into smaller rectangles, about
2 x 6 cm, to make about 40 biscuits in total. Place on the prepared tray
and bake in the oven for 20–25 minutes, or until crispy and lightly
golden.

Remove from the oven, dust each shortbread with the extra sugar and
transfer to a wire rack to cool. The shortbread can be stored in an
airtight container for up to 5 days.

ALMOND AND CINNAMON BISCUITS

Biscuits aux amandes et à la cannelle

Makes 24

If you like almonds and cinnamon, these biscuits are sure to please. You could prepare the dough ahead of time, but the biscuits are best cooked fresh, filling the house with a wonderful aroma that will make them hard to resist.

250 g butter, diced

125 g (⅔ cup) caster sugar

I teaspoon vanilla bean paste

250 g (2 cups) plain flour, sifted

I tablespoon baking powder

100 g (I cup) ground almonds

I teaspoon ground cinnamon

Put the butter and sugar in the bowl of an electric mixer fitted with a paddle attachment. Beat on medium speed for 5 minutes, or until pale and fluffy. Add the vanilla bean paste, beat to combine, then add all of the other ingredients, a little at a time, stopping to scrape the sides of the bowl to ensure you have a well mixed dough.

Divide the dough into two even-sized portions and shape into rough log shapes. Wrap each dough portion in a sheet of baking paper and use the base of your hand to roll into neat logs, 5 cm in diameter. Refrigerate for I hour.

Preheat the oven to 150°C. Line two baking trays with baking paper.

Unwrap the dough logs and cut into slices, about 2–3 cm thick, to make about 24 biscuits. Arrange the biscuits on the prepared trays, leaving room between each for the biscuits to spread. Press dough down with your hand to flatten a little and dock with the tines of a fork.

Bake the biscuits in the oven for 20 minutes, or until golden. Use a spatula to lift them onto a wire rack to cool completely. The biscuits can be stored in an airtight container for up to a week.

VARIATIONS: You can replace the cinnamon with ground ginger and use ground hazelnuts or shredded coconut instead of the ground almonds to vary the flavour.

BRETON BISCUITS
Sablé Breton

There are several recipes for this biscuit, which originated in northern France. Some use yeast in the dough, sometimes with a touch of cinnamon, but mostly they are left plain. They are the perfect biscuit for an afternoon coffee break.

500 g plain flour

300 g salted butter, diced and softened

200 g (1⅔ cups) icing sugar

2 free-range eggs

1 tablespoon baking powder

1 pinch of salt

1 teaspoon vanilla bean paste

½ teaspoon ground cinnamon

1 free-range egg, well beaten with a touch of milk, for egg wash

Put all of the ingredients, except the egg wash, in the bowl of an electric mixer fitted with a paddle attachment. Mix on low speed for 2 minutes then increase speed to medium and mix for 2 minutes to make a smooth dough. Roll into a ball, cover with a clean tea towel and refrigerate for 1 hour.

Preheat the oven to 160°C. Line two baking trays with baking paper.

Roll out the dough on a lightly floured work surface into a rectangle, about 1 cm thick. Use a 6 cm or 8 cm round or fluted pastry cutter to press out as many biscuits as you can. Re-roll any scraps of dough, refrigerate for 5 minutes to firm up and continue pressing out biscuits until all of the dough is used — you should make about 40 biscuits in total.

Arrange the biscuits on the baking trays and brush on the egg wash. Refrigerate for 5 minutes for the glaze to dry and then dock each biscuit with the tines of a fork. Refrigerate for a further 10 minutes. Bake in the oven for 15 minutes, or until golden.

CINNAMON SUGAR BISCUITS

Palmier à la cannelle

These biscuits, traditionally known as 'palmier', are supposed to represent palm leaves. You will find them in various sizes, but in France they are made to be quite small and dainty, which is my preference as well.

100 g (½ cup) caster sugar

½ teaspoon ground cinnamon

2 sheets butter puff pastry

2 free-range egg whites, lightly beaten, for glazing

Line two baking trays with baking paper.

Mix the sugar and cinnamon together. Brush the top face of each pastry sheet with some of the egg white and sprinkle some of the cinnamon sugar evenly over the top. Fold over the left and right edge of each pastry to meet in the middle and roll gently with the rolling pin to seal the sheet together. Brush with egg white again, sprinkle with some more cinnamon sugar and fold the left on top of the right fold. Repeat with the remaining pastry sheet and the egg white and cinnamon sugar. Refrigerate for 30 minutes to firm up.

Preheat the oven to 180°C.

Cut the pastry into 1 cm thick slices to make 36 palmiers in total. Arrange cut side down on the prepared trays so you can see the palm shape. Bake in the oven for 15–20 minutes, or until the palmiers are crisp and golden and the sugar has caramelised. Transfer to a wire rack to cool completely.

Palmiers can be stored in an airtight container for up to 1 week.

CITRUS BISCUITS

Sablé au citron

This is a plain biscuit flavoured with citrus. They are great to take on picnics as they travel well, but taste just as delicious served as a snack for morning or afternoon tea.

200 g butter, diced and softened

100 g icing sugar

1 free-range egg

finely grated zest of 1 lime

finely grated zest of 1 lemon

2 drops citrus oil (optional)

250 g (2 cups) plain flour, sifted

1 free-range egg, well beaten, for egg wash

Put the butter and icing sugar in the bowl of an electric mixer fitted with a paddle attachment. Mix on high speed for 5 minutes until pale and creamy. Add the egg, citrus zests and the citrus oil, if using, and continue mixing until well combined. Gradually add the flour on low speed to make a smooth dough. Gather into a ball, wrap in plastic wrap and refrigerate for 4 hours.

Preheat the oven to 190°C. Line two baking trays with baking paper.

Roll out the dough on a lightly floured work surface into a rectangle, about 5 mm thick. Cut the dough into small rectangles, about 2 x 6 cm. Arrange on the prepared trays and bake in the oven for 15 minutes, or until golden. Allow to cool on the trays for 10 minutes, before transferring to a wire rack to cool completely.

Citrus biscuits can be stored in an airtight container for up to 1 week.

NOTE: You can find a range of flavoured oil in specialist food shops. The citrus oils — orange, lemon and lime — are the best. A couple of drops are sufficient to flavour a biscuit dough, crème brulée or a sponge.

CHOCOLATE CHIP COOKIES
Biscuits aux brisures de chocolat

This is a basic chocolate chip recipe, which children everywhere will love. You can vary the biscuits by adding pecans, almonds, currants, dried blueberries, ground cinnamon, with or without the chocolate — the possibilities are endless.

200 g butter, diced

200 g (1 cup) caster sugar

200 g light brown sugar

1 teaspoon vanilla bean paste

3 free-range eggs

500 g (4 cups) plain flour, sifted

2 teaspoons baking powder

350 g (2 cups) chocolate chips

Put the butter, sugar and brown sugar in the bowl of an electric mixer fitted with a paddle attachment. Mix on high speed for 3 minutes until the mixture is pale and creamy. Reduce the speed to low and add the vanilla, then add the eggs, one at a time, beating well after each addition. You will need to stop from time to time to scrape down the sides of the bowl. On low speed, add the flour and the baking powder until well combined. Lastly, fold in the chocolate chips by hand.

Divide the dough into two even-sized portions and shape into rough logs. Wrap each dough portion in a sheet of baking paper and use the base of your hand to roll into neat logs 5 cm in diameter. Refrigerate for 1 hour.

Preheat the oven to 180°C. Line two baking trays with baking paper.

Unwrap the dough logs and cut into slices, about 2 cm thick, to make about 24 biscuits. Arrange the biscuits on the prepared trays, leaving room between each for the biscuits to spread — they will nearly double in size. Press dough down with your hand to flatten a little.

Bake the biscuits in the oven for 15–20 minutes, or until they are golden and have a crisp edge. Allow to cool for 10 minutes on the tray before transferring to a wire rack to cool completely.

VARIATION: If you prefer thick biscuits, double the width of each as you slice the logs and place in large egg rings to prevent the dough from spreading during cooking. You will need to increase the cooking time by approximately 5 minutes.

GINGERBREAD BISCUITS

Biscuit au gingembre

Makes 24

These biscuits can be cut into standard round biscuit shapes, but if you are offering them at a children's party, just cut them with kid's pastry cutters to make them more interesting.

2 tablespoons golden syrup

250 g butter, diced

300 g (1⅔ cups) dark brown sugar

600 g (4¾ cups) plain flour

1 teaspoon bicarbonate of soda

2 teaspoons mixed spice

2 tablespoons ground ginger

1 egg, well beaten with a touch of milk, for egg wash

Put the golden syrup and 125 ml (½ cup) water in a small saucepan and bring to the boil over mediuim heat, stirring to make a syrup. Set aside to cool.

Put the butter and sugar in the bowl of an electric mixer fitted with a paddle attachment. Mix on medium speed for 5 minutes, or until pale and creamy. Reduce the speed to low and gradually add the flour, bicarbonate of soda, mixed spice and ground ginger until well combined. Lastly, add the golden syrup mixture and continue mixing to make a smooth dough. Gather into a ball, wrap in plastic wrap and refrigerate for 2 hours.

Roll out the dough on a lightly floured work surface into a rectangle, about 3 mm thick. Transfer to a tray and refrigerate for 20 minutes.

Use a 6 cm round pastry cutter to press out as many biscuits as you can. Re-roll any scraps of dough, refrigerate for 5 minutes to firm up and continue pressing out biscuits until all of the dough is used — you should make about 24 biscuits in total. Refrigerate again for 20 minutes so the biscuits hold their shape during cooking.

Preheat the oven to 190°C. Line two baking trays with baking paper.

Arrange the biscuits on the prepared trays and brush over the egg wash. Bake in the oven for 15 minutes, or until golden. Allow to cool on the trays for 10 minutes before transferring to a wire rack to cool completely.

Gingerbread biscuits can be stored in an airtight container for up to 1 week.

ALMOND TUILES

Tuiles aux amandes

Tuiles are normally a very thin biscuit, shaped like an arch, much like a roof tile. They can be made plain or sometimes with flaked almonds. My recipe produces a much different result, making crunchy, substantial, satisfying tuiles that are highly addictive! If you make large tuiles you will not need to prepare a dessert, simply serve them with coffee or tea.

150 g butter, melted

250 g (1¼ cups) caster sugar

4 free-range egg whites

300 g plain flour

2 teaspoons baking powder

250 g (2¾ cups) flaked almonds

Preheat the oven to 180°C. Line two baking trays with baking paper.

Put the melted butter, sugar, egg whites, flour, baking powder and almonds in a large bowl and mix well with a wooden spoon to combine — some of the almond will break up and that is fine. Lift 1 tablespoon of the mixture onto the baking tray and pat down to flatten to about 2 mm thick — if you are making the large tuiles, use 3 tablespoons instead. Repeat with the remaining mixture.

Bake the tuiles in the oven for 5 minutes, or until the edges are golden.

Working with one tuile at a time, carefully lift the warm biscuits with a flat metal spatula and place over a large rolling pin or round bottle to press them into a nicely curved shape. Transfer to a wire rack to cool. If the tuiles cool down before you have a chance to shape them all, return them to the oven and gently reheat until they soften.

Tuiles can be stored in an airtight container for up to 5 days.

VARIATION: You can use desiccated coconut instead of the almonds.

MADELEINE BISCUITS
Madeleine

Makes 60 small or 30 large

The Madeleine is a classic French biscuit that requires a special mould to produce their classic shape. They come in two sizes — the small madeleines are for serving as petits fours, while the larger version are perfect served on their own with a cup of tea.

150 g butter, diced

4 free-range eggs

200 g (1 cup) caster sugar

150 g plain flour, plus extra for dusting

50 g (½ cup) ground almonds

2 teaspoons baking powder

finely grated zest of 1 lemon

icing sugar, for dusting

Melt the butter in a small saucepan over medium heat for 10 minutes until it acquires a golden colour and a nutty taste. Immediately strain into a small bowl to avoid burning and to remove any sediment. Set aside to cool.

Put the eggs and sugar in the bowl of an electric mixer fitted with a whisk attachment. Mix on high speed for 2–3 minutes until pale and fluffy.

Combine the flour, ground almonds, baking powder and lemon zest in a separate bowl, then gradually add to the egg mixture on low speed until well combined. Add the melted butter and mix until a smooth dough forms. Cover with plastic wrap and refrigerate for 2 hours.

Preheat the oven to 180°C. Lightly grease madeleine moulds with butter, dust with flour and shake the moulds to remove any excess flour.

Spoon or pipe the madeleine mixture into the moulds and set aside at room temperature for 15 minutes so they can rise a little before cooking. Cook in the oven for 8–10 minutes for the small madeleines and 2–3 minutes longer for the large, until golden and crisp. Allow to cool in the moulds for 10 minutes before turning out onto wire racks to cool completely. Dust with icing sugar just before serving.

Madeleines can be stored in an airtight container for up to 4 days. If you prefer a softer biscuit, transfer them to an airtight container immediately after they are removed from the oven (without dusting with icing sugar) — the steam from the warm biscuits will soften their exterior.

Golden, viscous, sweet
caramel requires some skill
to prepare — more timing
than technique — but will
give your dessert unique
appeal and a beautiful
texture

BIBLIOGRAPHY

All the recipes in French Kitchen are recipes I have used and developed over the years. They became personal, many inspired by my gastronomic travels through France and my years working in the kitchen. I also find inspiration in cookbooks and here are some that are very special to me, having educated me and made me passionate about great food and creative recipes.

Bertolli, Paul, with Waters, Alice, *Chez Panisse Cooking*, New York: Random House, 1994.

David, Elizabeth, *French Provincial Cooking*, New York: Penguin Books, 1960.

Oliver, Raymond, *La Cuisine: Secrets of Modern French Cooking*, Paris: Editions Bordas, 1981.

Olney, Richard (Series Editor), *The Good Cook* (European Edition), Time Life Books, 1978–1980.

Poilâne, Lionel, *Le Pain par Poilâne*, Paris: Le Cherche Midi, 2005.

Willan, Anne and I'Ecole De Cuisine, *French Regional Cooking*, London: Marshall Editions, Hutchinson & Co (Publishers) Ltd, 1981.

INDEX

ACKNOWLEDGMENTS

In the preparation of this book, I was fortunate to have the help of key members of my staff at Bathers' Pavilion and the huge support of an inspiring and dedicated team at ABC Books, HarperCollins. I would like to acknowledge the people that were critical in producing such a beautiful cookbook.

Kristy Frawley, my personal assistant was a treasury of advice, and an indefatigable manager who put order and sense into my handwritten recipes. She was a great link to the editors at ABC Books, managing all requests with poise and efficiency. Kristy has a great passion for cooking that was critical in guiding the flow and clarity of my writing; she understood the book as an everyday reader would, and made it all the better for that.

Phil Sajowitz, my longstanding executive chef at Bathers', also provided me with strong support. He understands intimately my style and wishes, and was an immense help in setting the base for many recipes and worked hard for many weeks on the testing and preparation. Phil's advice has made this book more focused and seamless.

My pastry team is full of talented pastry chefs, lead by Anna Polyviou, my executive pastry chef. They all contributed their knowledge and skills to many of the recipes, but special thanks must go to Melanie Haseltine, who ensured each recipe was tested to exacting results. Together we worked long hours on developing the methodology to provide clear and practical advice; her commitment to this project was inspiring.

I was also very fortunate to work with a team of superbly experienced publishing professionals. In William Meppem, my photographer, I found a true partner who was able to extract the best from me and drive the style and setting of each photo to evoke the beauty of every recipe. It is in no small measure due to William that the book is so evocative; his skills and vision are in full display in the beautiful pages, they are an expression of his talent.

Jo Mackay, my publisher, was the one person that drove this project from start to finish. She is a person of great resources and used every one of her skills to make this book what it is. She defined and developed the vision and guided me towards my strengths. She managed every detail, large and small, and steered everyone toward the final result. She deserves all my respect and appreciation.

At HarperCollins, Darren Holt's beautiful design brought the recipes and settings to life, and captured the atmosphere of what it is to be surrounded by good food and friends. Typesetter Graeme Jones ensured the text flowed beautifully and creative director Helen Biles kept a close eye on the design.

Lydia Papandrea as project editor managed a mass of detail and kept me and Kristy on a tight path. She extracted every missing instruction from us and made the book a beautiful flowing art work. Jacqueline Blanchard morphed my long recipes into clear and precise instructions that will help achieve better results in the kitchen. Jacqueline completely understood my writing and my way of cooking. She gently guided me to express the simplest of explanations.

I am grateful to Robin and Judy Crawford for making available their very special Hunter Valley house to complete the book in a stunning environment. Thanks also to Esta and Kevin who supported me at the farm.

Harani, my beautiful neighbour, was ready to lend me anything from her house when I was cooking on the beachfront. Thanks to Stefan from Scullery & Holz, who helped me finish my kitchen in a unique style, Rosemary at Aeria who lent us some beautiful ceramic artefacts, David at Glen Dimplex Australia, who provided my gorgeous Beiling cooking range and Sue Jenkins at Accoutrement for the beautiful kitchen pieces.

Finally, I have to say thank you to my family especially Yvette, my wife, who gave me the space and free run of our house to cook and photograph most dishes in this book. Only she understands my capacity to use every pot, pan, roasting tray, cooking equipment and utensil we have in the house — and we have quite a few! Thanks, Honey.

The publisher would like to thank the following retailers for the use of their lovely objects: Accoutrement, Aeria, Bed, Bath & Table, Burnt Orange, Lilley and Lilley, Lucienne Linen, Maison Bleu, Mosmania, Sista Life, Ruiz & Mackell-Wong.

The publisher would also like to thank Ana Maria, Caley, Céleste, Erin, Finn and Sasha and their parents.

First published in 2010 by HarperCollins*Publishers* Australia Pty Limited

First published in the UK in 2011 by
Jacqui Small LLP
An imprint of Aurum Press
7 Greenland Street
London NW1 0ND

Publisher: Jacqui Small
Managing Editor: Kerenza Swift
Cover and internal design: Darren Holt, HarperCollins Design Studio
Photography: William Meppem
Production: Peter Colley

ISBN: 978 1 906417 62 8

A catalogue record for this book is available from the British Library.

2013 2012 2011
10 9 8 7 6 5 4 3 2 1

Printed in Singapore